Alex is a professional chartered civil engineer with a keen interest in the arts—particularly drama and literature. It therefore comes as no surprise that Alex has chosen to write his first novel about the remarkable and dramatic life of an illustrious engineer from the time when Britain led the world in ingenuity and invention. This is the largely untold story of the father of one of the greatest, if not the greatest, engineers that Britain has ever known—Isambard Kingdom Brunel.

ALEXANDER WREN

The Other Brunel

AUSTIN MACAULEY PUBLISHERS®
LONDON • CAMBRIDGE • NEW YORK • SHARJAH

A CIP catalogue record for this title is available from the British Library.

ISBN 9781035807833 (Paperback)
ISBN 9781035807840 (Hardback)
ISBN 9781035807864 (ePub e-book)
ISBN 9781035807857 (Audiobook)

www.austinmacauley.com

First Published 2025
Austin Macauley Publishers Ltd
1 Canada Square
Canary Wharf
London
E14 5AA

DEDICATION

I dedicate this book to my former partner and friend Jennifer Hiscox, without whose patience, capability and undying devotion to the cause this novel would never have come to fruition.

ACKNOWLEDGEMENTS

With grateful thanks to the staff of the Library and Archive at the Institution of Civil Engineers for their assistance, the Brunel Museum in London and the SS Great Britain Archive in Bristol for providing the inspiration and knowledge to spur me on, and Loris Clements in providing essential input and assistance in the final editing of this historical novel.

CHAPTER ONE

THE GLISTENING, MEANDERING Seine stretched out before me. Morning light was now fully emerging from behind the houses and hills to the east. The charcoal moved effortlessly across the white paper, my hand feeling controlled by another as the harbour scene before me came swiftly to life on my page. Rouen was my home, and a place I felt a spiritual attachment to. I was in my element as I stood behind the easel: time had no meaning or consequence, as the past, present and future merged into one. Beside me, Baldoin scuffed the turf, sniffing the ground as dogs do. He looked up at me with wide eyes, reassuring me, as if I needed reassurance, of our special bond.

The harbour slowly started to come to life as stevedores and labourers went about their business for the day, loading and unloading cargo onto tall-masted ships and light vessels moored at the expansive quayside.

The light dimmed, as though a cloud had obscured the sun.

A gaunt figure approached from the edge of the bank. Sykes, my banker, looking dishevelled and ill at ease.

"I am sorry that I have failed you, Marc," he muttered through tight lips.

I looked on but said nothing; ignoring his pleading eyes and sunken frame, returning my eyes to the harbour scene in front of me. I began to imagine a beautiful expansive bridge linking the island of La Croix with Rouen; the image I was creating on the page before me slowly tracing the form of this structure—so magnificent in its presence and status, so entirely suited to its surroundings. A dream come to life.

Abruptly, the river water rose up in waves and cascaded over the grassy bank where I was standing, knocking me off balance...

"Marc my darling, wake up! There are officials from the Magistrate's Office, including an attendant constable, at the door with official papers for your arrest for debt." Sophia was tearful and confused.

I slowly came around from my slumped position over my desk. It was after eleven in the evening. Before me lay the letter from Rouen whereby I had been informed that, as I was not a member of the Government Corps of Engineers, my participation in the Rouen bridge project would not be valid. Emerging from my semi-conscious state, I was jolted into stark reality. This letter represented the new France. Politics of the State and new regulations now took precedent over private enterprise. My extreme disappointment when I first opened this letter was rudely reawakened; my heated passions and enthusiasms doused with cold water. All the work I had put in designing and detailing two structures, one of timber and one of iron, all gone to waste over a technicality.

I also realised that, still clenched in my hand, was the missive advising me that my bankers, Sykes and Company, were declared bankrupt.

I had been cast adrift on turbulent seas.

CHAPTER TWO

The King's Bench Prison, Southwark
May 1821

ANOTHER COLD, DANK night amplified the desolation and isolation of the stuffy room. Hard stone floors and the low brick and timbered ceiling restricted the very soul and stupefied the spirit. It had been but a week since my arrest and subsequent conviction. The magistrate at the King's Bench Court was brief and direct in his summing up. I could hardly plead not guilty with all the evidence of my slow slide into debt laid before me. But I did expect understanding and clemency; after all, had it not been the government itself placing me indirectly into this predicament by reneging on legitimate payments due to me?

My anxieties disturbed my sleep, but I was determined to find a way through this disorder. This was only temporary, I told myself. I rolled my body over and held Sophia as tight as I was able without disturbing her slumbers; her body soft, warm and welcoming under the blankets. She did not open her eyes. I regarded her face for a while; she had hardly changed since we were first wed. Despite the recent stress and strain, her skin was smooth and glowing. Her presence here was crucial to my well-being; her smile my light of hope at the end of a long dark tunnel.

But sleep, try as I may, was evading me this night. It had been only some ten days since we had entered this grim, grey shell, but already my spirits were failing.

I rose from my bed. The room was immersed in darkness save for the intermittent glow of a crescent moon through the sole small window by my desk; but there was sufficient light for me to clothe myself and kneel on the small mat by the furthermost stone wall.

I clasped my hands together and closed my eyes. Was it hypocritical of me to pray at this time? I seemed to contact God now only in times of need. I felt like a fraud. Yes, my family and I attended church together most Sundays to pay thanks and praise the Lord, but was that enough for the Almighty to have mercy on us and listen to our pleas? I had felt this way for a long time—probably ever since I renounced my Catholic faith. My decision had been made as a sign—an inner revolution of sorts—all those years ago in New York when my precious heartland was being devastated by its own bloody and repugnant revolution.

Perhaps my decision was made too hastily; although my hunger for religious conversion was also fed by my unrelenting and unfettering love for my future wife, who would never have been allowed to marry a man of my faith. Would God forgive me?

'This sad situation was misfortune, nothing more. It will pass. You have friends and influential people on your side—your family and others. You cannot fail to make good. But on the other hand this unfortunate situation has arisen as a result of placing your inventions and business endeavours above the expectations, duties and responsibilities you have to your closest family and friends.'

The argument continued in my mind. I implored myself to gather together positive thoughts but to no avail. I had no mind to pray, I needed to take a walk.

"My darling, where are you going?"

"Oh, Sophia. I am sorry to have awoken you from your slumber." I wiped my clammy brow with my handkerchief. "The truth is that I am of troubled mind and need to get some air."

"I understand, Marc." She never questioned my reasoning.

The heavy oak door creaked open onto the dimly lit corridor leading to the stairwell, admitting a draught of air which carried on it the odour of sewage. My foot narrowly missed the bucket of stale, pungent urine immediately outside the threshold. The scavenger labourers were late this week collecting this most prized of natural commodities to transport to the tanneries and wool merchants. Judging by the smell, the human excrement in the back yard was also piling up; awaiting sufficient quantity to be worth paying for the labour for removal.

Behind me, the ratchet clattered and the bolt thudded. Sophia was securing her isolation. I would use our secret knock to enter on my return.

I made my way toward the stairwell, picking up the muffled night cries and moans of my fellow inmates. In the gloom, I stumbled on the uneven floor as I approached the main stairs and made my descent. The echoing of human voices became louder as I stepped purposefully past the ale and porter bar, trying my best to avoid the scattering of men and a few women and children in various states of intoxication; some seated on the ground, others squatting or standing, partially blocking my route. A man in ragged clothing and with a mouth full of broken teeth barred my way.

"And where are you off to this fine night may I ask, sir?" he spat through foul, alcohol-fuelled breath.

I smiled as politely as I was able, without answering, managing to shoulder my way past and on to the other side of the building, increasing my pace.

"Sod you then…sir."

The clinking of bottles, slurred speech and forced laughter faded into the background as I briefly entered into the liberating open air before opening the door to the undersized prison chapel. A solitary man was kneeling on the front row of pews, looking up at the stained glass window. He heard my approach and turned.

"This is a late hour to seek the hand of God," he murmured.

I had been acquainted with the chaplain all too briefly upon my admission to this ghastly place, but I instantly recognised his long Roman nose and kind eyes, even under dim candlelight.

"I may say the same of you, *Mon Père*. But I recognise that your work never ceases, particularly in a place like this with so many waifs and strays to attend to and console through the power of the Almighty." The Reverend William Evans smiled. I continued. "I had sought this modest house of God tonight as I have deeply disturbed thoughts, and need to seek solitude to pray and ask the Lord for guidance and strength. But I am nevertheless assured and comforted by your presence."

I knelt by Evans and clasped my hands together.

"That is good to hear." He sent a sideways glance at me. "You are Marc Brunel, are you not?" His enquiring eyes met mine.

"Yes. It is good of you to remember me."

"The distinguished high forehead and professional air gave you away."

"We are all viewed much the same here by the law of the land, I am afraid."

"And in God's eyes, of course."

Abashed, I nodded.

"Now, what troubles you?"

I was reticent to allow this stranger into my confidence and open the door to my personal life, but he was a man of the cloth, after all. He could surely be trusted, and moreover particularly here in this humble house of God; an island of peace amidst the sea of incarcerated turmoil. I felt a sense that our Creator was eavesdropping. I took in the holy but meagre surroundings before considering my reply. This was not easy for me.

My mind returned to my youth. A naive, outspoken Royalist, my mouth got me into trouble with the volatile Parisian revolutionaries. But fortunately for me, help from my mentor and close family friend was at hand.

I began to speak...

CHAPTER THREE

Paris January
1793

THE SETTING SUN'S rays cut through the cold winter air as if to show that there was still hope for the future of this city stubbornly resplendent with royal buildings, rolling parkland and wide cobblestone avenues. There were all the familiar sights and sounds, but now things were different. The citizens continued to go about their daily lives apparently untroubled by the chaos and devastating events that were seething under the skin of a capital now infected by an epidemic of untamed proportions.

Jean-Claude Penoir made his way into the heart of the metropolis, struggling under the weight of a large hessian sack. This precious package contained newly printed pamphlets which bore the heading *'J'attends La Tête De L'assassin Louis XVI'.* He strode along undaunted, proudly wearing the white, red and blue cockade and spurred on by a combination of pride, excitement and the natural energy and exuberance of youth. The spirit of the determination of the poor and downtrodden was etched on his face. Although he was only a small cog in the huge unstoppable machine that was driving the revolution, he knew that his task of distributing propaganda was paramount to the success of the new people's council and the eventual overthrowing of the ruling classes.

Jean-Claude's journey on this sunlit afternoon took him from the printing works in the predominantly working-class area of the city on the left bank of the Seine, now firmly in the hands of the *sans-culottes,* to the cafés, streets and meeting halls along the Place de la Révolution on the opposite bank. He smiled to himself as he recalled that, until recently, the name of this thoroughfare had been *Place Louis XV*; place names and all references to royalty were now consigned to history as the fire of the uprising took hold. Jean-Claude had travelled this route many times over the past weeks. His blistered feet hurt from the cheap, ill-fitting shoes, his legs ached from the miles of walking and his woollen breeches chafed his skin; but making the people's voice heard had become Jean-Claude's personal crusade. The young man was doing this for his family and friends, many of whom were now giving time and effort to the cause in a multitude of other ways in parallel to his own. But most of all he was doing it for France.

Jean-Claude turned into a small side street off the main thoroughfare near the Palais-Royale and into the street frontage of the *Café de l'Echelle,* handing out his illustrated leaflets to all and sundry, not stopping to engage in conversation, but eager to be maintaining the momentum of the cause.

The decorative wrought iron chairs and tables of the café were occupied with the usual mixture of urban dwellers of all backgrounds and denominations, despite the unwritten restrictions on the clergy, foreigners and royalist sympathisers. As he glanced around, one person caught his eye; a man whose proud demeanour and confident air cut through the atmosphere as though his figure and presence were lit from within. But to Jean-Claude this person appeared uncomfortable in his attire of flannel breeches, bright blue cotton shirt and woollen waistcoat, not because they did not fit well, nor because they seemed out of place; it was as though the man had made a special effort to blend in with the prevailing mood, circumstances and fashion of the population at large. But it was his footwear that betrayed him, revealed in full as he sat with legs crossed; although worn and fairly unobtrusive, his expensive black leather shoes gave away the fact that he was probably not one of the proletariat, but who was he?

Jean-Claude had been coming to this café for months and he recognised many of the clientele, and even some senior members of the working-class council, either by name or by sight. He knew for a fact that he had never seen this particular man before.

The stranger was reading a copy of *L'ami du peuple,* which was partially obscuring his face. Jean-Claude was intrigued and, taking his bag off his shoulder, sat where he could keep an eye on the newcomer, but not before placing one of his crisp new pamphlets on the man's table with a forced smile and the dull thud of a firm hand.

The man took his time, letting his newspaper drop and thus revealing his face and shoulders. Jean-Claude guessed he would be in his mid-twenties. At first glance, his weathered skin and the rough texture of his hands gave him the appearance of a farmer. Maybe he was just a man up from the country for market day after all.

"Bonsoir, citoyen."

* * * * * * * * * * * * * * *

I haven't been to this part of the city before. In fact, I would not necessarily have chosen to come to this café, particularly at this time, *mais je n'avais pas le choix.* François, the head of the Carpentier family, my current guardian and mentor, has urgent business matters to address in the capital, and I, being of a naturally inquisitive and adventurous nature, could not help accompanying him, albeit with some trepidation. I was all too aware, through common knowledge and the passing of information within our level of society, that the metropolis was in the grip of a massive people's uprising and that a visit here could be dangerous, given our royalist sympathies and allegiance.

The leaflets that littered the streets, swept into the air by a passing breeze; the red, white and blue banners and flags flying from upper windows and hastily erected flagpoles; the occasional whiff of cordite on the air; the hurried and purposeful manner of the populace and clusters of men on street corners engaging in furtive dialogue are all testament to an undercurrent of restlessness. Anticipation, even fear, is in the air.

The last time I visited Paris was when I was just six years old; a year before my poor mother was taken from us. My father had brought me on the long journey from the *ferme Brunel* in Hacqueville on a market day to show me how a livestock market worked in a large city, and to work as a novice tenderer for the day. I can remember feeling both fascination and discomfort at the fast exchange of ideas of the auctioneers and their assistants going about their everyday business. Then, the boulevards and squares were busy with men of differing professional backgrounds; bankers, lawyers, government officials and the clergy, rubbing shoulders with the working classes. No longer.

The social order has changed completely, and my father would not have believed that today, in this city he had known and loved, no one even resembling a member of the upper class would dare show his face in public. He could never have imagined that *Les Jacobins* would have been able to take control of commerce so quickly, or that the church's enormous power would have been effectively eroded. I, myself, have difficulty trying to understand the momentous events that have occurred recently. With the king being held a prisoner in the *Salle du Manège* following the dramatic and bloody assault on the *Palais des Tuileries,* it seems to me that Paris, and indeed France herself, are embroiled in a bloody revolution the like of which I could never have imagined.

I feel it would certainly be wise to return to Rouen as soon as François has concluded his business affairs.

The café where I was partaking in afternoon coffee and cognac and busying myself reading a turgid piece of printed propaganda disguised in the form of a newspaper entitled *L'ami du peuple,* had started out relatively quiet and undisturbed when I had first sat down here around five by the local bell tower clock. But now the place was pulsating with the sound of social intercourse, the natural rise and fall of collective voice increasing as the afternoon turned to evening and the sun began to set and cast an orange glow on the square in front of me. Where in God's name was François?

I was jolted out of my reverie when I felt the shudder of a firm hand through my table. I was reluctant to look up for fear of being confronted by a drunken lout or other undesirable, but my inquisitiveness got the better of me, and I slowly dropped the paper to cast my eyes down on a newly printed pamphlet. It had an illustration of a guillotine with an executioner and several onlookers, one holding a severed head in his hands under a headline *'J'attends La Tête De L'assassin Louis XVI'.* My mouth ran dry.

I lifted my eyes and saw a young, bright-eyed boy of about sixteen years staring straight at me with a contradictory combination of smirk and raw innocence. He greeted me, not in a welcoming way, more of an inquiring one. He sat splay-legged, leaning back on his chair. I nodded in acknowledgement of his greeting but did no more than that. I was not in the mood for conversation and certainly not with this young upstart.

The air was becoming chilly as evening rapidly approached, and I made this, and my unease, my reasons for rising painstakingly and retiring into the warmth and thin welcoming light of the inside of the now busy café. But my friendly assailant followed me and persisted in making conversation.

"I don't recognise you as a regular here at this café, Monsieur," he shouted back to me as I approached the threshold of the glass-paned double oak doors marking the entrance.

"That's because I'm not," I ventured to respond, rather tersely, whilst only slightly turning my head in his direction.

I entered the dimly lit and smoke-filled café. It was occupied by a number of people in various stages of inebriation, partaking in their individual group motions for debate, some standing, some seated, some leaning against the solid mahogany bar. I was reassured by the social effervescence of city life and my mood improved. It was as if this café, just off the former Palais-Royale, epitomised Paris life but with the upper classes either missing or under-represented for fear of reprisal.

I leaned on the bar, opened my heavy overcoat and ordered a bottle of *vin rouge maison.* I noticed that my persistent comrade had also moved into the café and now stood beside me, still keen to engage me in conversation.

"Monsieur, I cannot help but think there is something familiar about you. Have you been in the city before?"

I felt obliged to respond, not because I wanted necessarily to continue the conversation, quite the opposite, but I felt that if I did not show a willingness to talk, I would appear suspicious, which, even to this citizen of such immaturity and little influence, might still leave me a little compromised.

"I have not been here for some time, so you are mistaken to think you may know me as you would have been too young when I was last here," I replied. "And I doubt very much if our paths would have crossed, as you appear to be from a part of this city that I would not necessarily have had a connection with, being the simple son of a farmer from a distant *département.*" The boy seemed to accept this explanation, but, after a pause, pressed on.

"So are you here on business then, Monsieur?"

"Yes, of an agricultural nature, if it is any business of yours, which I do not believe it is."

I grabbed my wine and glass and turned away from the bar, ready to take my place on a comfortable old leather chair that had just become vacant next to the main fireplace, where a welcoming if somewhat small log fire crackled. I removed my overcoat, eased my body into the armchair, rested my drink on the floor at my feet and gazed into the fire.

The warmth relaxed me and I drifted off once more into the recent past. I was sixteen again, being accepted as a cadet on the new French frigate *Maréchal de Castries,* and setting sail for the West Indies in the service of my country. I still have the quadrant of brass and ebony that I designed and made all those years ago with money reluctantly donated by my father. The glow of the fire made me reflect on these days, the red and yellow embers reminding me of the beautiful setting sun over Antigua and Barbados and the year-round summer warmth of the Caribbean. Truly paradise on Earth.

My gaze shifted to a middle-aged man with a full grey beard and ruddy complexion, who sat with friends around a small wooden table by the front bay window. He had been looking my way for some time, and I couldn't help noticing. He caught my eye and raised his head. "Marc?"

"*Oui, c'est moi,*" I replied politely but pointedly. "*Et vous êtes*?"

"You probably don't remember me. I'm Bernard Gautier. I used to own the farm next to your father's when you were just a lad growing up. But I still recognise the distinctive family nose and the high forehead. *Comment allez-vous?*"

I searched through my memory. "*Ah oui. Je pense que je m'en souviens.*"

"Come over and have a chat with me and my friends over a drink or two."

I was a little hesitant at first, but I realised that this man was indeed the man who visited my father's farm from time to time to share stories and offer his assistance, and I began to relax. I got up from my position of comfort and shook his outstretched, age-marbled hand.

"What a coincidence to find you here in Paris. *Pourquoi êtes-vous ici?*" he asked.

Even though I knew this man, I was still averse to telling him too much, as I would no doubt be overheard by many others, and he was with people that I didn't know.

"Here with a companion who has some urgent business to attend," I explained.

I sat on the edge of the white-painted wooden window sill, my legs partially drawn up to my body, with one foot on the table cross beam for balance and support, indicating that I did not intend to stay and talk for long.

"Ah, I see."

Bernard's two friends looked on. One had a mop of auburn hair, a rather mobile face with distinct laughter lines. His companion was somewhat gaunt and weasel-like, with thinning grey locks and dowdy dress.

"May I introduce my two friends, Monsieurs Taillefer and Perigot." I shook hands civilly with the Red Fox and the Weasel (as I had immediately labelled them in my thoughts), and turned my attention back to Bernard.

He leaned over close to my face, and uttered in a hushed, alcohol-infused voice. "You were always a rebellious boy. I remember your determination not to join the priesthood even though your father and family expected it. Your mind was on things of a more practical nature."

I glanced at his friends, to ascertain that what I was about to say was not being overheard. But the Red Fox and Weasel were engrossed in their own conversation. So I replied in confidence, "*Oui. C'est vrai.* I was never one to embrace the classics, they bored me. I was more interested in how things work, and mathematics and drawing. But my love of music still persists."

"Yes, you took up the flute, as I remember. Do you still play?"

"*Bien sûr,* it's been my close companion on many a voyage and adventure."

Bernard breathed in deeply. "This is not necessarily a good time to be in the city."

"No. I am aware of that."

The café was now filling up and the hum of voices was increasing. Our discussion moved on, lubricated by the alcohol, and I was surprised to look down at my bottle of wine to find it empty. We continued to converse, with Bernard's two companions merely nodding politely in agreement at our talking points or maintaining their own separate conversation peppered with the odd glance at the scene unfolding before them across the room.

There was a group of people standing at the other side of the café, who began to move some of the furniture around as if to make a stage for themselves. It gave the impression that some announcements were going to be made. Three or four of the group got up on the chairs to make themselves seen and heard more clearly. Each had their own small but attentive audience.

"At long last, our so-called leader and king is now held prisoner in his own palace, awaiting his trial for treason," the ring-leader announced.

A man on another chair confirmed, "As you may have read from the pamphlets and newspapers today, *la Convention du Peuple* will pronounce sentence for our poor, unfortunate Louis."

This was met with laughter and cheers from many of the listening throng, followed by loud applause. Each subsequent outward expression of defiance and violence against the government was met with encouraging fist-waving. I was astonished that the authorities and ministry should permit such nests and hotbeds of sedition and revolt. Not only was the café now full, but there was also a growing crowd at the doors and windows, craning to listen to the speakers taking their opportunity to turn the screw of rebellion and anarchy in no uncertain terms.

"Vive la France! Vive la revolution!" went up the cry.

I simmered with frustration at this intolerable situation, and, no doubt fuelled by the considerable amount of alcohol I had consumed, could no longer contain myself. I angrily blurted out, partially under my breath but with sufficient volume to be heard; *"Vous aurez bientôt* à *invoquer, comme autrefois, la protection de la Sainte Vierge, a furore Normannorum libera nos, Domine!"*

My outburst unfortunately coincided with an almost unnatural stillness and silence in the air, as if an angel of the Lord had just passed by. Time seemed to stop.

I was shocked to hear my own voice echoing back at me, as though this utterance had not been from me but from someone else standing at my shoulder. I had used the words of the bold inscription on one of the entrance gates to the city of Rouen when the city had been temporarily invaded by the republican insurgents in August. It warned that the people responsible for this revolution would face a summons through the blessed spirit of Sainte Vierge to the judgement of God for all its sins and transgressions.

I could feel the full blush-heat on my face and the sweat on my palms. In my state of inebriation and anger, I had stupidly exposed both my royalist sympathies and religious upbringing. I felt stripped to the skin. But, since I had uttered those words of condemnation with such vitriol, now I had no choice but to at least show I could stand firm and stoic against the rebels, and imprudently against all odds.

Bernard looked at me in horror, but at the same time nudged his friend to his right.

"Have you been sent by the king?" one reveller shouted at me.

"*Cet homme est un sympathisant royaliste*!" yelled another.

Fingers were pointing at me and fists were being raised.

I looked over to the entrance door. My missing chaperone, mentor and friend, François Carpentier, had arrived and was standing on the threshold, shaking his head.

Just then, the Red Fox arose and deliberately strode over to the thronging mass. What was he doing?

"*Mes amis. Citoyens.* Pay no heed to this idiot! He is just baiting you and is much the worse for drink. Please let us reconvene with dignity and reflection. The revolution is fully set in motion. We do not need to make trouble in our own house."

The wind of storm appeared to be quelled, at least temporarily.

"That man is *Citoyen* Taillefer, a member of the People's Assembly, Marc," Bernard whispered in my direction. "You are very lucky I am here, and that he is a friend of mine. I suggest you leave immediately for your own safety."

I nodded acceptance, and moved, weak on my knees and heavy of heart, to the door where François waited.

"Leaving so soon?" the young boy I had encountered earlier exclaimed, from his position leaning against the bar. "Just when my comrades were warming to you, too." I caught sight of his dirty face and smug smile as I brushed past in haste without answering.

"*De Dieu, qu'est-ce que vous pensez*?" François muttered as he grabbed me by the arm and hastily led me away from the café, along the now crowded pavement outside, barging our way through the melee as we made for the welcoming space and cold fresh air of the darkened street.

"*Mais où* étais *tu*?" I demanded of François, while hurriedly wrapping my overcoat around my body and breaking into a brisk walk to keep up with him slightly ahead of me leading the way.

"Never mind where I was. Why did you have to get involved at the café? You know full well what is going on in this city, and you leave yourself wide open to the whims of angry people."

"I'm very sorry, I couldn't help myself." I exuded my words through shallow intoxicated breaths that permeated the night air in wisps of vapour, and made me sound like a callow youth. "Where are we going now?"

"We are *en route* to a friend of mine's inn, La Petit Gaillard Bois, but a short street away, for temporary shelter and safe haven."

We hurried onwards, walking at pace but not hastening so as to avoid the impression that we were running away from something. In a city on the brink of civil war, where people were now being arrested or murdered on a daily basis, drawing the attention of observers would not be sensible.

The sound of our footsteps echoed through the lonely street, lit only from the windows of cafés and dwellings along the east side of the *Palais Royale.* It was as if the whole of this sector of Paris had been sucked into the *Café de l'Echelle.*

At first, I was confident that we had made a fortuitous escape, but soon we heard the sound of angry voices. I turned momentarily and saw three or four men pursuing us, quick of step and gasping hard and deep into the night sky.

I tapped François on the shoulder. "*Nous sommes poursuivis*!"

"*Oui, je sais,*" he barked. "Not far now."

Our brisk walk turned into a trot. François turned sharply into a small lane on the right, with a Gothic-spired grey church on the corner, its façade disfigured and stained glass windows smashed. I followed a couple of paces behind. I saw a discreetly visible cast iron inn sign, reflecting what little luminosity was to be had, jutting out from the cold stone façade of the three-storey block of buildings running down the left-hand side of the street.

Our pursuers were gaining on us.

We entered a narrow alleyway between buildings. François pulled a large cast iron key from his coat pocket and turned it in the lock of a bulky, bronze-studded timber door. We stumbled into the vestibule of a small but exquisite inn house. My senses were reawakened by the heady scents of ale and brandy and the distant sound of men's debate.

Shutting the door firmly behind us, we paused for a minute or two in an attempt to catch our breath.

"My friend Henry and his wife own this place," said François. "They live in the rooms above and are expecting us, although not quite in this heated and dishevelled state."

CHAPTER FOUR

Rouen

February 1793

AN ABUNDANCE OF steam rising from my horse into the chill early morning air told its own story. I had ridden this strong and trusty mount at a gallop for nearly all of the ride from Paris, mostly in darkness, only stopping to give the sweating creature water from the small tributaries of the Seine that I encountered on my journey. I must admit that I helped myself to the refreshing liquid too, such was my thirst and dry mouth.

I was relieved to be at last in familiar and comforting surroundings. The soft leather saddle loosened easily as I removed it and handed it to Emmanuel, the stable boy, who hung it up with the bridle and stirrups on the timbered wall of the stable.

"*Bienvenue. Bien de vous revoir, monsieur,*" he said, smiling.

"*Merci,*" I replied. "*Est-ce que Monsieur Carpentier est de retour?*"

"*Oui, il y a une heure déjà.*"

"*Je suis très content.*"

It was no wonder that François arrived before me. He was a fine horseman and knew the route from Paris better than I, so, despite his being senior to me by a generation he was always going to win the race, if race it was. We had become separated at some point within twenty kilometres of Rouen, but by that time I was familiar with the local countryside and routes, so was not too concerned that I may get lost.

The last few days since I had been obliged to beat a hasty retreat from the Parisian café had been taxing in the extreme, but also strangely exhilarating. I realised now that I had overstepped the line and just hoped that François bore no grudge.

Leaving the stables, I cast my eyes down the long gravelled driveway and spreading lawns of the fine country home, now awakening with the early light of morning. The perimeter pine trees swayed in unison to the chill westerly breeze. I breathed a deep sigh of relief as

I took in this welcome sight and inhaled the distinct odour of cow dung that was, for me, so evocative of the Rouen farmlands. I made my way slowly along the stony drive to the imposing, tall-chimneyed brick and flint-walled house which I knew as *Chez Carpentier*.

My arrival must have been observed, as the handsome oak door was already being held open for me by a liveried servant. The marble-tiled entrance vestibule awaited and I removed my sweat-laden heavy coat and handed it over to be placed on one of the high, ornate brass hangers. I was reassured by the warmth and lavish splendour of the familiar interior of this *grande maison*.

"Ah te voilà, mon cher ami."

I turned around, in the midst of easing my gloves from my hands, and there was François beaming at me. We embraced and kissed each other on either cheek. Further words were not needed at that moment; our mutual happiness on reuniting was obvious.

"Enfin! Tu as rencontre une jolie fille en route, peut-etre?" François jokingly enquired. I just shrugged.

Mme Carpentier looked on, smiling.

"Allez, faisons ensemble un petit déjeuner!" he proclaimed as he led me through the hallway, past the impressive central winding staircase, into the *salle à manger,* where the delicious aroma of cooked meats wafted in the air and reawakened my appetite.

* * *

"I'm afraid that the uprising has spread throughout France now, Marc," François explained through mouthfuls of *porc et œufs brouilles,* his face partly in shadow from the bright speckled morning sun that beamed in through the glass-panelled bay window. "I have heard that barriers have been erected around Paris, and Robespierre has commenced a *'règne de la terreur'* in the city against any considered to be loyalist or constitutionalist."

"Will no one stand up to him? What about the army and navy?"

"The generals and senior ranks have been arrested and are awaiting trial for treason. They have been replaced by supporters of the commune."

"Treason against our king? *Non!* He is still the reigning monarch."

"Louis now awaits his fate and inevitable execution. Pamphlets and newspapers from Paris are being circulated throughout the principal cities of France, inciting violence against royalists."

"Are we under threat too, then?"

"We are making the necessary arrangements to protect ourselves," François replied.

I needed to get some rest as the journey on horseback and our hurried escape had made me quite tired. I felt a headache starting to pound through my temples. I adjourned to my bedroom; my racing mind burdened with this troublesome news. Once in my room, I kicked off my boots, loosened my britches and *blouson* and briefly admired the view from the oriel window. The cloud shadowing the low rolling hills in the distance threatened rain.

As I lay on the bed and attempted to drift off to sleep, I could hear all the echoes and creaks of the house around me: the patter of feet and the sound of distant voices on occasion coming near, but not quite entering my resting place. The house was constantly busy with Monsieur Carpentier's family and visiting friends, but today the normally soothing sounds of human activity were more pronounced. It seemed that more than the usual number of visitors were present. I could hear female voices rising and falling, resonating through the house. If I were not feeling so fatigued, I would rise up now and see who it was that were assembled here, and introduce myself.

I twisted my body and leaned over to where my book and glass of water stood on the bedside table. My throat was still very dry, and I gulped down the water. My mind began to wander as I thought of the dreadful things that were happening now throughout France, like a thick smoke suffocating the farms and towns; all in the name of the so-called people. My old home, *la ferme Brunel,* would be among them. What fate would befall Father now? He would probably just carry on as accustomed. That was his way; the stoic, unshakeable characteristics that I inherited and yet ironically also rebelled against.

Pressing my fingers into my temples, it was as though I could feel my brain getting tighter in my head as the throbbing increased. And so I lay, neither sleeping nor active, just drifting into my own world of thoughts and imaginings. Stark images of bloody revolution, conflict and pain. The crying voices. The guillotine.

CHAPTER FIVE

The King's Bench Prison, Southwark
May 1821

SOPHIA STIRRED UNEASILY in the cell bed. Half-awake, she reached out for Marc, but her hand fell only on the cold and empty space where his body had lain—when? It seemed some hours ago when he had left for a walk with a troubled mind, but she couldn't be sure. She knew she dare not venture from the bleak protection of this room on her own to be amongst the criminals and vagabonds that dwelt on each corner—especially in the night. But where was Marc?

She began to feel concerned and uneasy, but at the same time she maintained that deep emotion, borne from the years she had known this man and had become so close to him that she almost felt like she knew him better than he knew himself, that he would be safe. Nevertheless, she would wait up and listen for the door.

Donning her heavy nightrobe, she looked out onto the drab city skyline, ominous and imposing under dim light and framed in part by the prison's tall boundary wall.

Raindrops pattered and rolled down the glass pane.

Her mind floated back to her youth, when she had first felt similar mixed feelings of dread and expectation.

* * *

Plymouth Harbour
December 1792

She stood breathless and exposed to the elements as the light winter drizzle began to fall from grey skies. Just sixteen, she was a diminutive figure against the square-rigged masts and full sails of the brig. The westerly wind tossed her dark brown curls as she held on to her billowing skirts and tried to hold back her tears.

Sophia could barely bring herself to wave goodbye to the members of her family who had made the short journey with her by carriage to the port. Her recently widowed mother stood on the quayside, stern and resolute. Too stern, her young daughter felt, but typical of the spirit with which she had coped with raising a large family.

Closely hugging her mother, and sheltering her from the elements, was her dearest elder brother William. Also here to witness Sophia's departure was Sir Frederick Rogers, the Member of Parliament for Plymouth and a close friend of the family, who had acted as guardian to the children since the death of their father. As usual he was resplendent in long coat and instantly recognisable by his perfectly tended handlebar moustache.

She would never forget how very supportive of her mother this man had been through difficult times. Her elder brother had also played his part; taking it upon himself to look after all his siblings. Although he was apt to tease Sophia, he loved her dearly and, both because of her bright personality and the fact she was the youngest, she was his favourite. Although William's cautious smile and stoic stance did nothing to reveal his love for her, she was still reassured by the strong connection mirrored in his gaze and familiar rosy cheeks as the merchant ship eased its way from port and the waving figures gradually melted into the misty distance.

Sophia remained in the cold and spitting rain, her tears and the rivulets on her face now indistinguishable. She wondered how much she had been crying, but steadfastly reminded herself that she was on a great adventure. The opportunity to visit France and learn the language was one to be relished and enjoyed, and it was essential that a young lady of her standing in society should acquire a practical knowledge of the language.

Despite this, Sophia could not help but think that the timing of her visit was not ideal. Though no more than rumours, news of unrest and revolt amongst the people of Paris at this time had reached England. Whether talk of the troubles was deliberately suppressed so as not to disrupt the important trading relations that England enjoyed with France, or whether it was just national naivety at a time when her country was buoyant and had a strong fleet, she did not know. But she was sure that her family would not willingly and deliberately expose her to danger. Her voyage was now a *fait accompli.*

La Manche had turned choppy, and her stomach had churned with the constant rocking and rolling of the shallow-drafted sailing vessel ever since they left the natural shelter and rolling hills of Plymouth Bay. She felt embarrassed when eventually the seasickness enveloped her slight frame and she vomited over the side, in front of other passengers and crew. She had hoped that, being one of four daughters and nine surviving children of a seagoing father and an agent to the Royal Navy, she would have inherited his sea legs, but not so. Sophia was therefore grateful, after many hours at sea, to see land, and to spend a few hours docked at Le Havre before following the meandering Seine inland.

As the ship heaved to in Rouen, she first caught sight of the grand sandstone wharf and, behind it, her sharp eyes scanned the cobbled streets and the sprawl of medieval half-timbered houses dominated by church spires. The tucked-away lanes were dimly lit by the morning sun as it struggled through the low cloud.

The smell of leather and woollen goods intermingled with the pungent animal scent of livestock and attendant horses, with many people busying about this efficient but quaint port. This was very definitely foreign soil. The manner and purpose of the gathered throngs revealed very little of the political and social upheaval that was now spreading through France. It seemed to Sophia that the only natural and obvious connection between Rouen and the French capital, other than sharing the same cathedral name *Notre Dame,* was that they shared the same river.

She was met with a welcoming embrace from the Longuemars, who were waiting for her on the quayside at the foot of the ship's gangplank. The couple appeared to Sophia to be in their early forties, and their clothes were of expensive cloth and well cut; their presence exuded importance. Friends of the family, they were to be Sophia's hosts during her stay in France. Although the Longuemars had never met her, they recognised Sophia instantly from the brief description given to them by her brother William.

Their smiles were warm and welcoming as they greeted this stylish, graceful young Englishwoman, and Sophia felt fortunate to be benefitting from the kindness and hospitality that had been promised by her family. William had also told her that the Longuemars were fluent in English, and well-travelled individuals in the gainful employment of the West India Company.

"Did you have a good journey?" Mme Longuemars enquired while her husband took charge of Sophia's baggage.

"Oui, merci," she replied, blushing away the lie, before hurriedly adding, *"Un petit mal de mer, c'est tout."*

A fine phaeton waited a short distance from the quay, with two beautifully groomed chestnut mares chafing nervously in their harnesses. The sight of such splendour attracted the attention of several local men who, after a lengthy inspection, shook their heads but then carried on with their business.

* * * * * * * * * * * *

"Et maintenant, le verbe dormir; je dors, tu dors, il dort..." Madam Longuemar's voice faded into the background as Sophia lost concentration; though not before she thought how apt a verb that was, given her current weary and heavy-eyed condition. The journey to Rouen from England had been drawn out and arduous.

Once she had been in the charming and opulently furnished three-storey terraced *maison* rented by the Longuemars for the best part of a week, Sophia had begun to feel at home. She spent many hours in the rear *salon,* book in hand, gazing through French windows at a well-stocked but winter-ravaged garden, and listening to the sounds of the busy port in the near distance. *Le Gros Horloge* astronomical clock's chimes resonated through the town, marking the unhurried passage of time.

This afternoon, Sophia's recent memories of home, family and her sea crossing were preoccupying her thoughts; until she realised that the two local French girls, Monique and Michelle, who usually joined her, were missing. She was disappointed by their absence as their conversation and blossoming friendship were already improving her French and, by the same token, the French girls' English. Maybe they had been delayed in some manner.

"Sophia. Have you understood what I have just said?" enquired Mme Longuemar.

"Yes of course," Sophia lied, through bleary eyes.

"I perceive that you are still fatigued from your recent journey here. Perhaps we should cease for the day and continue again tomorrow," Mme Longuemar suggested gently.

"Merci, Madame. I think that would be advantageous."

"Hopefully tomorrow we can visit the town so that you can experience the sounds of the language at first hand and we could also attend mass at the Cathedral. But for now, we will retire for dinner.

I think a reviving bath and an early bedtime will make you feel in better health in preparation for our small excursion."

"Yes, madame. Thank you for your kindness and consideration."

* * * *

Despite Sophia's homesickness, she already felt safe and cared for, albeit she particularly missed her younger sisters, with whom she was accustomed to share her experiences and secrets. But Sophia had confidence and capability beyond her years.

She slowly rose from her ungainly and cramped position in the bath water, stepped out and gathered up the waiting towels. The cold enveloped her body instantly and she began to shiver. An unpleasant sensation of fever ran through her. She hoped this was not going to be the onset of an illness. She had only just arrived!

Wrapping the deep cotton around herself, she dried her skin as best she could and sat on the cushioned bedside chair opposite the mirror on the wall. Still feeling weak and faint, she lit a candle and held it up to her reflection; to her dismay her skin had developed an ashen hue and her eyes were unusually swollen.

A sudden loud knock on the bedroom door startled her.

"*Sophia, puis-je entrer*?" She recognised the voice instantly.

"*Oui. Bien sûr.*"

Mme Longuemar opened the door and entered the bedroom.

"Oh, Mme Longuemar. I was just about to retire. I'm sorry but I am afraid I am feeling quite unwell. Thank you for preparing the bathing water for me. *Vous êtes très aimable.*"

Mme Longuemar's deeply furrowed brow betrayed a profound grief and despair.

"I am sorry to be the bearer of this news, but Monique and Michelle are dead."

* * *

The phaeton four-wheeled carriage drawn by the two chestnut mares shook and rattled its way at a relentless pace before turning sharp left on to the narrow country lane. Sophia was huddled under the fold-up hood at the back, sheltering from the cold wind that whistled through the open sides. Her body was firmly wrapped in long winter coat and scarf, her head almost totally hidden by her soft woollen bonnet tied tightly against her slender white chin.

Her time in Rouen had received an unexpected and severe setback. Monsieur Longuemar sat opposite her as her chaperone and guardian, a blank, resigned expression on his face as he gazed out into the countryside, his body rising and falling with the ruts on the track.

Sophia's heart was heavy and her head pounding, her now severe influenza made worse by the news that her new French acquaintances, Monique and Michelle, having been accused of Royalist sympathies, had been dragged into the street by a mob amid shouts of '*a lanterne*' and murdered.

Sophia had learned that the Revolution was now spreading like wildfire, and that many of the senior officers in the French army and navy had been arrested and guillotined by the revolutionaries as suspected royalists. The Longuemars, alarmed, felt they had no choice but to flee France and return, via England, to the West Indies, lest they too fall under suspicion and suffer a similar fate.

Sophia, however, was in no fit state of health to undergo a long sea voyage, and had no choice but to remain in France for the foreseeable future. Given the catastrophic events unfolding around her, this made her extremely nervous, but, though disheartened, she was acquiescent to providence.

Monsieur Longuemar turned to Sophia and smiled politely. "Our friends the Carpentiers will look after you now, Sophia. They are a good family of upstanding status and well respected in the local community. They know you are coming."

CHAPTER SIX

The King's Bench Prison, Southwark
May 1821

I KNEW THAT the pattern of the knock at our door was instantly recognisable to Sophia. I had made it so. It was our security.

"Marc! At last!"

We embraced on the threshold and stepped, hand-in-hand, into the room. Our room; my penance. The dull thud of the door closing resonated in the corridor outside.

"I was worried. You have been away for some time."

"Yes. I am sorry, my love. I lost track of time. I sought refuge in the prison chapel. I had to try and clear my mind, and I found solace and empathy through a comparative stranger, but a God-fearing man—a man of the cloth no less—in whom I decided to confide."

Sophia did not question my motives or even enquire as to who this individual was, but it would not be difficult for her to guess. Time has not altered her youthfulness and beauty; this dreadful experience has not wearied her. She simply gave me that look—the same heartfelt gaze I had experienced all those years ago when we first met at the Carpentiers' *grand maison* in Rouen...

* * *

The next layer of brushed oil paint had hardly set on the canvas when I became aware of another presence in the room. My first attempt at still life was being scrutinised. I turned to see a beautiful young lady with dark brown hair, fine features and delicately powdered skin smiling politely at me. She was dressed in a long, blue satin dress, pinched neatly at the waist, and spoke French with an attractive and soft English accent.

"I think you have captured the light on the fruit very well. *Vous avez l'air d'un grand artiste!*"

"Merci, mademoiselle." I probably stared at her too much; she began to blush.

"Comment vous appelez-vous?" I stammered somewhat rudely.

"Sophia. I have been invited to stay here for a while, *par la gentille famille Carpentier.* Unfortunately, the family with whom I was staying on the other side of Rouen were obliged to flee France. My poor health prevented me from leaving with them and returning to England."

"I am sorry to hear that. But you certainly look in the best of health now".

"Yes. It is behind me. Thank you."

She inclined her head very slightly before taking her leave. My fleeting encounter with this charming young lady had left an indelible mark on my heart and mind.

I turned to Madame Carpentier, who had simultaneously entered the salon, and whispered, *"Ah, quelle jeune femme ravissante."* But Madame Carpentier was neither amused nor encouraged to say anything in approbation of my obvious enthusiasm.

Her stern expression spoke a hundred words. *"Oui, mais elle n'est pas pour toi."* I attempted to look suitably chastened, but I was not to be put off that easily.

* * *

Winter turned to spring, and early summer showed itself through the budding of the bright green leaves on the trees and the colourful flora in the borders of Chez Carpentier's resplendent gardens. This house had been my home from the age of thirteen, when I arrived here from the Seminary of St Nicaise in Rouen to continue my formal education in mathematics and science. The Carpentiers became my family.

As the trees blossomed, so did my love for Sophia. We walked many a time hand-in-hand through the expansive manicured gardens, conversing about inconsequential matters; we shared our experiences and hopes for the future; we touched and kissed in quiet corners. Her beauty of form, her English reserve but adventurous character, possessed an irresistible attraction to me.

Sophia reciprocated my affections in many ways. She looked on admiringly despite my almost adolescent attempts to play the harpsichord in the salon and my equally amateur approach to painting. But my enthusiasm for life was enhanced through her. I cannot remember any time in my life when I felt happier.

Despite our walks being largely restricted to the grounds of the manor house, our love knew no bounds. The family had recently acquired a Red Setter by the name of Baldoin. I had taken it upon myself to assist in the training and well-being of this animal, as I had been brought up with dogs on the farm, enjoyed their company and loved their simplicity of thought and instinct. We laughed at the dog's antics and boisterousness when we played with him on the open lawns. And with Sophia's encouragement, I also resurrected many of the skills I had acquired when I lived on the farm, indulging in joinery and cabinet-making.

In time, Sophia Kingdom took me into her confidence as her background story unravelled. A daughter of a naval family, her father's early death left her to be brought up by her mother but under the wing of elder brother William. She had come to France to learn French with friends of the Kingdoms, but her stay with them was cut short as the Longuemars had to flee France under threat from the *sans-culottes;* two local young girls who were well known to them were murdered by the revolutionaries one night in the town. The Carpentiers, as friends of the Longuemars, obligingly took her in.

We tended to take our security for granted as we appeared remote from the troubles that were grumbling on in Rouen and enveloping the rest of France, so this news came as quite a shock to me—particularly to a young and vulnerable woman.

However, at least fate had taken a hand and brought us together.

"Are you not homesick?" I enquired as we meandered through the gardens on one of our after-dinner sojourns.

"Yes, a little," she said, a fleeting solemn moment in her eyes. "I miss sharing my secrets with my younger sisters and the warmth of my mother in Plymouth. I miss William too—but not his teasing!"

As a God-fearing man, I very much missed attending mass on a Sunday at the glorious Notre Dame Cathedral. I longed to give my respects to the clergy and honour the Almighty, praying He would see us through these troubled times. But this house of God, like so many now throughout France, was closed and boarded up indefinitely by order of the Republicans.

I made only the briefest of visits to the town as and when necessary, for provisions or just as a break from the house and its surroundings; sometimes with Sophia on my arm, when she felt she had the courage to do so, and sometimes with Baldoin in tow, but always dressing in a manner that would not draw attention to myself and my standing in society.

To say I did not heed the warnings of the personal repercussions that might occur on my visits would be false—I was all too well aware of what was happening now in France, and the tide of revolution—but I would not be restrained by the *sans-culottes,* nor be diverted from my Catholic beliefs and politics. On one such small excursion to the docks, I was idly sketching the river frontage and storage warehouses, Baldoin by my side, when I was approached by two officious strangers who had been unloading cargo from a berthed clipper. They asked my business on the portside.

"If you are asking if I am a citizen of this town, then yes I am. *Mais mon chien, par definition, est aussi un citoyen.*" I replied, a little defiantly, to the 'patriots'.

Providentially I don't think that they possessed the mental capacity to reason that I was being ironic, and left me alone. But it was a warning to me, as if I needed to be reminded, that the tide was turning.

Fortunately, the disturbances and troubles in the city had not yet reached as far as the rural peripheries and the Carpentiers' homestead, despite François' being so noteworthy through his professional status as American Consul and his membership of the prosperous classes.

This came as no surprise to me, as his eminence was more than balanced by his pragmatic attitude and moderate, conciliatory nature. He was appreciated and respected by many local residents of all social classes for work he had carried out in the community. He, therefore, was not an obvious target for the revolutionaries, but the tucked-away, exquisite and opulent manor house, albeit set in rolling arable farmland, was.

* * *

It was from the high, grassy banks flanking Chez Carpentier that I first saw them coming. What initially appeared to be merely a fragmented and disorganised rabble revealed itself, through a cacophony of shouts and drum beats, to be something far more menacing. Revolution had arrived on our doorstep.

I wasted no time in ushering Sophia, the young children and the dog into the safety of the house before standing firm by the portico main door. François was already at the head of the gravel driveway when I returned, his head semi-bowed in disappointment and resignation at the impending trouble. He was joined by two older male members of the family, Professor Dulague, my tutor of many years, and four local dignitaries and friends; one of whom I recognised, from my days as a cadet, as the French navy Vice-Consul Monsieur Pontier.

"It seems that the barricades and the *Corps de defense locale* have failed to serve us in this instance," François murmured, staring fixedly towards the high pillared, wrought-iron entrance gate.

From my vantage point, I could see the area immediately in front of this gate and to the perimeter railings beyond begin to pulse with the movement of maybe thirty or so men on horseback and on foot, all jostling for position, some armed with swords, others with batons. The mob's volume rose, the sounds of stamping feet, human voices and excited horses building. Then the assembled republicans parted rank like the waves of the Red Sea to allow their ringleader and spokesman to take centre stage at our gate.

I felt particularly uneasy at this situation. Although I was more than aware that an invasion of this type was looming, it now came into sharp focus. Up until now we had been living under the convenient delusion that what was happening to France would somehow evade us, and that the uprising would disintegrate into chaos before normality would eventually be restored through the army or royalist groups banding together. But stark reality now shook us out of our complacency.

"*Monsieur Carpentier*!" The man in a loose blue chemise and distinguishing red, white and blue roundel cried out, his ruddy face framed by the bars of the gate.

"*Oui. C'est moi,*" François shouted into the air in the direction of the gate.

"*Il faut que je vous parle.*"

"On whose authority do you come here *en masse* and uninvited?" François' question was met with some amusement by the assembled horde and an insouciant shrug from the speaker.

"Monsieur Carpentier! Do you not know what is happening in France now? The people are in control! Not the rich and privileged friends of the king. Please step forward. I wish to inform you more about recent events."

The man's tone was superficially gracious but with an undercurrent of menace.

"Monsieur Carpentier. We do not wish to make our attendance here too uncomfortable for you and your family through force, so please come to the gate where we can speak more, shall we say, privately." More sporadic laughter from sections of his cohorts.

François took his time to look around at his assembled throng on the threshold of the house, as if for approbation. But none was forthcoming, so he turned slowly before setting off down the gravelled drive. Cheers rang out from the crowd of rebels as he approached the gate. I felt my stomach turn and beads of sweat trickle down my forehead.

Words were exchanged at length between François and the rabble's leader. All was out of our earshot, but we could see that this dialogue was strained, with the majority of what was said coming from the other side of the gate. It was as if an ultimatum were being issued. A paper was produced and handed to François, who read it briefly before handing it back through the bars of the gate.

After more discussion, the mob eventually dispersed. The head of the Carpentier family looked up and held his gaze to the cloudless summer sky for a few moments, turned, and trudged wearily back to us. When he was a few feet from us, he forced a smile, which was swiftly replaced by a stern expression and a brow as furrowed as tilled earth. Tears were forming in his eyes.

CHAPTER SEVEN

The Chapel, The King's Bench Prison, Southwark
May 1821

"SO YOU SEE, *Mon Père,* all was not well. Despite the fact that I had been extremely fortuitous in meeting the woman who would one day become my wife, the troubles in my country grew large; threatening our very livelihoods. I, amongst others, became a targeted man."

The unassuming prison chapel was a more welcoming place this morning. Not just from the familiarity I now had with it, but by sitting at the pews and sensing a connection with God. A spirit prevailed. What windows there were, high up in the brick-vaulted ceiling, let in a welcome natural light, giving the whole blessed chapel ambience and warmth.

"Your story is very compelling, Marc. They must have been very difficult times for you. But tell me, where and when did you begin to feel disconnected from Our Father?"

Reverend Evans was a kind and sympathetic listener. His whole demeanour lent itself to a genuine and sincere interest in my history and past circumstances.

"The interminable guilt I felt, and still feel, in turning my back on my family, my closest and dearest friends, and the love of my life to whom I am now wed and who shares my humility, devastation and depression here in this very gaol."

The Reverend paused before he gave his considered reply.

"There are many here who have fared far worse than you, I can assure you. Although your experiences are no doubt painful, you are testament to the privilege of a strong mind and a capable, resolute determination to succeed. I know, from the details given to me by the marshal, that you are a professional engineer of some standing and respect in English society, and that you remain well-connected. But I can see from your expression and demeanour that there is something else on your mind."

"Yes." I dropped my gaze to the stone floor. "I believe that leaving my loved ones behind was the start of my denial of God, and my inevitably turning my back on Catholicism and the church of my father. My life has caught up with me. My penance is my incarceration here in this Godforsaken gaol."

After a pause, this good man looked into my eyes. "But it seemed that all agreed that you had to leave France, for the sake of your future and wellbeing. Your closest made a difficult decision and you accepted your fate. But that was because they loved you."

A tear came to my eye.

"Tell me more." Evans leaned in to me.

* * *

Rouen to Le Havre
July 1793

The muscular brown beast bumped and rocked me in the saddle. Snorting breaths and the rumble of hooves permeated the early morning mists as I steered this strong and agile animal deeper into the tree-lined bridleways and brushwood that flanked the Seine. I was again a fugitive from the outstretched grip of revolution.

After the traumatic events of yesterday in the drive frontage of Chez Carpentier, François called the whole family and any friends present into the salon for an urgent conversation. It was clear that the days of continuing to reside at the family home were now numbered. The *bonnets rouges* had issued an ultimatum, and the threat of violence, postponed due to the accumulated 'respect' that François had earnt with the local public, remained clear and present.

I knew that the royalist community were attempting to fight back, as columns of men from Brittany and Normandy were joining others from Bordeaux and the Loire to press forwards to Paris with the avowed object of rescuing the republic from its own tyranny.

But despite the deep attachment I had to my country, and my loyal spirit, I could neither entertain the prospect of a career of war nor ally to men who had stained their hands with sovereign blood. Besides, I really had little choice. I was horrified to learn from François that my name was on the long list of '*ennemis du peuple*' printed in the *Journal Républicain* handed to him that afternoon by the mob's spokesman. Bastards.

The reins grew uncomfortable in my hands due to the heavy riding I had endured since leaving Rouen, but, now that I was some distance from the city, I started to ease my grip and allow my steed to break its gallop and return to a canter. The last time I had ridden out was with my beloved Sophia in the countryside near Rouen. I pictured her face and imagined the scent of her body as my mind wandered to the times we were together. We would be reunited, that I felt sure, and I would honour her and devote myself to her in marriage forever. The image of her pretty smiling face and expressive hazel eyes would stay firmly in my mind, and console me on long lonely nights.

I was suddenly jolted out of my thoughts. Something had disturbed my mount. She began to pull uncontrollably on the reins and gather speed rapidly. I glanced around but could see nothing untoward about us. Nonetheless, the horse was now heading off the main thoroughfare into the thickets and wooded glades skirting our route. I attempted to draw her back on course, but this had little effect and we continued at speed on the rough ground and beneath low-boughed trees. We were bound as one—horse and rider—and her energy and desire to escape from whatever had frightened her was irrepressible. As we jerked and vaulted our way onward, and I struggled with the reins, my saddle began to slip and caused me to become off balance, but I felt I was starting to bring the stallion under control...

...the gloomy, musty-smelling room confined me. The portraits of many of my forebears glowered down at me, their eyes following me around the room. I tried the door again, but it was firmly locked by my father. He had the habit of confining me in here as a form of punishment when he considered I was falling short on my classical education.

I sat on the chair by the small casement window and tried to glimpse the arable countryside beyond the farm buildings in an attempt to divert my mind and to seek calm respite from my plight, but the stern stare of the portrait of the abbé above the stone fireplace bore into the back of my neck and troubled me deeply. Escape from this entombment was impossible, but I decided I had to do something.

The heavy hardwood table was nearly impossible to manoeuvre for a diminutive boy of only eight years of age, but, using all my pent-up strength, I managed, inch by inch, to drag it across the timber-boarded floor of the room. Despite the noise I had made doing so, I was sure that the abbé had not noticed anything different about the room as his stare continued to be fixed, but then I notioned that I saw a look of horror emerge on his wrinkled and pompous face. Clambering onto the table, I removed my pocketknife from its sheath, slowly and deliberately. Around the brow and under the lids I cut and sliced until the offending eyes were gouged out one by one, the victim showing no obvious pain or remorse.

Unexpectedly there was the familiar sound of a key turning in the lock of the door and it was suddenly flung wide open, the sunlight streaming in, my father silhouetted against the world outside.

"Marc! Que se passe-t-il au nom des dieux? Qu'est-ce tu fais*? This is the last straw. As soon as I can make the necessary arrangements, I will be dispatching you to the Collège à Gisors, where you will be taught discipline and learning the hard way by soldierly means."*

I knew that this school produced army officers and dressed their pupils in military uniform with cocked hats, regimental swords and powdered wigs. I shrugged at my fate, and showed more remorse to my father than I actually felt.

"Oui, Papa," I uttered under my breath, as I cast my eyes downward, more in introspection than in shame. An empty silence pervaded the room, followed by a gradual emergence of birdsong. My head suddenly felt weighty, and I became aware of a strong luminosity attempting to enter my now-closed eyelids...

...I woke to find myself lying on my side in tall grass amongst thickets and brambles, dappled bright sunlight shining through the canopy of trees above my head. I arose to a sitting position, held my head between my knees, and breathed deeply, rubbing my right arm, which felt bruised; otherwise, I felt no pain, just a dizziness of head and momentary disorientation. Looking around me, I realised I was alone in the copse. My only company was chirping wild birds and the gentle rustle of the leaves on the trees as the light breeze eddied its way through each branch and bough.

My horse was nowhere to be seen. I was crestfallen, as the realisation that I was probably still some miles from Le Havre hit me.

I carefully rose to my feet, brushing myself down and patting my body up and down to check that I was not hurting anywhere else. *Mon Dieu! Mon passeport! Mes bagages! Que devais-je faire?*

I took a few steps over the uneven, fern-covered ground and was relieved to find that I could walk easily and comfortably without encumbrance. I surmised that I wasn't too far from the *Cours de Daville*—the main thoroughfare to Le Havre—as I could hear the intermittent sound of horses' hooves beating the ground through a clearing some metres to my right. I discovered my discarded hat, sat it on my head and made for the road. My dishevelled but otherwise intact saddle bag lay upturned in the long grass, my clothing and personal items strewn across the ground. I carefully and painstakingly restowed the contents and slung the bag over my shoulder.

This was no time to feel remorseful, but I realised that without transport I had little security from my pursuers, and worse, that my chances of arriving at the port before my ship set sail looked in jeopardy.

I pushed my way out of the tangle of grass and low branches onto the two-cart-wide loose stony ground that constituted the now empty highway, and started to walk in the direction of my destination. Before long, I heard a rattle and clop behind me, and a twin horse-drawn coach pulled up at the side of the track in front of me. The head of a middle-aged man in a tightly curled grey wig emerged from the side compartment; his face, at first appearance, seemed vaguely familiar.

"*Vous êtes perdu, m'sieur*?"

"*Oui*," I replied, warily, as I had to be on my guard with strangers, regardless of the fact I was reasonably assured that anyone travelling by this means had some status and civility. "My horse threw me and I am now without means to get to my destination," I explained.

"*Où vas-tu?*" he enquired further.

I approached the carriage on the nearside to engage the man in conversation more closely. It was then I realised that this was Gaspard Monge, the mathematician, responsible for the many mathematical and geometrical methods that I had studied and followed throughout my six years at sea as junior officer cadet. When I was only sixteen years of age, I had seen him inspecting the *Cadets de la marine* in the same port that we were heading for now. I felt somewhat honoured, and blessed my good fortune to be in his presence.

"Le Havre," I lowered my guard now with confidence and returned the wide-eyed, high-foreheaded gentleman's interest with a keen attention.

"*Quelle est votre activité là-bas*?"

"I am to join a ship bound for America with the responsibility of purchasing grain for the Navy."

I have lied rather nervously, I thought, as I observed the other occupant of the sumptuous carriage. The driver, from his raised position seated at the front of the coach, looked on with mild disdain as he held on to the long reins and steadied the restless horses.

Monsieur Monge scrutinised me for a few moments before opening the door to his carriage and, with a half-smile, inviting me in.

* * *

We spoke on friendly terms for the whole of the shuddering and bumping day-long journey to Le Havre. The other male passenger, who was of similar age to M. Monge and resplendent in navy uniform, looked up only briefly from his book to acknowledge our conversation. I kept my counsel as best as I was able as I was still conscious of my possible exposure in light of the revolution sweeping France. I certainly didn't wish to risk more needless confrontation and difficulty, which might compromise my emigration.

The French countryside rolled by as I continually repositioned my body to gain the most comfortable seated position in the tight interior of the cab, adjusting to take in the views, but my back ached with the strain. Our journey was punctuated with stops for refreshment at the roadside and these provided a welcome opportunity to stretch my legs.

We had much in common to talk about, particularly the mathematical theories and practices I had learnt which were fundamental to engineering, and my enthusiasm for sketching and technical drawing that complemented them. He shared my keenness, and we were able to discuss many aspects of the profession, in particular the descriptive and differential geometry which enabled me to translate the images of three-dimensional objects on two-dimensional paper. A technique I used to great effect drawing ships' components and mechanisms during my time at sea as a junior officer in the *Marine Royale Française.*

It became evident through conversations and a glimpse I had of the official papers he was holding, that Monsieur Monge was now Minister of the Navy, and he was travelling to Le Havre as part of his responsibilities in the design and construction of gun and gunpowder factories. The engineering drawings on parchment that he carried were testament to that.

At times, his weary face took on a boyish mien. It was clear that he was enjoying my enthusiasm for his subject, and I felt honoured to be spoken to as an equal. I could not help but be aware of the other passenger looking on, but not joining in our animated debate, just nodding and grunting in approval when he thought necessary. Nevertheless, his very presence was a little unsettling.

CHAPTER EIGHT

Le Havre
July 1793

LIBERTY WAS THE quality of life that I deeply wished for the true upstanding citizens of France; I prayed for them to be free from the ugly, raw oppression and the menace of their own people. The men who were endowed with dignity, social standing, respect and an education would ultimately succeed in overthrowing this subjugation. The next generation would benefit from the strength and wisdom of these forebears, who represented the very foundation of French society. There would come a time, very soon I was sure, when France would awaken and shoulder arms against this tyranny, rip out the heart of Robespierre's regime and dismantle his instruments of death. But unfortunately, although I had the will and the desire to do so, I was advised, and felt in myself, that I could not risk joining this noble cause and thus subjecting myself to the way of life of a vigilante.

The Liberty was, by chance, the name of the moored American tall-masted brigantine of around 150 tonnes—my ship. She looked resplendent in the evening light, her giant white sails slowly being unfurled from her two masts and flapping gently in the breeze. I had spotted her almost at once; she was the impressive, wide-keeled vessel that awaited me and would see me on to a new life on a new continent.

I stopped momentarily on the crest of a grassy hill overlooking the port of Le Havre and observed the busy panorama before me. I counted four ships at berth, tethered by thick hemp ropes looped over the waterfront bollards: another square-rigged ship albeit not of the same type; a schooner with fore-and-aft masts and rigged sails; and a three-masted barquentine. The most impressive vessel was, without doubt, a frigate with a single gundeck, designed for commerce-raiding and reconnaissance, which cast a disconcerting, almost threatening shadow on the wharf.

I turned and bade farewell to my fellow voyagers on the coach journey and hastened to the wharf. The dockside was alive with the swaying and shuffling of the dark-skinned, muscular stevedores, as they loaded and unloaded bales of cotton. These poor men, some of whom were shackled, were under close supervision; each of the white foremen barking instructions had a cat o' nine tails firmly gripped in a strong fist. I snaked my way through the gaps and open lines of the assembled throng of passengers and ships' crews, all eager to make the necessary arrangements to embark on their seagoing voyage.

I overheard disjointed snatches of dialogue. It was clear that many of the people gathered had waited some time to board but were still being turned away by the captains of the ocean-going vessels, who were reluctant to set sail across the Atlantic before filling the ships with valuable cargoes. Whether this was the normal daily dock routine or whether the demanding and hectic scene I saw before me was a symptom of the menace of the rising people's revolution and the need for exodus, I could only surmise.

I continued to push my way through the gathered multitude. The piles of baggage and stacks of offloaded cargo in crates, cages and timber boxes that peppered the quayside to my ship threatened to trip me up, but I hurried on, knowing that, from the position of the sun in the sky alone, the time for sailing was fast approaching.

The gangplank of The Liberty was being hauled up by a burly sailor when I eventually reached the dockside where she was berthed. I had difficulty catching my breath as I attempted to raise my voice in order to announce my presence to a crew member.

"*Je suis Marc Bourdoir*. I am to board this ship for New York and report to Captain McCormack." I remembered to use the pseudonym I had chosen.

A gravelly, English-accented voice bounced its way down from the poop deck, "Ah Monsieur Bourdoir, we've been expecting you—but not quite this late."

I looked up and saw a square-shouldered figure in a grey blue uniform standing above me, pocket watch in hand. "*Oui, désolé pour mon retard*...err sorry I am late," I responded, almost forgetting that I was talking to an American. "An accident befell me on my journey here which caused me some delay."

"Hmm. Tell me, sir, before I permit you to board, what is your business here?"

"To purchase grain for the French Navy on the instructions of Monsieur Blanc."

Captain McCormack's stern expression softened somewhat as he nodded to the sailor on the lower deck. The long timber gangplank swung back into view as it was lowered onto the quay. The well-rehearsed introduction and exchange of coded dialogue I had learnt with François and communicated to The Liberty's captain had worked as arranged in advance via François' friend, the American Vice Consul in Le Havre.

I stepped onto the waiting ship, my eyes wide at the welcoming sight of the yardarm of the mizzen mast, the upper and lower decks and rigging dotted with men hastening about their tasks. I was filled with relief. I was again going to sea; this time not as a raw cadet but as a man who had absorbed much about life and destiny.

I was met by Captain McCormack at the head of the narrow steps leading to the upper deck. His large hand grasped mine in a vice-like grip.

"Welcome aboard, Marc."

His deep-set blue eyes and weather-beaten face confirmed to me that this man had spent most of his life at sea, and his confident air and demeanour gave me some comfort at a time when my mind was still racing from recent events, including my escape from my beloved France. McCormack's manner and tone were respectful from the onset, almost as though I was being treated as a valued commodity, despite my being his junior by some years and less experienced not only in seamanship but in worldly ways.

I could sense that we had the beginnings of a good amity and understanding which would be useful. I knew I had to work my passage by assisting him and his crew in the everyday operation of this magnificent ship. The prospect of the long voyage ahead—six weeks if the weather was set fair, up to fourteen if we encountered storms and rough seas—did not at all daunt me, as the experience I had gained in my time on expeditions in the Caribbean when I was an *élève officier junior* gave me a feeling of assurance and familiarity. I gazed up at the billowing sails set against the almost cloudless, dark-blue sky. My fervour for seafaring and love of sailing ships were instantly rekindled.

* * *

Through dark-rimmed eyes I looked in the mirror at the moving image behind me of my desk in my cramped cabin below deck. These last few days had wearied me physically but not in strength of mind. I smoothed my index finger over the small scar at the junction of my hairline and forehead, a legacy of a threshing tool accident on the farm when I was seven. Touching this, the only blemish on my face, gave me a form of comfort.

The gentle rocking and swaying of my body to the familiar roll of the waves stimulated my mind with thoughts of my future life, destiny and my current plight, but most of all of the loved ones I had left behind. Clasping my hands together, I closed my eyes and prayed to God for them all, and for my safe passage across this vast ocean. My Sophia's beautiful features drifted into my consciousness like a light, warming wind on the air.

Despite my somnolence and momentary introspection, I was buoyed by the emotion of being at sea again, and my spirit of adventure remained untrammelled. I stood up, stretched my arms and yawned widely, tasting the salty air and the scent of damp timbers. The water lapped and splashed against the ship's bow almost in rhythm with the soap water I spattered on my face from my wash bowl, as I gazed through my porthole at the rising light of dawn. A new day and a new horizon now. Would I be successful in my life? If success is marked by courage, a willingness to discover and expand on one's knowledge and then put that knowledge into practice in innovative and useful ways, then success would be in my grasp. Science would be my solace along the route and engineering my close companion.

Tugging open the cabin door, warped through years of sea dampness and use, I emerged onto the narrow corridor separating all the sleeping quarters and made my way to the galley further aft. The passage opened out to a raised floor crowded with tables and chairs, the smell of cooking on the air. There were around thirty passengers on this ship, mainly male, and ostensibly of wealthy disposition and respectable background, attired in a patchwork of cloth of many types and colours which reflected their differing backgrounds and characters. All were émigrés like me.

Pharoux and Desjardins, two portly men of my generation and of means and wisdom, sat in close discussion at one of the tables, their expressions shifting from waves of frowns to raised eyebrows through the changing tide of their debate. I had had the briefest of contact with them on the voyage so far—just a polite introduction and some small talk—but sufficient to know that we had a lot in common as educated men of principle with a sense of adventure. Pharoux was more demonstrative than Desjardins, but they both conveyed a real sense of mutual purpose and a confidence born from brevity of word and expansiveness of imagination.

"*Messieurs, bonjour. Comment allez-vous aujourd'hui*?" I pulled up a chair and sat immediately across the table from them.

"*Ah, Marc. Bien dormi*?"

"*Oui, merci.*"

The bright reflection of the morning sun from the starboard port-holes was in their eyes and complemented their infectious, cheery demeanour. A parchment map showing the northeast coast of America was spread out in front of them, their coffee cups holding down the rolled-up corners. My knowledge of this part of the New World was limited, but nonetheless sufficient for me to recognise the area of this land and its topography at first sight.

"*Cette carte me semble intéressante*," I ventured.

Desjardins leaned forward. "Yes. We are considering surveying a large tract of land between the forty-fourth parallel on the course of the Black River and Lake Ontario. It has potential for parcelling out for sale to migrants who may wish to settle on this new frontier."

"May I endeavour to propose some ideas that I have in mind regarding the existing waterways and navigable rivers—a subject where I possess a little engineering knowledge?"

* * *

The ship's callipers made their mark by my steady hand on the hemp fibre paper chart spread over the captain's table. My pencil line plots confirmed that since leaving port we had hugged the French coast, proceeding with the tide on a mainly westerly bearing.

McCormack looked on from his stooped position gazing over the green-inked French shoreline and beyond to the open Atlantic, his imposing figure silhouetted against the light from the huge paned glass window at the stern of the captain's quarters. I glanced up and past him to catch sight of the receding Brest Peninsular with its jutting cliffs and sea-foamed rock islands as if in a picture frame in a gallery.

The ship gently heaved and swayed as we continued to sail close-hauled to beam reach as the moderate prevailing westerly wind sought us out, with the point of sail being continuously realigned. I turned my body, and through the open door the sails were billowing and lifting like giant white wings, making the best of travel speed in relation to the true wind direction over their canvas surface. The ship's crew were working hard, clambering over the rigging like ants to make sure that the mainsails and foresail were brought under control and hauled into their most advantageous positions.

With the ship finally about to leave the French shores behind and head off into the open Atlantic, more adjustments to our heading would need to be made to take into account both wind and the major oceanic currents. Planning in advance for the effect they would have on the ship's speed and tack was my responsibility, under the watchful eye of the captain.

I reached for the ship's sea tables of currents and wind strengths on the shelf behind me and went about calculating our optimum point of sail and knot speed using the vector analysis that I had learnt as a cadet to determine the apparent wind velocity. I knew that the ship's own velocity would generate an equal and opposite wind which adds to the true wind to become apparent wind. I set about my task with McCormack looking on. I also knew that this seaman would not have used such mathematical analysis for this purpose—relying only on instinct and experience—but I was determined to complete this nautical process and compare the results with his intuition. His puckered brow did nothing to hide his doubt and scepticism of my methods.

Suddenly a cry went up from the crow's nest. "Ship spotted on the starboard bow." The captain immediately made a grab for his telescope and strode for the quarter deck. I followed.

"A fully square-masted frigate is approaching us at some speed from an upwind direction," McCormack uttered. He then handed me the bronzed spying instrument to share his observation. The oval of lens glass framed her shapely bow on the distant horizon, with sails swelling like balloons against the generous breeze. She appeared very similar to the ship I had observed at harbour in Le Havre with an imposing single gundeck and uniformed officers manning the bridge. Could it be the very same vessel?

"I think you had better go below and make sure your papers are in order, Marc *Bourdoir,*" McCormack half-smiled in recognition of my pseudonym, but my good mood was rapidly turning into anxiety.

I hurried to the lower deck and the familiar surroundings of my cabin. My hessian bag sat innocently in the corner. I fumbled through the inner pockets and sleeves, emptying out the contents on the floor and bed. My sense of dread was realised as I quickly confirmed that my pass document was missing, which I had half-expected, probably lost in the undergrowth when I fell from my horse on the ride to Le Havre some days ago. *Que faut-il faire?*

The captain's quarters were now well-known to me, so I wasted little time in locating the small storeroom aft which housed the sea-maps, charts and ship's logs where plain sheets of parchment were also to be found. I determinedly set about my task with quill in hand: ink glass, jotter and wax seal set to one side. It was my only chance, but time was on my side as I had estimated that the frigate would not be close to engaging us at her current speed for two to three hours.

McCormick returned. "Marc? Have you not found your official papers of identification?"

"*Non, Capitaine.* They must have gone astray when I was separated from my horse on the way to the port."

McCormick's weather-beaten face disintegrated into a deep frown, his sigh melting into the background sound of the surf.

"*Ne vous inquiétez pas. Tout ira bien*—all will be fine," I hastily reassured him. "My document comprised a single letter of recommendation signed by the American Vice Consul in Le Havre with an addendum page to the Director of the American Grain Company as formal introduction as I remember. So, with a little application and ingenuity I am confident that I can reproduce it."

The Captain grinned at my self-assurance. "From what I have seen so far from the sketches you have produced when on board, I know that your engineering drawing skills and cartography are of the highest standard. But if you have to forge your document, let me afford you some advice," he uttered simply and reassuringly. I was happy to receive his help.

* * *

The six-man rowing boat pulled alongside the starboard side of The Liberty, and uniformed officials began to climb the rope ladders to the upper open deck. I stood under the shadow of the main mast as The Liberty's officers formed a short line of courteous welcome. Hands were shaken and pleasantries exchanged, led by McCormack. One by one, the émigrés were called forward from the lower decks to present their papers when requested, for scrutiny. I noticed something strangely familiar about the officer leading this inspection, but from where I stood my view of proceedings was somewhat obscured by rigging and the bodies of other members of the crew, so I could not make him out clearly.

I was one of the last asked to step up. I shakily held on to my rolled-up manuscript with sweaty palm and made my way over to the other side of the deck. No more than a few feet away from the visiting entourage, I suddenly realised that the senior figure was the same person who remained silent in the coach I had shared with Monsieur Monge on the way to Le Havre. My heart sank.

He looked me straight in the eye. "*Monsieur*?"

His stare made time stand still. All I could hear was the lapping of the waves and flutter of sail amidst the silence of the wide ocean. I felt sure that he had recognised me, as through the cold steely look there was a momentary compassionate glimmer in his eye, but he uttered nothing. He reached out his hand for my document, but I felt my arm freeze before it creaked into life. The binding red string was untied and the paper unfurled in his hands. His scanning up and down was brief. He handed the paper back to me with a small knowing nod that communicated so little outwardly but so much to me.

"Tout est en ordre, monsieur."

* * *

... The Seminary's Superior, Monsieur Rosterue, looked down on me.

"Marc! Pourquoi avez-vous vendu votre chapeau de collège?"

The sweat began to build on my brow and hands. The floor came up to face me.

"I'm sorry but I must admit that I used the money to purchase a special tool I had seen in the cutler's window, to assist me in my carpentry, monsieur."

The Superior looked at me critically and sighed, turning to face the open window briefly before coming back to my eyeline.

"Marc. Since arriving here, you have shown artistic talent together with an analytical mind and application I have rarely seen before. But this is an ecclesiastical college. You are here to learn the classics and church matters. Your father still harbours thoughts of you becoming a priest."

A tear slowly trickled down my cheek as I shifted my body position in the undersized upright chair.

"Mais je ne veux pas faire cela. I have always drawn, and wondered how things work and are put together. Even my holidays have been spent sketching local buildings and chateaux."

"But Marc, you must also concentrate on what we are teaching you."

A silence fell in the room, as though time was pulling a veil over our discussion.

Monsieur Rosterue paced up and down for a while, stopped and pulled his fingers down his face.

"I will speak to your father about this. Not in a disciplinary way, but in a manner that will hopefully assist you in your future studies and academic life. I know, as well as do you, that your natural abilities and aptitudes lie in other directions not catered for by this learning establishment."

The Seminary bell began to ring in the corridor outside to mark the end of the current lessons. Its hollow, high-pitched sound slowly getting louder and more familiar...

I woke to the sound of the cabin closet door banging open with the sway of the ship. The ship's bell!

I rubbed my eyes and raised myself hastily from the hard divan. My stomach felt leaden from the heavy evening meal and rum I had consumed a couple of hours earlier. I hastily rearranged myself and put on the thick overcoat that I had purloined from a fellow passenger. It was my turn to take the watch up on the open quarterdeck with the ship's petty officer and check our course.

The mid-Atlantic sky was clear and starry, and a welcoming, fresh south-westerly breeze was steering the ship along its unwavering course for the New World. I pointed the ship's brass sextant at the heavens and fixed my sighting on Polaris in the Northern Hemisphere. I was immediately reminded of how much I missed my own dear ebony quadrant that had stood by me in my years as a cadet with the French Navy. It was probably now still sitting idle, but with pride of place, in the *salle à manger chez Carpentier*, where my dear Sophia would be now. I prayed she was in comfort and safety.

I returned to the candle-lit captain's cabin and calculated our position line on the ship's nautical chart spread out on the large plan chest, marking the point with my compass—forty-one degrees fifteen minutes north of the equator, thirty-eight degrees thirty minutes west of Greenwich, England. I knew that we had passed the Azores and were well en route.

We had been at sea for twenty-eight days already, our sailing time delayed due to rough seas, with many of the émigrés suffering *mal de mer*, but my hardened seafaring stomach and constitution showed no sign of such troubles. The captain had indicated the total crossing time to be approximately six weeks, but I knew that in reality it would take far longer.

CHAPTER NINE

The King's Bench Prison, Southwark
May 1821

MY GLOOM AND depression were lifted from me dramatically today. My dearest first daughter Sophie came to visit us!

The embarrassment of our surroundings and circumstances was instantly shaken off like shackles from our legs the moment her bright young face lit up the gloom. My joy knew no bounds. All feelings of desolation and resignation disappeared in an instant.

"Father!"

We kissed and caressed for many minutes; our eyes spilled forth the tears of joy and sadness melted together—all we three bound by unbridled love. The prison chaperone stood by for a moment and then left the room, partly from embarrassment and partly perhaps from his sense of duty elsewhere, leaving us to talk and share news together.

"Having you here, albeit briefly, has brought great joy to your mother and me."

"Yes, that is plain to see, Father."

We laughed for the first time in what seemed like months.

"I am just grievously disappointed that we should have to meet here and under these depressing circumstances."

"Yes, I know, Father. But hopefully all will be resolved in your favour very soon. We are all working hard to get you rightful clemency and released from here as soon as possible." Sophie glanced at her mother, who nodded and smiled reassuringly.

"I too have not wasted any time in writing to my influential friends, fellow engineers and politicians to see sense. I have been harshly sentenced to serve my time here, for debt by a government who, ironically, are my major debtors." My anger began to rise.

"Please, Father." Sophie embraced me again.

"I have brought some important letters for you. No doubt some responses from your pleas for help are amongst them."

She handed me a wad of correspondence of all shapes and sizes. I hastened to sort them into piles on my desk, when I noticed one where the seal had already been broken. I recognised it instantly. It was one of the old missives I had written from America when I fled from France. I started to re-read it.

"Is everything all right, my love?" My wife could see the consternation in my face.

"Yes, all is well."

Memories of my isolation and adventures in the New World came flooding back, and the correspondence between François and me while bloody revolution raged in my home country.

"Sophie. This letter was sandwiched between others in the bundle that you were kind enough to bring me here today. I would like you to return to our home, go to my private office and bring me the rest of them. They should all be marked with a red waxed sealed as this one." I held the letter up for clarity. "Here is the key to my desk."

"But why should you want them here, Father?"

"This one seems to have gone astray, and these records are of great sentimental worth to me. I cannot afford to lose them. Hopefully you can locate them."

* * *

37 Hanover Place
New York City
Saturday 7 September 1793

My dearest François

I trust this letter finds you in good health and security, but God knows what has transpired with your household and my dear Sophia since my leaving. I have made every effort through our mutual connections to ensure that this missive reaches you. Not a day has passed without my reflecting deeply on you all and the fate that my beloved country is now facing under the tyranny of the revolution. During my lengthy voyage here, I prayed at the end of each day for your well-being. I would inform you that I remain of good heart and strength of mind despite the sometimes tempestuous seas and strong winds that have carried and harried our progress in equal amounts. The captain was a fine, if not somewhat coarse and weather-worn, man of little word and a tendency to treat his crew quite harshly at times, in order, he said, to get the best out of them. But nevertheless I was constantly reminded of the spirit of your kindness and influence whilst on board, as I was treated with some respect by the captain and politeness by the officers, despite being a mere émigré.

I am now, at long last, landed on these shores after an arduous sea voyage lasting some ten weeks or more and am temporarily residing in an adequate lodging house owned by one Mrs Wilson. I do not intend to stay here long as my surroundings are not particularly suitable, and despite being somewhat buoyed by my presence in new lands far from France, I am in isolation and separated from the comfort of the French émigrés whose company I had become used to on my voyage. Also, the threat of being transported back to my homeland is as real as ever. It shows how far-flung our cultural influences stretch around this globe that we fell afoul of a small French squadron from St Domingo sheltering in the harbour on our arrival. As our rowed landing boat passed their ship, shouts were exchanged and accusations made about our being a cargo of royalists. Needless to say, we bade a hasty retreat once on terra firma to escape from these bandits. As you can imagine, this presented a none too pleasant introduction to a new country.

For myself, naturally I have had a lot of time for moments of deep introspection and have lingered long and thoughtfully over my situation and your plight. I felt guilty leaving you all behind but I know I have your full support in my venture and future professional career. You and your family have been a major influence in my life and I will never forget how much you have done for me in so many ways both as a friend and mentor.

My path and destiny are clear to me now. You know me very well, my strengths and my weaknesses; how I'm passionate about many things, science and mathematics but also the arts. I already consider that I have set myself well, with your valued assistance and influence, for a naval career, but I have a little way to go, I believe, to prove myself at the highest level. But prove myself I will and do you and my family justice for the faith and confidence you have all placed in me.

I have carefully placed this letter in the hands of the trusty McCormack, the captain of the worthy sea vessel Liberty that transported me safely here. I hope it eventually finds the safe harbour of your outstretched hand.

May God be with you and your family. Please also place a gentle kiss on my dear and beloved fiancée Sophia's rosy cheek for me, and inform her that all is well here. She never leaves my thoughts.

I am and remain always, your loving nephew.

Marc

3321 Bolein Street
Philadelphia
Thursday 26 September 1793

My dearest François

Mon cher ami. I know not much time has passed since I wrote my last letter to you, and although I still await your response, I am conscious of the difficulties that will arise in transporting my words to you through so many hands and over such a wide breadth of the ocean that separates us. I just hope that my previous and this dispatch do reach you eventually and you will in time, for my comfort, confirm your safety, which I entrust to God as every day passes.

I have moved to Philadelphia where I feel more at home amongst a fledgling French community. This is already a thriving and model municipality—described as the 'Mother City' by many of the local population. Long straight avenues and elegant buildings reflect the affluent and distinguished American society here as well as their ever-present optimism.

My evenings have been largely spent in the backroom of a bookshop owned by a Monsieur Moreau de Saint-Méry, where I have engaged in lengthy discussions with compatriots, including a crafty and charismatic individual by the name of Talleyrand who is entertaining but not entirely trustworthy, I consider, although he shares my opposition to the revolution, or so he says. Perhaps you know of him?

I have also been in contact with two financially well-endowed fellow émigrés, Messrs Pharoux and Desjardins who were also my compagnons de voyage on The Liberty. M Pharoux, it seems, is an architect and surveyor of some repute, and I was received by them both with all courtesy, kindness and generosity during the voyage. I believe they liked my originality of thought and amiability and are now considering inviting me to join them in surveying a tract of land extending some twenty thousand acres on the course of the Black River and Lake Ontario to purchase and parcel out to migrants.

I am excited by the prospect and the opportunity to show how qualified and capable I consider myself to be for this challenging project. But these gentlemen now reside in Albany, which is some miles distant from here, so it will not be long before I put my research and musings to one side and commit myself to the long and hopefully not too arduous journey ahead.

However difficult the travel may be, this represents an enterprise and abundant exercise for my body and spirit and holds out some prospect of future remuneration so that I may be able to husband my savings for any emergencies or contingencies that lie ahead.

The daylight hours are starting to shorten but my thoughts of your continued plight back home lengthen in contrast. My mind is like a beehive abuzz with excitement at the potential and prospects in this new country.

Philadelphia has a more formal approach to postal services, and with the help of a fellow émigré and his contacts in France I have entrusted this letter to him in the confidence that this will reach you in all haste.

Though my days are occupied with reading and socialising with the French community here, it makes for no substitute for the company of your family and the knowledge that you are all safe and well including mon amour Sophia.

May God protect you all from danger.

Tu me manques beaucoup, au plaisir te revoir.

Marc

Chez Carpentier
Rouen
France
12 February 1794

My dearest Marc

I trust this letter fi you in good health and spirit.

We received your letters from New York and Philadelphia in mid-December and I am naturally very pleased that you are making such extraordinary progress on new horizons in a young, emerging country. If only we were with you.

I am reluctant to tell you too much of what is developing here as some is mere talk and speculation and some borne out through evidence. I'm sure you will have heard many rumours and whisperings from the French community with whom you are now fraternising. You may also have been party to animated discussions concerning aff s here in France and our current plight. We are entangled in a web of confusion and confl but I must reassure you that our family is coping admirably with the attendant tribulations. When I refer to the family, I also must include Sophia as she is very dear to us all.

I apologise for not writing to you sooner but communications, particularly written, have been very diffi to issue, with every letter being at risk of interception and scrutiny. It is only through my trusted contacts—offi s and friends in the Admiralty—that I have faith that this missive will get through.

To put matters plainly to you, the country remains in the grip of revolution. Every person at our level of society is understandably anxious and at the beck and call of the Sans-Culottes led by Robespierre who instigated a 'reign of terror' here within a few weeks of your leaving. Word has it that he has been ordering the executions of any former associates, confederates who contradict him or indeed anyone whom he considers to be a threat to his own authority.

Naturally I have done all I can to protect myself, my family and Sophia from the angry tide of these atrocities but it has not been easy. I regret to inform you that I was imprisoned myself for some time but recently released unharmed thank God. I hasten to add that I was made comfortable and fed adequately during my incarceration but the episode placed a huge strain on the Carpentiers, as you can imagine. I tell you this because I do not want you to hear this second-hand from a stranger, but rather from my pen.

If all has gone to plan as a result of your meeting with Messrs Pharoux and Desjardins, I expect you are no doubt in Albany now and either preparing for, or well on your way to, your expedition and survey along the Mohawk River. I trust this is the case as you are a determined and capable man. Je suis fi de toi et de votre esprit courageux.

You are constantly in our thoughts; your vision and spirit shine through our dark days and give us hope for the future. The future, God willing, where we shall all be reunited. Sophia prays daily for your safe return and she warmly embraces you from across the ocean, as do I, naturellement.

May God keep you and protect you from all ills.

Votre ami le plus cher.

François

42 Duke Street
Albany
New York
Tuesday 25 March 1794

Dearest François

I have just returned from my venture with Messrs Pharoux and Desjardins and I was both delighted and excited to see your letter awaiting me. To say I was thrilled to receive it is quite an understatement. Even to reacquaint myself with your handwriting, not to mention your heartfelt words, has afforded me contentment and great joy.

These initial feelings of happiness as I hold your precious missive between my fingers, knowing the long distance that this document has had to travel, have been counterbalanced with my strong feeling of regret for your circumstances.

Naturally I am deeply distressed to hear of your imprisonment at the hands of the sans-culottes. What right do they have to treat those at our level of society who are responsible bastions of our culture, and have worked hard for their living and gains, with such contempt and malice? They have little regard or respect for France and yet have the audacity to fly the tricolour with a pride and passion that manifests itself as aggression and anarchy. I can scarcely contain my anger at the thought of this monstrous injustice. My blood boils at the thought of their treating you in such a manner.

For my part, I am fortunate to have found a wonderful climate of safety here, now I have escaped the clutches of Robespierre and the revolutionaries. Undeniably my swift departure at the time and under such circumstances, leaving you and ma chère Sophia far behind, trouble my mind almost constantly—particularly during my sleeping hours. I can do little to eradicate my feelings of selfishness and guilt over my escape. I feel almost a coward because I did not stay and fight against this tyranny, I should have organised myself and addressed the plight of the country with honour and pride as I'm sure so many others are doing now against the tide of revolt.

My heart aches and my eyes fill with angry tears when I think of what I might have accomplished had I stayed—at least in protecting my immediate family and friends. You must understand that my venture here is often clouded by deep regret. I know that your advice to me to flee to America was sound; indeed, without your help I could not have succeeded. Although it was not easy for me to accept my destiny at the time, I am aware that this illustrates both the tenderness and care you have for me and your unselfish and unswerving character. As a friend of many years standing, I know you are an extremely well-connected, upstanding man—a pillar of society who is both admired and revered by family, friends and also officers in our once proud navy. It is a disgrace that our beloved country is now in the grip of despicable people who are not fit even to 'nettoyer vos souliers.'

You know that my outer stoicism often conceals the true feelings within my heart. I often have to suppress my natural emotions—the ones that are typical of an effusive mind and reveal themselves in the gesticulations of a passionate Frenchman—but that does not mean that I feel the hurt and despair less than any other of our brave compatriots who are now under threat.

There are occasions when I seriously question my presence here. But it is my work, amongst the French community and this exciting and new land of opportunity that inspires and allows me to draw a temporary veil over the problems in France. I know you believe that of me, and hopefully my recent activities illustrate this.

The venture presented me with a wonderful opportunity, both to experiment with new engineering practices and to explore this wondrous country. Our party was well equipped with guns, axes, tents and supplies for the long and eventful journey from Albany along the Black River. We covered enormous distances by various means of transport—horse-drawn gigs, flat-bottomed boats worked by two red Indian guides with paddle and pole and even German-made sledges when the snow lay thick and glistening on our route.

Pharoux and Desjardins were gentlemen throughout. Rough, almost impassable roads with cold and wet weather conditions confronted us for the large part of our travelling and survey work. However, we were undeterred, and the daily challenges of mud and rain made our bond of friendship even stronger. I was excited to have the good fortune of being able to undertake surveys using triangulation methods and new instrumentation which undoubtedly aided our progress.

Even in those backwaters, one could ascertain a European influence. There were Dutch and English fortifications and isolated dwelling houses of stone and timber construction and a few French émigrés already taking residence here on the banks of the river.

I was beset by emotion at one stage when we were rounding a small creek in our canoe, the bank being hidden by rich foliage, French children's voices were suddenly heard resonating through the air. "Viens, Papa, Maman. Voilà un bateau." There in the back woods was a family who had fled from the horrors of the revolution, supporting themselves with the work of their own hands and the forbearance and kindliness of wild and lawless natives. We landed and exchanged words on the news in France, and the confidence shown to this family by the indigenous Indians was extended to our party.

Back at last in Albany, we are all now established as co-directors in this project and are planning to board a river boat in the next few days bound for New York. We shall take with us our findings and plans which we are hoping to discuss with influential men in the city who, we trust, will support us and invest in this venture.

May God continue to guide and protect you all from danger.

Marc

231 Holland Avenue
City of New York
Tuesday 29 April 1794

Dearest François

Some time has elapsed since I heard from you, which gives me some concern. I have information from the émigrés here in New York that life is still very difficult in France, so I am perhaps not entirely surprised that letters are failing to get through or that more important matters have taken precedence with you. I simply continue to hope and pray that you, your family and my dear Sophia remain relatively safe and well.

The French community here and word from Pharoux and Desjardin's families and friends back in France says that all English members of the population are being treated as spies and are in peril. I deeply hope Sophia is not implicated and is kept away from the fray. If any harm were to befall her, I should never forgive myself.

I have been busy here, as always. The meetings I have had with many influential men of power and worth, thanks to my fellow countrymen and fraternising with contacts through my fellow directors, have been almost too many to count. But one of these gentlemen is exceptional—a wealthy New York merchant by the name of M. Thurman, whom we met on the riverboat to New York when we unfortunately became stranded on a sandbank on the Hudson River. Although he initially showed interest in our scheme of forming a navigable waterway along the Mohawk River to link New York to the Great Lakes, his enthusiasm waned when he realised that we ourselves would be the immediate beneficiaries as the canal would be effectively flanked by our company's newly owned land.

Undeterred, we devised a new plan to form a navigable river and canal between the Hudson River and Lake Champlain, thus opening up a trade route by water between New York and the St Lawrence instead. This new proposal was met with approval from M. Thurman who has now agreed to finance the project survey, and so we will soon be off on another adventure, God willing.

I must say that I am impressed by Thurman. As an American loyalist and a true gentleman, he has sincere sympathy for our counterparts in France. I have often shared quiet moments with the man, when he has comforted myself and others with our sorrows and anguish and has often ministered to our needs and those of the French community here.

In short, he is emerging as a valued friend. In addition to discussing the practicalities of our project, I am able to confide in him as with no one else here and open my heart on matters dear to me. He is very much like you in that respect, and has much of the strength of character and wisdom that you possess.

I feel that I have risen to many of the challenges the assignments have so far presented to me, to the extent that M. Pharoux has strongly confided in me, and as a result placed me into the hands of M. Thurman directly over all engineering matters. I trust I am now well-respected both as a man of competence and as a character of force and responsibility, admittedly as a result of circumstances, but nonetheless now in a position best calculated to promote and control my own happiness. If I can achieve this by conferring lasting benefits on my kinsmen and fellow businessmen and professionals here, then this happiness will be of true worth.

May God be with you and protect you all from danger.

Je t'embrasse.

Marc

Chez Carpentier
Rouen
France
25 July 1794

My dearest Marc,

Thank you for your letters. I take it that you have sent two and no more since I last wrote to you.

It continues to be diffi to send letters through to you, but, in this instance, I am able to bring some good news. Robespierre has fallen from power, thus marking the end of the tyranny. Rumours are that he has been hoist by his own petard as the National Convention of men around him eventually succumbed and rebelled. It was inevitable as they saw close compatriots and colleagues being guillotined needlessly and cold-bloodedly as Robespierre became elevated as the sole remaining strong man of the revolution. He recently introduced a new 'law', which abandoned the façade of justice and the right to call witnesses, leaving the courts as merely places for condemnation and sentencing. Thousands of French citizens have lost their lives as a result.

It is perhaps too early to say, but we are hopeful that our worst days are now behind us and that some semblance of order will now slowly emerge. But it will take time; corruption, greed and unrest will remain at the feet of the people who have gained control of France for some time to come, I fear.

I did not tell you before for fear of unnecessarily distressing you, but at the height of the perils Sophia had to reside away from us at Gravelines Nunnery, as to remain here as an English girl would have put her at risk. Thanks be to God that yesterday we were reunited with her here at the house in Rouen, where she was greeted avec beaucoup de câlins et baisers. We had missed her deeply. So you see that your love is back in good hands now. Sophia has not been too troubled by her forced departure from us, but she is clearly happy to be with our family once again. She speaks often of you, and with great aff

Judging by your last letter you are obviously making some signifi t progress with many infl tial people in American society. You have always been a very hard-working, enthusiastic and capable young man, ever willing to explore and experiment. In some ways, I envy you. You are now reaching a level of maturity that always held promise throughout your childhood and early academic life. You are of an age where your youthful exuberance and energy will complement your natural intellect and experience, so it is hardly surprising to me that you are rapidly gaining positive results for your endeavours. Through your infl on others in high standing and prominent areas of society you are cultivating citizens who can make a real diff ence to this world.

There are no guarantees for success in life, but your natural abilities in science and the arts, together with an adventurous and unswerving spirit such as you possess will signifi tly improve your chances. The fact that you mention no setbacks, illnesses or anything that would have stood in the way of your endeavours is to your credit and speaks volumes for your indomitable spirit and strength of mind.

I am very pleased that all is working out well with you on the American shores so far, but I am far from surprised. Please keep me updated with your progress as I am excited and buoyed by your progress. God knows there are enough dull days here, and your letters are like a ray of sunshine through the gloom. You are the continuous and vivid vision in all our thoughts, and your love Sophia longs for the day you will return to her arms and once more be together.

May God keep you and protect you from all ills, and grant you continued success in all you do.

Votre ami le plus cher.

François

231 Holland Avenue
City of New York
Sunday 2 November 1794

Dearest François

I have read your letter of July with unbounded joy, as I always do, but particularly on this occasion, since I not heard from you for some time, and was quite concerned. Knowing that you, your family and my dear Sophia are now in better spirits, and that the climate of oppression appears to be lifting, has pleased me more than I can express. My heart beats for you all.

News has reached us here of Robespierre's latest outrages against France. Let us hope that now he has been displaced, his unchristian calendar and price controls will die a similar death. Though I also hear that the new Directorate is more interested in military conquests than in the interests of its citizens.

Naturally my thoughts and attention wander often towards events in France, but concentrating on my work very much assists in helping me temporarily to put those worries to the back of my mind. Indeed, the commitment and focus I put into my endeavours here provide a distraction from the travails back home. That is not to say that you, my family and friends that I left behind, are not ever-present in my thoughts, and Sophia deep in my heart. I am still plagued by guilt as I feel so safe and contented here in the land of the free, compared with your difficulties in Rouen. I fight through my work to become a hero, not the coward I sometimes, in my lowest moments alone with my thoughts, believe I am.

As I mentioned in my last letter, the survey of the Hudson River and Lake Champlain went largely to plan, much to the joy of my 'homme sage' M Thurman who continues to afford me full support as a valued friend and engineer.

Many notable events took place when I visited the survey team and Indians en route, none more so than when I was forced to kill a very lively and threatening snake on Rattlesnake Island in Lake Champlain. In retrospect, I should really have taken more note of the name of this isle before venturing forth with such gay abandon!

My brief on this project, through M. Thurman and with the approval of Messrs Pharoux and Desjardins, is to discover means of improving the navigation of the rivers. I am therefore applying my best skills and innovations to the means of removing or bypassing natural obstructions, realignment of the route and evading falls, swamps and cataracts. This involved my designing and commissioning, amongst other considerations, machinery and hoists mounted on barges using strong cabling, temporary pyramid-shaped timber platforms and catch nets to provide the elevation and horsepower needed. I have attached a sketch of the arrangement that I am particularly proud of, to illustrate my mere words more vividly. You know I have an affinity with sketching and drawing.

This project has appealed to me in many respects and through it my natural abilities in drawing, instrumentation, engineering and the arts have all cohered. Because of this, I realise that I have a deep and abiding calling for a future in civil engineering, and from now on I shall be making every concerted effort to expose myself to similar challenges along the way. Please accept that I shall never turn my back fully on the joys and experiences I have enjoyed in my formative years as a naval officer cadet, as these memories remain precious to me and have proved to be valuable in building my character and independence. I have you to thank for that, mon ami. My mind is alive with ideas and formulations. I now dine well and in exalted company; my health is good and I am strong of mind and body. I have the Lord to thank for all of this, and my family and friends to honour as part of the process of life and living.

Amongst the many 'irons in the fire' that I have at the moment, M. Pharoux, in his capacity of architect of some renown, and myself have recently entered a competition to design a new Capitol building for the American Congress in Washington, which I am very excited about. This will be a project which has to reflect the dignity and majesty of Congress whilst being practical in its layout as a council chamber with accommodation to match. I am inspired by the Palace of Versailles in this venture and our early drawings and plans look quite magnificent and certainly meet the criteria set.

I am determined to make a name for myself here for the benefit of all God-fearing men and women and am motivated by your travails and the hardships you are suffering in equal measure with my drives and energy.

May God continue to be with you and protect you all from danger.

Je t'embrasse.

Marc

231 Holland Avenue
City of New York
Sunday 29 March 1795

Dearest François

It has been some time since I last wrote to you. Forgive me. The winter months were not kind to me, as I succumbed to a fever for a while and was confined to my bed for several days. Thankfully that did not spoil my Christmas, which was spent with friends and acquaintances here, the highlight being the gathering at the main square which was festooned with decorative lighting and colourful banners. The Americans seem to want to do things on a large scale, which is impressive but bears no comparison to the time of festivity and the cosy surroundings and bonhomie of Chez Carpentier which I still miss deeply—particularly at that time of year. The city church of St Mary was equally resplendent with the luminosity of candles and the cherubic faces of the choirboys when I attended mass on Christmas Day. I trust you all had a similarly pleasurable occasion—as much as your circumstances will allow with France still mired in volatile times. The memories of Christmas and my malady are fortunately now shrouded in the mist of time. If anything, my short bout of sickness made me more aware and respectful of my health and condition, given my inclination to lead an energetic and adventurous life. I now take regular early morning and late evening brisk walks in the suburbs and park areas of the city as exercise for my body and mind, which I have found is an excellent way of harnessing collective thought and personal considerations.

Alas, my competition attempt at the design of the great council chamber in Washington, although meeting with approval for its arrangement and grandeur, failed on the grounds of practicality of build and economy. I had held high hopes, perhaps on reflection unwarranted, given the paucity of my experience in this field, but my confidence remains high for future similar endeavours. I have come a long way since sketching the churches and sizeable domestic buildings as a youth in Normandy! I have been given notice, however, that my design was of a sufficiently high standard to warrant further consideration—not for this grand building but instead for the Park Theatre in the City, which I am particularly excited about.

I have already met with two émigrés—M. Savarin, a barrister, and a Baron de Rostaing, a French nobleman, who are both leading figures in the arts of drama and music as well as key figures in the production and direction of this venture. There may even be an opportunity to accommodate a cameo stage appearance from me to pander to my ego at the grand masquerade that is planned for the opening!

Please write to me again soon. Despite news of the travails you find yourself under in revolutionary-plagued France, your letters are always a joy to receive and provide great solace and comfort to me in equal measure.

You are always in my thoughts and prayers.

Je t'embrasse.

Marc

Chez Carpentier
Rouen
France
Saturday 25 July 1795

My dearest Marc

Thank you for your letters. I trust this one reaches you safely and fi you in good health. I have read with keenness and a certain envy of your exploits and achievements in New York and beyond.

We are all well here. The new Directory is in control of this country now, and although the reign of terror has ceased, and Robespierre is no longer, there still remains unease amongst the populace as the dust from the recent past settles and we begin to breathe freely again. Although people in every sector of society can go about their business with increased assurance and some confi ence, we still feel that we are treading on eggshells as the political, economic and social basis of France enters into another bewildering phase. We are like a ship with strong rigging and large sails but with an unpredictable course. When all will resolve itself, only God himself knows.

I am deeply sorry to learn of the sudden death of your close business partner, patron, collaborator and friend M. Pharoux. To die under such tragic circumstances whilst undertaking survey work on the Black River is so heart-rending, and the impact of his passing without having reached his potential, and so young, must have shocked you to the core. I imagine that you are still questioning why he should want to risk his and seven of his companions' lives attempting to cross this river in the immediate vicinity of the great falls. We shall perhaps never know; but you must not dwell on this tragedy or place any blame upon yourself. I entreat you to give up your prayers to him and trust to Divine providence that you yourself were elsewhere and concerned with other projects at the time.

Your diversifi into the design of notable buildings and the respect you are obviously now gaining from higher circles, as a result of your direct involvement, commitment and contribution to the infrastructure of New York, speaks volumes for you. I am pleased that you have found your niche as an Engineer. When I think about your childhood and your natural inquisitive mind, it is hardly surprising that your life ship is now sailing on this bearing. The nautical analogy is not by accident!

Back to matters closer to home here: I have recently become increasingly uncomfortable over the degree of security that the basic postal system that we have enjoyed through troubled times now off s despite the change of regime. Call it just no more than a feeling in my bones if you will, but it may be that I will have to be more sensitive to the timing and the route by which these letters are sent to you, for fear of repercussions on my family and Sophia. I am sure you will understand. Please continue to write to me as your letters always represent great joy and freedom; qualities of life we yearn for here. I am more assured that the arrangements for post from your side of the Atlantic through my established and trustworthy sources remain secure.

May God keep you and protect you from all struggles and perils.

Votre ami le plus cher.

François

Naval Cottages
Plymouth
Tuesday 29th March 1796

My dearest Marc

I trust that this letter fi s you safe and well, my darling.

François has told me all about your journeys and the many successes you have enjoyed in your ti in Albany and then New York while I was in Rouen. I am naturally very proud of you. Your eternal spirit of opti and resourcefulness has no doubt been the foundati of your success—the same positi e and jovial character and strength of mind I experienced in those warm and cloudless summer days when we strolled arm in arm in the gardens of Chez Carpenti Marc of the sensiti e touch and the warm heartf lt embrace. How I miss those ti s, and your endearing presence.

As you can see, I am now returned to England, back in the bosom of my family. France under the revoluti proved to be too dangerous a place for me and my fellow countrymen and women, as we were essenti y treated as spies, and as such were subject to abuse and maltreatm François and his family did their best to shield me fr the worst of the atrociti s and protect me fr personal harm, but there was a period during the reign of terror when I experienced extreme discomfort in the hands of the rebels away fr Rouen. Thank the Lord, I am safe now.

The Carpenti s were wonderful to me and I will always be indebted to them for their generosity of mind and pocket. On tw occasions, they nursed me back to health when I was weary with fever and aching limbs; the second ti more recently when I returned to the house weak and dishevelled fr some extremely diffi experiences in strange and perilous surroundings. Before I embarked on my journey back to my homeland, these dear fr s ensured I was strong enough to undertake such a venture.

The last tw years in France were more diffi for me than I could have imagined. There will no doubt be a ti in the future when I shall feel able to reveal more of those circumstances, but, for the ti being, please be assured that I remain strong and have put all memory of my plight behind me.

Needless to relate that, through all of this, the memory of your kindly face and beauti expressive eyes, that I brought to mind on so many occasions, kept me safe and comforted. My heart yearns for you now as it did so much in my darkest hours, Marc.

Not having you near me to comfort my soul with your joie de vivre and love left a chasm in my thoughts. I attempted to fi my ti with embroidery and dressmaking tasks; I learnt French and undertook household duti s—including taking the dog for walks. They all proved to be pleasant diversions, but no substi for being with you.

Yours in kind and sincere thought,

Sophia

The Engineering Council Chambers
City of New York
Thursday 22 September 1796

Dearest François

Many letters have passed between us since my taking up residence permanently here in New York, and a lot of water has passed under the bridge. As you may imagine, I have been courted on many occasions by émigrés and French compatriots alike to return to France. However, my inclination is to remain here in America to make the best of the numerous opportunities that have presented themselves to me, and to forward my career as an engineer and professional man, until hostilities subside in France.

I am assured from our exchanges of correspondence that your safety and that of your family and friends has improved somewhat since the days of Robespierre and his tyranny; and I accept that my mother country is now entering a new phase of her political, social and economic existence through the Executive Directory which, it seems, has brought better stability. The word here is that France has gained allies with Holland, and both Russia and Austria, who have now acknowledged the power of our newly emerging country. All of this is still not sufficient to compel me seriously to contemplate a return, as France does not yet offer any real security for me personally, and there seems little prospect of the establishing of a political freedom that I consider essential through a proper constitutional and trustworthy authority.

The new power-brokers lack discretion and the wisdom to rule as they are unlikely to grasp the true principles of effective government. They have started to roll a snowball down a hill and this snowball has gathered momentum but they are unable to control or stop it. France without liberty and freedom, such as I have experienced and enjoyed here through the council of Washington, cannot have progressive growth or a tangible hope for the future; America has opened my mind to all this.

Whilst I accept this, I know that the love of my life is away from those shores—safely returned to England, thank God—and I know that my future will be inevitably intertwined with hers; but where and when we will be reunited, I cannot be sure, whether on English or French soil, but with the help of my will and that of the Almighty, we will.

For my part, I have been entrusted by the citizens of New York with the designs of the sea defences, wharfs and quays of the waterfront between Staten Island and Long Island—the 'Narrows'—developing the good work already carried out by my predecessor, a French officer of talent and experience by the name of Major L'Enfant.

Through this work and my other associations and successes in the design and construction of other notable city infrastructure, I was very pleased to be officially admitted to the privileges of a citizen of this great city, culminating in my most recent appointment as Chief Engineer for the whole of this ever-expanding metropolis. My cup runneth over.

I have in recent times applied myself to the preparation of designs for a cannon foundry—the first of its kind in this State—some elements of which represent a new branch of engineering to me, as I will have to apply some ingenuity and innovation to the present system of hollow iron castings which I feel is far too inefficient and can be improved upon. Without being tied down and having the licence to solve problems presented to me without the shackles of authority (as I have enjoyed many times already here in America), I am confident that I can put in order a process and establishment for casting and boring ordnance which will be unrivalled, and which will demonstrate my capability in mechanical and process engineering to boot. I am conscious that manufacturing is very important to the economy of any country whilst providing gainful employment to many.

I am always delighted to be able to share with you the details of my work here; my enthusiasm occasionally gets the better of me, but you know me very well and you understand my passion and ambition. It is strange to say, but I feel that I am being guided to my destiny by a light that illuminates a path before me. This light is both conscious and subconscious and offers me solace and comfort in my professional and personal life.

I continue to consider myself extremely privileged to be working here in New York. The opportunities afforded to me here have been plentiful, challenging and compelling. The people and dignitaries alike have treated me with a kindness and respect that I can only have dreamed of. Many of my fellow countrymen feel the same pride in our new homeland. I know that the time will come when I shall leave these shores and venture upon new horizons and challenges and settle down to the security, encouragement and familiarity of family life with my beloved Sophia. I trust in the Almighty that this time may come soon.

May God continue to be with you and protect you all from danger.

Je t'embrasse.

Marc

231 Holland Avenue
City of New York
Tuesday 21 March 1797

My Darling Sophia

Please accept my apologies for not writing to you directly since my arrival here in America. As you no doubt know I have been communicating with François as regularly as we are both able, given the circumstances in France and the focus and responsibilities that have been thrust my way. That is not to say you are not ever-present in my thoughts. In fact, there is not a day that passes where I do not reflect on your face, your touch, and the scent of your body. To dwell for too long on the heartache I feel at our separation, although it would be deep and sincere, would only make me melancholic and sad. Thus, my exertions and adventures in my professional life help to provide a welcome light diversion from the dark cave of despair and depression I feel without you.

I experienced sleepless nights imagining your situation when François recently informed me that you were torn away from the comfort and security of the Carpentiers in Rouen, just for being English and therefore labelled an enemy of the people. It made my blood boil and my pulse race to think of the way you may have been treated, despite François easing my mind through his assurances. Forgive me for feeling this way, but we hear so many stories and rumours here in New York.

I know the circumstances and haste of my departure from Rouen and my deliberately turning my back on the country of my birth were a shock to all (none more so than I), but I also know that you understand and were fully accepting of my choice, my love. In fact, to my mind, I had no choice. The country was being overrun by vagabonds and usurpers and was no longer a place for an outspoken royalist and professional man such as myself, his future no longer in his own hands. Our bond and relationship are built on love, deep affection and fidelity—actual human emotions and qualities which are not reflected in the now dominant political and social force that has held France to ransom.

When the time is right here for me to move on, and the opportunity presents itself, I will make all speed for us to be reunited; I can assure you of that. This is my pledge to you, my Sophia, from the bottom of my heart as your suitor, lover and fiancé, in both anxious and excited anticipation. We have laid strong foundations for our life together. There is no one else for me, Sophia. Your grace, adorable nature and English patience shall be the rocks on which I will build our future.

Je t'embrasse avec une profondeur de passion.

Your Marc

Chez Carpentier
Rouen
France
Sunday 10 February 1799

Dear William

I bring you, as Sophia's ward and guardian, some wonderful news. As I am writing this, Marc is on a sailing ship bound for England to be reunited with your sister Sophia!

He has fi given up the notion of returning to France, a country still in the throes of great political, social and economic upheaval. It was inevitable that Marc would seek his destiny away from these shores, to be reunited with the true love of his life. I know he will perhaps fiit diffi to adapt to the friction that has surfaced between our nation and that of your homeland brought about through the Jacobites, and illustrated through Sophia's regrettable experiences here. But Marc has secured and enjoyed the friendship of many infl tial people with links to America, France and England, so I am reassured that, with the help of these dignitaries and with God's grace and you and your family's understanding, he will surmount any prejudices that may come his way. He has always been a determined individual, and the lure of England and the love of his life were just too great to refute.

I can also inform you that he has taken an additional forthright and determined step to being accepted in your country, as in the last year in America, Marc converted to Protestantism. As you can imagine, this was initially diffi for me to accept as his decision eff ely denied his French roots and the Roman Catholic faith which had served him so well during and beyond his formative years. However, I have had to resign myself to it.

I know he was also infl in this choice by the knowledge that senior members of the professional community in New York held posts in the city that were deliberately reserved for Protestant communities that no doubt had Puritan origins.

I imagine that your family would not entertain Sophia being wed to a Catholic at a time when almost the whole Roman Empire is drawing swords against England and its allies. I did anticipate this situation arising, as you know from my previous letters to you; so I trust my interventions have achieved something in smoothing the way for Marc and your youngest sister to be together in marriage very soon now. Despite the numerous failings of the world in which we now live, this couple are undoubtedly destined to be together forever. And I am as excited as you no doubt are at the prospect of her being connected with the Brunels.

I know that you are more than aware of how successful Marc has been in America, culminating in his progression to the exalted and much-respected position of Chief Engineer in New York. Success breeds success, as Marc has been socialising and working alongside very infl tial and wealthy members of the upper echelons of American society. One such man was a Major General Alexander Hamilton—a distinguished aide and former trade secretary to President George Washington himself. Marc made his acquaintance at a dinner arranged by his friend and fellow émigré M. Delabigarre, who had just returned from England. Marc and Hamilton were united by temperament and an instinctive distrust of our republican France which is now unfortunately waging undeclared war on America.

The leading topic of conversation, as I understand it, centred on the recent successes of the British Navy at Camperdown and St Vincent. M. Delabigarre enlarged on his interest in the supply of materials of ships of war and in particular the manufacture of ships' blocks. He acknowledged that the current methods of production of these important components were outdated and failed to keep up with the huge demand. Marc, being the progressive and inventive man that he is, suggested ways of addressing the defects and has devised a new 'mass production' system based on observations of similar production facilities he devised at his Cannon and Ordnance factory and his plan for a 'shaping machine'.

He is bringing his plans and papers with him on invitation from your very own HRH Duke of Kent, whose acquaintance Marc initially made in New York through notable letters of introduction from many eminent individuals. I understand the Duke has strong connections with France, as his brothers are the Duke of Montpensier and the Count Beaujolais, and thus he immediately had a strong affi with Marc and his pleasing personality. This has led to Marc receiving a letter of introduction from the Navy Minister of your Prime Minister Mr Pitt's government—one Earl Spencer.

I believe Hamilton is actually travelling with Marc on his journey to your shores, and is due to put into your port of Falmouth in the fi st week of March. I am sure you will join me in wishing Marc a safe and comfortable voyage and trust you share my anticipation of noteworthy times to come.

Incidentally, before I bring this missive to a close, are you aware that the Directory in France has been overthrown? It appears that governance of France will soon be in the hands of a prominent military man, who covered himself with glory serving as an artillery offi before rising through the ranks. It is even rumoured that he will eventually become First Consul. His name is Napoleon Bonaparte.

Please communicate with me as soon as you are able after the event of Marc's arrival. I shall be pleased to know all that transpires.

François

CHAPTER TEN

The King's Bench Prison, Southwark
May 1821

I SHIFTED THE pile of drawings and calculation sheets to one side of my desk. Pen in hand, I began my day's work, running through a scrawl of equations and sketches necessary to build a new type of steam engine; one that would regularise steam power and enable that power on a greater scale to be achieved. Maudslay would help with the prototype and eventual manufacture, as always. He is overdue a visit too, I mused.

My projects were one way I could lose myself and take my mind from the stifling containment of this room and my sentence—correction, *our* containment. The other way was to share intimate moments with my darling, dedicated Sophia.

I looked across at her seated at our table preparing the food so graciously brought up to us by our household. We could not bring ourselves to sit and eat with the other inmates—there was no effective segregation, and typhus was rife. Some days ago, we had been concerned that we were also infected, as the signature headaches and fever took hold. I even developed a rash on my arm that persisted for two days, but good fortune blessed us, and all eventually passed quite quickly, although it was difficult to avoid the germ-carrying fleas and lice that pervaded everyone's clothes here.

I broke off from my work and sat near to Sophia. We held each other closely.

"Marc, together we can overcome this confinement and look forward to better times, I am sure. You know William is making things happen outside these walls."

I nodded and began to muse about the time I first arrived in England from America; when I met with her elder brother William before moving on to greet Sophia for the first time in over six years. A bright smile returned to my face as I recalled being both apprehensive and excited in equal measure.

* * *

London
March 1799

Beads of condensation chased their way down the leaded glass window, almost as though they were racing the droplets of rain on the outside of the pane. My index finger traced a letter 'S' on the misty glass surface. Sophia would soon be in my arms again. My pulse raced.

It was an unseasonably cold afternoon here amongst the connecting hamlets that made up the ever-expanding and spread-eagled metropolis of London, but the warmth inside the coach house was a welcoming comfort to my bones after the long and bumpy coach ride from Falmouth.

I felt a smile coming to my face. This was the realisation of a boyhood dream: to visit England and experience its rich past and culture at first hand, being more than aware of the historic connections with France and this island nation. I had always considered England to be a land so different from France in many ways. The English were frustratingly more reserved than the Gauls, and their often direct form of dialogue and stiff attitude gave them the appearance of being stuffy and unsociable.

It is not until one digs deeper, or befriends a fellow of this country, that one realises this is often just a polite show of indifference—a façade to hide the real person—almost as if the revealing of any emotion is considered a serious betrayal of the soul. Very strange. William Kingdom, Sophia's elder brother and guardian, I imagined, was such a man. Despite the fact I had never met him, the words we had exchanged by letter during the latter part of my six years in America gave me the confidence to believe that this was a man of both maturity and honour. But all that would be revealed today.

I pushed my empty tea mug, and the china plate spread with oatmeal biscuit crumbs, to one side, and reached deep into my trouser pocket to locate the few coins I had remaining to pay my bill. The whiskered, ashen-faced innkeeper cast his eyes away from the other customers leaning against the solid oak bar on my approach. His face was almost having an argument with itself, and bore a contradictory look of both concern and kindliness as I approached.

"Ah sir, do you wish to pay?"

"Yes, please."

I handed out the ready money requested.

"I wish to make for the north side of the Thames—to Somerset House. Do you know of it?"

"Yes, sir. Being a Londoner for all my life, I ought to." He broke off and looked me straight in the eye. "Do I detect an accent not necessarily connected with these parts?"

I felt a little taken off-guard. I did not think that my French tones were completely undetectable but believed that they had been suppressed somewhat by my years in America. I was conscious that France and England were currently in conflict and that my presence, and that of my countrymen, would not always be met with a warm welcome on these soils.

"Yes. I am originally from France, but have just returned from America."

"Good for you, sir. But may I offer you some small words of advice?"

He leaned over the bar, glancing sideways at the drinking men either side of him to check he was not being overheard, and addressed me in a low voice.

"Now, I don't necessarily speak for myself you understand, but your kind are not always welcomed here. Best you keep a fairly low profile if you don't want to bring trouble on yourself."

I returned his gaze. There was a brief silence between us as the background hubbub of the assembled seemed to become more audible, almost like a hiss in the ears. An acknowledgement of our respective positions was made without further exchange of words.

"Thank you for your counsel, sir," I replied. I was not exactly dismissive but nevertheless cautious whilst retaining my dignity. "Now, would you be kind enough to proffer further advice on the best means of getting to my intended destination? I had considered walking, but the weather conditions are foul today and look set to remain so."

The man leaned back, and sucked in a breath.

"There are hackney carriages that run regularly from this side of town over the river via the Westminster or Blackfriars bridges. The drivers wear colourful livery and are easily spotted, and you can wave one down and enquire of the fare before you get on board."

He added. "Mind you, they have started to be more of a nuisance than a service to London now, if you ask me. These Hackney Hell Carts, as we now call them, are in their hundreds; thronging the streets causing congestion and more horse shit everywhere they go."

I smiled back in mock-empathy, grabbed my baggage and made my way into the damp, grey street.

The clatter of wheels on cobbles from the numerous carts and carriages resounded from the stark stone buildings. Through the misty rain people came into sharp focus and drifted out again as they went about their business in a purposeful and hurried fashion. I pulled the heavy collar on my overcoat tight to the underside of my neck and looked for a sheltered place to stand and await my transport. The wide porch entrance to a bay window-fronted shop came into view as I too strode meaningfully with the others; the rain moistening my brow and hands, I advanced on my intended dock.

As I turned to face back into the street, I felt the lower reaches of my coat being pulled. At first, I thought I had snagged my clothing on the cast iron railings that stood either side of these premises, but as I looked down, I was confronted with the dirtied face of a young urchin in ragged clothes with outstretched hand. "Please, sir, can you spare a copper for my dinner?"

The plight of this child was clear for all to see. I made all haste to reach into my pocket for change but as I looked up a single horse-drawn carriage with a liveried figure in attendance approached my side of the road. At that very moment, two shabbily dressed men with menacing looks crossed the road toward me. I speedily approached the carriage and waved and shouted attention as he pulled over.

"Where to, sir?"

"The riverside entrance to Somerset House, please," I hastily replied, as I climbed clumsily inside the raised interior, nearly tripping over the seat and throwing my bags in the rear. I didn't even have time to request the fare—I had no choice but to escape from the immediate dangers of common street life.

"My, we are in a hurry!" The driver snorted as he tugged the reins and the horse pulled round and off into a slow trot. I glanced back and saw the two men with arms folded, and the young vagrant, gazing in my direction, disappointed I was not to be another of their victims.

The ride was bumpy and shaky and the noise from the clatter of the hooves and wheels of this carriage, the rain and other vehicles made conversation with the driver impossible, which suited me. The sweat on my forehead and my flushed skin seeped up from within my overheated body despite the rain and cooling breeze as we clattered through the streets. The last time I remember experiencing a predicament such as this was when a similar adrenalin rush pumped through my veins as I made my escape by fast horse from the besieged Chez Carpentier household some six years ago now; my eyes filling with tears of sorrow.

Now they were tears of joy. Joy at being in England and the expectation of re-joining my darling Sophia, whom I had missed so deeply since our desperate and painful parting. Completing my transition from motherland to a bold new frontier in America, to making my name and gaining acceptance as part of English society would, I accepted, not be easy as a Frenchman. Nevertheless, my and Sophia's lives would be forever entwined, and my destiny would now be firmly rooted in these shores.

The drizzly rain dribbled off the edge of the hood of the cab onto my boots as we passed stark grey stone and timbered buildings with tucked-away, narrow cobbled lanes on our route to the north bank of the Thames. Some of these buildings had stood since medieval times and were showing signs of decay and distortion. Gaps appeared between adjacent properties where demolition had been necessary, and there were clear signs that London's expansion and regeneration were gathering pace, as construction work was in evidence everywhere you looked. Such a contrast to New York's wide avenues and light and airy buildings, where everything was about invention and building new—starting from a clean sheet of paper with a grid system of roads and byways.

I was jolted forward in my seat. We had come to a halt on the entrance to Westminster Bridge.

Many horse-drawn carts, coaches and carriages had come together on the approaches to the low-arched sandstone portico that marked the entrance to the bridge.

"Sorry, sir, but the traffic here going into the city at this time of day is always heavy. We may have quite a wait until we are able to cross."

* * *

The decoratively corniced vaulted ceiling lent purpose and standing to the well-lit hall of this national building where I sat in isolation watching the dignitaries and public alike go about their business. I was informed by the commissionaire on entry that the Navy Office was located toward the rear of Somerset House, which was borne out by the list of all resident public offices and chambers on the large marquetry laid board adjacent to the sweeping staircase that dominated this part of the building. I waited to be called by William Kingdom.

The contrasts in the city north and south of the river were clearly drawn. The south side seemed more a collection of villages connected by main thoroughfares, whereas, once one arrived at the north bank, the density of buildings and traffic denoted a more lively commercial and domestic conurbation, with the architecture reflecting more prestige and importance.

The small puddle that had developed on the marble floor at my feet was testament that I was slowly drying out from my inclement weather journey through the metropolis, and my temperament and frame of mind were warming too at the prospect of finally meeting the man who would be reintroducing me to the love of my life.

"Mister Brunel?" A bespectacled man with inquisitive eyes and furrowed brow stood before me. "Would you kindly walk this way?" He turned and made small but precise steps in the direction of the staircase. I followed, suddenly aware of my odour of damp and my slightly dishevelled appearance which contrasted with his smart, dark grey suit.

After my scant luggage was placed, together with my greatcoat, in temporary store in a side reception room, I made my way, not up the staircase as I had expected, but through high-ceilinged ground floor corridors, which snaked their way into the building's interior. My guide kept two or three paces ahead of me, walking briskly and determinedly without even looking behind to check on my progress. The sounds of my footsteps were out of step with his and echoed through the almost empty, darkened tunnel.

I heard the distant sound of hammers and saws, and noticed that some walls remained un-plastered, and that areas of floors were laid bare. This building was obviously still a work in progress.

We eventually came to a sturdy oak door. My chaperone knocked and smiled politely; duty-bound rather than anything sincere.

"Come in."

I was shown into the burgundy-carpeted interior, facing a large bay window which looked out onto an inner garden courtyard resplendent with mature trees and shrubs and gravel paths. The rain had abated now and a spring glow filled the wood-panelled room. The figure behind the expansive desk rose to his feet.

"Marc Brunel! How wonderful to meet you at last!"

I advanced to meet this tall, lean and be-whiskered gentleman robed in dark grey flannels and waistcoat. William Kingdom was not as I had imagined him to be, but the image in one's mind is invariably different from the reality. There was a dusting of grey in his thick mop of hair and his pronounced cheekbones and wide eyes gave him a knowing look. At first glance, I could see no resemblance to Sophia in her brother William, but it had been such a long time since I had seen her, I may have been overlooking obvious likenesses.

As a Frenchman, I felt compelled to hold this man by the shoulders and at least touch cheeks, but my advances were cut short by an outstretched hand and a firm shake. I compromised by grabbing his forearm with my other hand. We looked each other straight in the eye.

What seemed like an age, but can only have been a second or two, passed. He turned and sat on the edge of his desk with arms folded.

"How was your journey?"

"It was a voyage of over eight weeks in some testing weather and occasional high rolling waves, but I'm used to that. I gained my sea legs some years ago as a cadet in the French navy so I am equally at home on land or water. The coach journey up from Falmouth was fairly uneventful, but I did meet with some English 'hospitality' here in London, when I was reminded in no uncertain terms on two occasions that I was a foreigner in a city that houses its fair share of vagrants and xenophobes. This is quite a contrast to America, where class distinctions are not so well drawn and the mix of culture is the lifeblood of an emerging nation."

I had not necessarily meant to be so outspoken so soon into our conversation, but my Gallic spirit and natural tendency to give vent to my thoughts dominated my speech. It was as though I could hear my own words echoing back to me.

William nodded: "I'm afraid that it is something that you will have to expect from time to time here. As you know, relations are none too cordial between our nations, and the French that are here are sometimes targeted, as ill-feeling abounds—certainly in the lower classes. However, I can assure you that Frenchmen of repute and high pedigree who will no doubt contribute to the economic success of our nation will be held in high regard and their interests will be protected."

William uttered these words as if rehearsed, though I suspect given his position in the British Navy Board it wasn't the first time he had spoken in such a manner and under similar circumstances.

"Please take a seat. You must be tired after all that travelling." He ushered me to a Chesterfield on the other side of the room under the bright watercolour seascape reproduction. "Would you like a drink?"

"A small brandy would suit, thank you."

He sat next to me, leaning in my direction as he handed me my glass.

"Your good health," he smiled.

"*À la vôtre*!" I replied, with raised eyebrows. He didn't rise to the bait.

Another pause: William looked to the ceiling and collected his thoughts.

"What are your first impressions of London?"

"I found a great contrast in the urban environments going from north to south. The city here on the north bank is business-like and more resembling a metropolis. London also seems to be a work in progress, as I see buildings being demolished and a lot of new construction taking place. Westminster Bridge is looking fine, but I hear that London Bridge is old and narrow and the masonry is crumbling and falling into disrepair. The horse-drawn traffic struggles to cross, partially from the bottleneck but also due to the vast number of hackney carriages converging on this principal crossing of the Thames."

"Yes, you are perceptive. The problems have been recognised. The Government has recently passed an Act limiting the number of licences issued, but it is now getting out of hand. The newly constructed Blackfriars Bridge further downstream has helped ease the flow, but Westminster Bridge takes the share of the majority of traffic with London Bridge."

He rolled the brandy around in his glass before speaking again. "You may have heard that a competition has been opened to design a replacement for the medieval London Bridge. Our own Thomas Telford and the Scot, John Rennie, have put forward plans. The City awaits finance and the most practical way forward. Perhaps if you had arrived here some six months ago, your name may also have been included."

The manner and tone in which these words were uttered put me in a quandary as to whether this was a compliment to my engineering prowess or a slight on my questionable timekeeping. I decided to ignore the remark and respond with a shrug of the shoulders and a smile. The main subject I wanted to introduce as soon as possible came forth.

"How is Sophia?"

William glanced away from my eyes and studied the inner courtyard through the window, before turning and delivering his reply.

"She has been well enough here back on familiar soil in the bosom of her family. The timing of her going to France was far from ideal given the upheaval and in which your country was, and is still, immersed. It was a period in her life that she will never forget, for various reasons—some positive, some negative. The Kingdoms owe a huge debt to the Carpentiers for protecting her and ensuring her safe passage back home. Our prayers were answered after much pain and discomfort for all."

I expect the look of disappointment on my face on hearing this political reply was as sincere as the churning I felt in my stomach. I nodded in agreement and empathy.

All I could bring myself to say in the silence that followed was, "Yes, I felt deeply for her too, all the time I was away from her. Not a day passed without my heart feeling heavy and a tear coming to my eye."

Sophia's elder brother looked deep into my eyes for a moment, his own eyes watery and expressive. He reached into his waistcoat pocket and withdrew a handkerchief.

"I long to see her and hold her, and, if you would allow me the honour, beg you for your sister's hand in marriage."

William acknowledged my heartfelt words with a small nod and smile.

"Sophia knows you are coming, but not the exact timing. She is lodging with me at the moment in St Mary Newington on the south side of the Thames. She is naturally very pleased at the prospect of meeting you again after all this time. She has grown into a very capable and beautiful woman, but then I would say that, wouldn't I?"

I laughed, and we embraced.

William was neither warm nor distant, but always treading the path of politeness and courtesy. Whilst I had not expected him to welcome me with open arms, I was somewhat taken aback by his initial reticence, but now I could detect an undoubted warmth there.

"But come, Marc, you must be tired and in need of sustenance. Drink up your brandy, and let us move on to a fine restaurant I know, where you can tell me more of your adventures in America, and we can get to know each other a little more."

It was obvious he was taking his role as Sophia's guardian very seriously (a little too seriously, I ventured) in the absence of her late father, but I accepted it all with a good grace. For now, at least.

CHAPTER ELEVEN

St Mary Newington, London
April 1799

FOR THE FIRST time in many weeks, I felt clean, refreshed and of smart disposition. I had at long last bathed in warm water and soap and enjoyed the luxury of clean linen sheets on my bed. The first-floor rooms that William had so kindly arranged for me in St Mary Newington, just a stone's throw from the quaint parish church, were comfortable and light and had pleasant views onto the avenue and parkland below.

I took a long gulp of the fresh spring air that permeated the room through the open window. My body felt invigorated, my mind at ease, and my heart light, as excitement grew in me at the prospect of being reunited with my beloved Sophia.

I tightened the silk stock around the neck of my crisp cotton shirt, donned my recently purchased royal blue overcoat, lifted my top hat off the stand at the foot of the stairs and made for the front door at the opposite end of the narrow hallway.

The morning sun assailed my eyes as I entered the street and began my leisurely walk to William Kingdom's residence, making due reference to the plan I had drawn with William's assistance when we dined together on the first evening of my arrival in London.

This district of the city was pleasant and expansive, with a true character of its own. The cobbles and sandstone buildings reminded me of Rouen, where I had first met the love of my life. Was it really similar, or was my mind making an association as a result of my buoyant feelings of anticipation?

It was a Saturday, and although this part of the town bustled with people, horses, carts and smart cabs, the whole atmosphere was leisurely. The professional man in his many guises was well represented in this manor, and many women on the arm of their spouse wore a colourful tied bonnet and free-flowing dress. Fashion was obviously changing; giving the individual the opportunity to express him or herself and providing insights into private lives as a consequence. It gave me some enjoyment and distraction to fleetingly attempt to guess the occupation and domicile of some members of the public as I went about my way.

I stopped again to re-consult my small hand-drawn map. The next right by the draper's shop on the corner, onto Carrick Street, and then the second left into Broad Avenue, and I would be there. My pace quickened in anticipation.

After my initial experiences and impressions of this metropolis, I was slowly starting to feel more at ease with myself and my surroundings; more secure and comfortable as a foreigner in the capital city of a country that was now taking up arms against my own. But as I no longer felt connected with a France that was being restructured socially and reformed politically, I considered I was already taking on the persona of a token Englishman.

I had turned my back on Catholicism in favour of the Protestant faith, not only as a rejection of post-revolutionary France, but also to gain acceptance in English society as a committed, hardworking and innovative engineer who could truly make a difference to this country's economy and future standing on the international industrial stage. I knew, too, that I would not be accepted by the Kingdoms to be a worthy suitor and future husband to Sophia without making sacrifices and changing some of my inherited French customs and manners.

I will always be French and proud of my country, but things had moved on. Now was the time, for the sake of my future destiny and peace of mind, to take an international perspective on life and awaken my soul to this new horizon. I had decided that I had no intentions of returning to France. The opportunities to succeed here as a professional engineer and valued member of English society were present and real. My love for Sophia was deep and sincere and her worth to me on a grander scale than I even realised in myself.

I had reached the front door of the terraced house. The solid brass knocker moved easily upward in my outstretched hand, before coming down firmly with a double rap on the rebated brass plate.

* * *

The courtyard garden could have been claustrophobic, but the attention to detail in the small space, with roses climbing the high masonry walls, and terraced paved and grassed areas, made one envious that such a modest space could be designed with such panache.

This enclosure was sheltered from the noise of the street by the house, and the pleasant tinkling of a piano resonated. From where this welcoming sound was emanating was difficult to tell, but it appeared to be coming from the upper storey of either this, or the house next door. I had not heard music like this played so well in some time.

It was in this peaceful and restful place that I sat in patient silence on the timber bench by a small apple tree, having been politely ushered there by William with an index finger placed firmly over his lips. Sophia would be down soon.

The clouds were slowly being sent on their way by the mild breeze, as the birds chirruped their welcome. I turned to face the house and, through the open window of the sitting room, caught sight of William chatting with an older woman whom I did not recognise, before they both disappeared into the depths of the room.

As the warmth of the sun and background noise of urban life combined with the piano and birdsong to massage my soul, I closed my eyes. Despite my raised levels of awareness and expectation, I felt myself drifting into sleep.

The piano had stopped playing. I opened my eyes. There, standing on the threshold of the wide-open French windows, were two women, hand-in-hand, stock still, smiling in my direction. One was the mature woman I had seen earlier in the house, the other a beautiful female form in a gauzy cream-coloured dress that tumbled seductively over her shoulders and breasts. I stood up. This was my Sophia! Of course, I remembered her as the teenage girl I first met all those years ago in Rouen, but this picture of femininity was now, whilst still retaining her girlish charms and coquettishly smiling face, a mature woman of some twenty-three years. I was dumbstruck; and she was tearful.

"Marc!"

Her chaperone let go of Sophia's arm, and my love held out her hand for me to kiss, which I did passionately and lovingly, her delicate fingers enclosed in mine.

My heart soared. No words were necessary. We gazed deeply into each other's eyes and the world was at peace, and at my feet.

"Marc. I am Sophia's mother, and I am very pleased to meet you at last. This is a very special day for the whole family. We have all learnt so much about you, your family and your successes in America, but also so much from Sophia herself about the short time you were together in France"

"I am very pleased to make your acquaintance, Madam Kingdom." I nodded and took her hand too.

"Shall we sit down?"

With Sophia's small hand in mine, we all made dainty steps toward the bench where I had been previously seated. I was naturally overjoyed, and relief and contentment washed over me like a sudden April shower.

Madam Kingdom was first to break the silence. "We shall have much to talk about later I am sure, Marc, but for now I have to go indoors to discuss the luncheon arrangements with cook." She nodded and smiled at Sophia and me before disappearing into the house. We watched her leave the garden before turning to face each other.

"My dear, you look more beautiful than ever. The days have been long and the pain of separation deep in my bones. There has not been an hour when I did not yearn for your touch and long for your kiss. My darling, I have been looking forward to this moment for what seems like a lifetime."

"I too have waited impatiently for this very moment. You have taken on the look of a man with great wisdom with that noble high forehead of yours and your deep hazel eyes—just as I remember them."

"My destiny is here with you now, in England. With you at my right hand, I know your influence and support will drive me on to great things. I am so happy to be with you." I caressed and kissed her hand again. "America was a wonderful experience for me, but with us being reunited I have all I need to make our life together very comfortable and successful."

"Oh Marc! Your presence here brings me so much joy. I knew that you were on your way but was not informed by my brother that today would be the day. It is such a wonderful surprise." Sophia's tear-damp cheek touched mine as she leaned forward and we embraced. Her lavender scent wafted in the air; her body warm next to mine.

I had never felt so happy. We moved on to discuss many matters in brief, including our time apart. Our innermost feelings began to be laid bare, and I felt now was the time to enquire.

"Your brother William has been most welcoming to me, although I cannot help feeling that he is holding something back, almost as though the sense of duty in him is dominating his natural instinct to be friendly to me. It may be the fact that this is the first time we have met, and that the newness of our first encounter combined with my being French has caught him a little off-guard."

Sophia broke from my gaze and looked over my shoulder. A long silence ensued.

"I am sorry, my darling, if I have said anything to upset you. That was not my intention."

"No, no, Marc. It had to be spoken of at some time, so, if it would please you to talk of it now, so be it." She regarded me with moist eyes. "William bears no grudge, but still feels that the timing and nature of your departure from France was ill-advised. I was left without you, a young English girl exposed to the difficulties of living in a country in turmoil. My brother, rather harshly, considered that your actions were not those of a man who professed to care deeply for me."

I gasped and cast my eyes downward. I tried to speak, but Sophia put her finger to my lips.

"Please Marc, let me continue. I know that we discussed this issue at great length with the Carpentier family and that, although you were very reluctant, your immediate emigration was the right decision. You know you had my blessing in that." She drew a deep breath. "Unfortunately, things became rapidly worse for me from that time on. I had to spend a prolonged period away from the security of the house at Rouen through no choice of my own and in fear of the tyrannical mob that was overturning France at the time. There was a time that I was in fear of my life. I have not fully related my experiences to anyone to date, and perhaps I never will."

"Oh Sophia!" I held her hands tightly. "I knew from François' letters that you had all experienced difficult times but not such as this. I share your sorrow and am truly sorry. I do not blame William for feeling as he does. Hopefully time will heal this whole unpleasant episode in our lives, and we can move on as one. I love you."

We kissed.

The diamond solitaire ring slipped easily onto her finger. "I shall formally ask William for your hand in marriage. We shall be wed as soon as I have found better accommodation more suiting a woman of your standing and beauty and a man of my good virtue and fortune!" The tears of sadness gave way to tears of joy.

William suddenly appeared at the open French window. "What's all the commotion here? Is there something I should be aware of?"

"Please join us, brother," Sophia uttered whilst drying her eyes with her handkerchief.

William, as we had planned, carried the silk-bowed box that he was keeping for me under his arm.

"Thank you, William. A little something for you, Sophia!" She untied the bow and opened the box. At first, she couldn't quite make the iron contraption out. A cogged wheel and levers connected small riveted vertical plates with small hoppers either side. When the wooden handle at one end was turned the plates moved up and down, making the piece come to life.

Sophia looked at me quizzically.

"My dear, our card shuffling days are over!" I laughed as I produced a pack of cards from my coat pocket and placed them in one of the side hoppers. As I turned the handle, the cards made a whisking sound and the machine turned them this way and that until neatly dispensing them in the hopper on the other side, ready for dealing.

"Quite ingenious!" Sophia joined with my laughter.

At that moment, other members of the Kingdom family appeared in the garden; Sophia's other brothers and sisters with her mother and close friends. We both stood up and acknowledged their presence on this proud day. The celebrations had begun.

CHAPTER TWELVE

The King's Bench Prison, Southwark
May 1821

"FROM MY POSITION, this specification for your improvements on the marine steam engine will be a challenge to manufacture and will take time, but it is entirely possible, perhaps with a little modification along the way."

Henry Maudslay carefully examined my drawings. He was as bright and positive as ever. I was very pleased that he had visited me here in gaol. It was like being with an old friend—which he was, of course—as well as with a professional man who had proven over the years his ability to move my designs off the drawing board and transform them into beautiful machines.

He knew what to expect, finding me here in these dire surroundings. Apart from the introductory quip about my choice of hotel (and a handkerchief to the nose when the occasional waft of stale air passed through our modest domicile), he remained undeterred. In fact, his presence gave us both quite a lift; not only because we were partners in a new project but because he brought life from beyond these walls of containment.

"Yes. I have made provision to recycle the fresh water used specifically for generating the steam by use of a condenser. The volume of fresh water in the boilers, as you can see, will therefore remain the same."

"Excellent, Marc. I am pleased to progress this to fabrication, when all is ready."

Ironically, had it not been for my French connections, I might never have made the acquaintance of this trustworthy and knowledgeable man. More than can be said of his rival, Mr Walter Taylor.

* * *

Bedford Street, London
October 1800

Time had passed so quickly. Our wedding on a cold and bright November day at St Andrew in Holborn had been the crown- ing glory of my life. I felt fulfilled and blissful the moment we said our vows, and the gold token of our love and commitment to a life together glided so easily onto Sophia's finger. A petite, bijou apartment in south London suited our immediate needs, but soon after our moving in we discovered, to our great joy, that Sophia was with child. I sensed that we would soon be rapidly outgrowing our home. In addition, I found that my many professional projects were also taking up a great deal of room in my office. Life was indeed moving forward apace, I mused.

I slid my set square to one side on the drawing board, revealing the full extent of my work. The top of my mahogany plan chest was a mass of engineering plans, sections and details, some of which I had brought from America, but most as a result of spilling out my developed thoughts and ideas for the new manufacturing process. The notion that an automated method could be devised to increase production as well as providing a more accurate and better-machined block was a compelling one. This was my aim. The working model that would be produced from these drawings would sell the case effectively and simply.

My fellow émigré here in London, de Bacquancourt, introduced me to a gentleman by the name of Maudslay some months ago. Maudslay was a likeable man of immense capability, having been apprenticed to the outstanding craftsman Joseph Bramah, and our partnership and understanding had grown through mutual respect and trust. His apprenticeship, practical background and enthusiasm dovetailed well with my analytical and thorough engineering approach. We shared the same goals and passions. I must also say that we made very good drinking partners!

Spending time with Maudslay at his works gave me the unique opportunity to slowly and methodically make subtle suggestions for potential changes to his manufacturing process and machinery which I would then reflect back into my designs—it was in effect the complete reverse of an engineering evolution, but I was driven on by the feeling that I was always at least one step ahead of what was happening in front of me. Most of the machinery on display in Maudslay's workshop would inevitably make its way to Taylor's Works in Southampton, but two 'model' machines had pride of place in a side workshop area for modification as my design developed and the assembly and testing took place in parallel.

I reached down and rubbed the base of my back. My high perch was not the most comfortable arrangement, and continually leaning forward to apply pen to paper in fine detail produced a dull ache.

I was also still somewhat fatigued from the long coach journey back from Belper, Derby, where I had had the pleasure of being shown around Messrs Strutt & Co works amidst the numerous workers hard at their tasks at their looms. I observed they had adopted my contrivance for winding cotton into balls where there were about twenty spindles on one swing.

Whilst I was pleased that my invention had quickly been met with wholesale adoption by the factories in this country, I had neglected to secure the benefits of this invention by patent; such was the triviality with which I had viewed its inception and application.

But I had much bigger matters on my mind. The wife of the owner had praised me and the new efficiencies of the process and jokingly suggested that I ought to invent a means of relieving ladies from the wearisome employment of hemming and stitching.

I had, in fact, been working on such a contraption while in America, and the patent for this device had already been secured through my background work. When I informed her, she was quite surprised and immediately set about researching the device through contacts in the textile industry, particularly in Ireland, where I knew that it was employed hemming cambric handkerchiefs and stitching linen drawers, shirts and jackets.

Returning my mind to the present, I considered my current predicament as I gazed through the open window overlooking the chequered gardens and allotments below. These rooms in Bedford Street were not particularly spacious but were sufficient for my work and for Sophia to go about her household business as she began to settle down and relax. She had her brother and his family members nearby and was always fully supportive of me and my tendency to spend most of my waking hours working at my desk and drawing board.

I was now making haste with detailed engineering drawings of the machines I was designing for the mass production of ships' pulley blocks. Henry Maudslay's fabrication workshops in Wells Street were just a ten-minute walk away; one of the main factors in our moving here from Canterbury Place, Lambeth.

I caught the sweet scent of rose next to me.

"Marc. I am sorry to interrupt you, but you are meeting Mr Maudslay and Mr Bentham in Wells Street in half an hour."

"Yes, my love. I had not forgotten."

She looked longingly into my eyes and laid her hand on mine. "I still find your French accent very appealing."

I laughed and kissed her on the cheek.

"Remind me about these blocks, and why they are so important to the Navy."

I was happy to expand on things as Sophia always took an active interest in my work.

"You have, no doubt, observed them at various positions in the rigging of a sailing ship. A slotted sheave is enclosed in a cheek or shell and is fixed to the end of a rope line, to a spar or to a surface. The blocks perform the function of either simply changing the direction of a line or forming a tackle where there is a proportional increase in mechanical advantage if one end is attached to a load rather than the fixed end of a tackle—in other words, it makes it easier to haul up a load by hand."

Sophia prevented me from saying any more with a hand on my wrist.

"Thank you, Marc. Yes, I can now imagine it, and I can also see that your enthusiasm for this project is undaunted!"

"I consider it important that engineers have the ability to explain things in simple terms to the general public."

She mockingly slapped the back of my hand, and we both laughed again.

Sophia was blooming. I had never seen her look so well and vibrant. Her eyes were clear and meaningful as they gazed deep into mine. I caressed her passionately, whilst being careful of the pronounced bump in her midriff. I remained overjoyed at the prospect of our first child. She was my wife, dear friend, confidant and lover, and would endure until the end of time. We kissed.

I collected a selection of my drawings and notes and made for the office door and landing.

* * *

The word 'workshop' did little justice to Maudslay's empire. His rise, in just a few years, from mere apprentice to master of the expansive fabrication metropolis that lay before me was testimony not only to his ability as a mechanical technician of extreme talent, but also to his achievements as a businessman and major contributor to the manufacturing hub of this country. England should be proud. There was no doubt that this man and his facility would prove the worth of the new block-making process that I had been working on for so long.

"Good morning, Henry." I shook his grime-engrained hand firmly.

"Marc. Good to see you again after all this time."

"Ha. Yes, it must have been all of a week since we last met!"

Henry Maudslay was a man with a receding hairline and a stare which invited inquisition; not unlike my own. An impressive forehead was a distinguishing feature of the Brunels, so I felt a comfortable kinship when in his presence.

Maudslay readjusted the high collar on his waistcoat and hitched up his generously cut breeches (he had a habit of doing this before moving off from a standing position) and harkened me through the main factory building to his office at the rear.

The brick and iron-trussed building was adorned with clanking pulleys and flywheels that, through a system of chains and leathered belts, fed the power from the solitary large steam engine housed in the engine house nearby. Smaller gantries and cranage raised the heavier iron-machined components for transfer to the next assemblage area, and cylindrical containers with pipes and valves whispered and whistled the oil lubricants and water supply to cool the hot machines.

Flatbed carts and portable trestles decked the workshop floor; some being pulled by young boys to transport finished components, others stationary, awaiting stock. The recent remnants of the days when all power was provided by horse were evident, with spent bridles and now redundant rope tethers hung from walls, and shallow troughs ran the length of the brick tiled floor to convenient gulleys.

We walked side-by-side, step-by-step along the corridors between the lathes, mechanical presses and numerous other individual machines which clacked and hissed their welcome as I passed. The operators barely had time to lift their eyes from the job in hand, as they carried out their work with diligence and precision. A fully working factory, with a familiar smell of hot oil, grease and sweat, buoyed my mood. I felt both excited and a little apprehensive on finally meeting the individual who ultimately would be instrumental in the success of my project.

"Sir Samuel Bentham, may I present to you Mr Marc Brunel."

The man standing before me ran his hand through his mop of greying hair, widening his gaze with high, mobile eyebrows. He took a stiff military stance as he thrust his hand forward to initiate a positive but brief contact with mine. I had heard through my peers that this was a man of high integrity and standing, rising to his current position of Inspector General of the British Navy by working his way up from an apprenticeship to a master shipwright in Woolwich at the age of fourteen. He had become a bastion against the corruption and maladministration in the Navy that had threatened the very core of the service (and ultimately the lives of British seamen), where the system of awarding lucrative contracts was blighted by bribery, thus producing substandard and often dangerous products. Here was a man of strong mind and character who was not necessarily credited openly for his efforts as they exposed the Admiralty to some startling truths.

His presence here was testament to the importance of the pulley block machine to the Navy. More importantly, it acknowledged the achievements of both Maudslay and me in designing and fabricating the machine which made possible the improved and more efficient process of manufacture.

"I am very pleased to meet you, sir."

He looked me up and down. "I have already heard a lot about you, Mr Brunel. Your naval background and successes abroad in engineering, both mechanical and civil, and the invention of many instruments, devices and machines, do you proud and articulate a great deal about you. It is good to meet you face-to-face. As a French émigré you must find it difficult sometimes to reconcile the differences between the cultures of our nations and the fact we are now at war with Napoleonic France; but then again without the latter, ironically, I would not be in attendance here today to view your machine at first hand."

"Yes. It is difficult for me sometimes, sir, but broadly speaking I have found people have been more welcoming than not, and in many instances have warmed to me and I to them." I looked at Maudslay, who nodded and smiled lightly in acknowledgement of our particular friendship and partnership. "Thank you for coming here today."

Bentham smiled. "Not at all. I have heard many good reports concerning this machinery you have created between you, and the fact that you have formed a worthy alliance."

He picked up from Maudslay's desk a newspaper and waved it in the air before opening it at a pre-marked page, "*The Times* has quoted you as 'laying the foundations of most extensive engineering establishments in the kingdom, and in which, perhaps, a degree of science and skill has been combined and applied to mechanical invention and improvement scarcely exceeded by any other in the world'." He paused to fold the paper and place it back on the desk. "Grand praise indeed! Although how this newspaper can be confident of your excellence on a global scale I am not assured."

We all laughed.

"But then again, that is precisely why I am here. There is now considerable pressure on the number of pulley blocks required by the navy at this time. Every British man-of-war is fitted with approximately fourteen hundred blocks, excluding reserves in case of damage or replacement, and our Navy needs to ensure consistency of supply. This is something we cannot be assured about, given that only three establishments in Britain have the appropriate facilities to manufacture such blocks. Taylors of Southampton have the main contract, as you well know, Mr Maudslay, as you are supplying the machines from here for them."

Maudslay nodded.

"As you probably know, I have already conceived a system of machinery for making blocks myself, and in point of fact have recently installed a twelve-horsepower steam engine to drive the necessary woodworking machinery at Portsmouth Dockyard. But it is with curiosity and intrigue that I would now like to see this machine, and make up my own mind as to its potential and capability of performing mass production."

"Then let us go and view this machine in operational mode." Maudslay offered.

In a corner of the noisy workshop stood the working model of the morticing and boring machine which would make the lignum vitae hard timber oval shell and circular sheave components that made up the completed block. Maudslay fired it into life, with the assistance of the machine's attendant worker.

"We have applied a slide rest instrument to a turning lathe such that the direction and the motion of the cutting tool can be controlled with great accuracy, resulting in absolute and consistent precision, ease and rapidity," I said, as the components began to be produced steadily and accurately, sliding out of the side metal shelf at the other end of the contraption.

Bentham picked one up and examined it. "You say you've applied for a patent for this already, Brunel?"

"Yes, sir."

"Well, the next step will be for you to recommend this to Earl Spencer, the Navy minister, with my approval. I shall also make an admission to the Lords of the Admiralty in order to facilitate full trials."

"Thank you, sir. We are most pleased."

Although I did not mention this to Bentham myself, I considered that I was obliged to also contact Taylor's in Southampton to offer them my new machine, as they already had an established business in this field and may want to avail themselves of my ideas in order to improve their production methods. I would speak with my brother-in-law who was now Under Secretary to the Navy Board, as no doubt through his connections with the Admiralty he would already be in contact with the company. An approach directly from me would risk being ignored, as Mr Taylor may consider my introduction to be solely on commercial lines.

CHAPTER THIRTEEN

Woodmill Works
Southampton
5th March 1801

Dear Kingdom

I am favoured with your letter of the 2nd inst, and I should have replied yesterday but I had not time.

Your brother has certainly given proof of great ingenuity, but he is not acquainted with our mode of work. What he saw at Deptford is not as we work here. I will just describe in a few words how we have made our blocks for upwards of twenty years—twenty-five years to my knowledge.

The tree of timber, from two to five loads measurement, is drawn by the machine under the saw, where it is cut to its proper length. It is then removed to a round saw where the piece cut off is completely shaped, and only requiring to be turned under the saw. The one, two, three or four mortises are cut in by hand, which wholly completes the block, except with a broad chisel cutting out the roughness of the teeth of the saw, and the scores of the strapping of the rope.

Every block we make (except more than four machines can make) is done in this way, and with great truth and exactness. The shivers are wholly done by the engines, very little labour is employed about our works, save for the removing the things from one place to another. My father has spent many hundreds of guineas a year to achieve the best and most accurate mode, of making the blocks, and he certainly succeeded; and so much so, that I have no expectation of anything better ever being discovered, and I am convinced that will never happen.

At the present time, were we ever so inclined, we could not attempt any alteration.

We are, as you know, so much pressed, and especially as the machine your brother-in-law has invented is as yet untried. As you well understand, inventions of this kind are always much different in a model than in actual working practice.

Trust me in this, my dear Kingdom.

Yours in great truth

Samuel Taylor

* * *

I pushed the letter away across my desk in disgust. This was a great disappointment. There would need to be a change in plans that would affect both me and my family.

I heard the cry of our young child's innocent voice from a distant room and smiled. All was well with my world. The leather seat squeaked as I rose and made for the drawing room where my wife held little Sophie.

"Ah, Marc."

I took our young, beautiful and frail child in my arms. Her skin smelt so clean and new, just as three-month-old babies do. My joy was unbounded.

"Have you finished today for lunch?"

"Er yes, yes." I looked away.

"I see there is something on your mind, my darling. Would you like to share it with me?"

Sophia juggled with the attentions of our dearest little one as I began to offer an explanation of my mood. I handed her the letter. She unfolded it and began to read.

"Young Mr Taylor is a very impudent and silly man with little foresight to improve his process. He is carried solely by tradition and a blinkered overconfidence; 'qualities', if one were to label them as such, also exhibited by his father."

"Oh, how do you know his father?"

Sophia looked a little embarrassed and shy, before confessing: "When you were away in America, he propositioned me."

I was quite shocked. It would have been strange if a beautiful, intelligent and well-connected woman such as Sophia would not have had any suitors since her return to England, but I was nonetheless taken aback.

Sophia continued. "Obviously I turned him down immediately." She gazed into my eyes. "You are the only constant in my life, Marc. I spent long days waiting for your return. You know that I would never have seriously considered any other man's hand in marriage in favour of yours, Marc, my darling."

I collected myself. "Yes. I have always been assured that that was the case, but this is a little disconcerting to hear, particularly at this time."

Sophia kissed me. "He is a very impudent man and not fit to clean your shoes. If he does not want to improve his process and embrace the assistance of one of the most cultured, endearing, engaging, dashing and capable engineers of this century, then that is his loss."

I laughed, and my heart soared at her words. Modesty notwithstanding, I was starting to feel that, through my connections and early successes particularly in America, I was increasingly becoming accepted as intimate of the landed ruling class in this country. Sir Samuel Bentham was fast becoming a friend and confidant and had introduced me to eminent and influential men of science, including Messrs Babbage and Faraday.

I was naturally very happy that Sophia was so gushing with praise and support for me. However, in anticipation of the approval of my machine by the Lords Commissioners of the Admiralty, we would almost certainly have to uproot to Portsmouth, in order that I would be able to fulfil my vision and set up my own works with Maudslay's help. I just hoped that she would accept that. I imagined that she would, but I wasn't going to take anything for granted, particularly when it came down to her well-being and that of our future family and lives together.

I would aim to supplant Walter Taylor in two ways now!

CHAPTER FOURTEEN

The King's Bench Prison, Southwark
May 1821

I WOKE UP with a start. My pillow was damp with sweat, and as I came around in the semi-darkness I became aware that the shouting I had heard in my dreams had actually been cries from Sophia in her sleep. My disturbed night had made it difficult to separate the sounds of my dreams with the stark reality of our dank and cold confinement.

I turned back the covers and lit the candle on the side table. Sophia was sitting upright on the edge of the opposite side of the bed whimpering. I rested my hand on her shoulder. "My darling! What is it?"

She remained facing away from me but reached back to hold my fingers. "All is well, my love. I have just had a terrible dream."

"Oh, my dearest. Let me console you," I seated myself next to her, putting my arm around her and bringing her close. Beads of perspiration sat on her forehead and ran down her reddened cheeks. We sat for a few minutes, the silence of the night punctuated with the pre-dawn bird chirrup and the clop of hooves and clatter of a cart from a distant street.

"You seem to have had more than one of these disturbed nights now, Sophia. What is troubling you so? I want to help you, but I must first understand what is causing you this distress. It upsets me deeply to see you this way."

She at last turned to face me. Her lightly swollen pink eyelids and deep frown told their own story. This was something serious and concerning to me, as her wellbeing was foremost in my mind. Thus it always was and always will be. Her transitory poor disposition and sad mien did nothing to dispel my deep love and affection for her; in fact, it fuelled my adoration. My eyes filled.

"Thank you, my darling. I know you have my best interests at heart, but this is very difficult for me."

"Yes, I can understand, but please confide your anxieties to me so that I may help in any way I can."

She looked away momentarily and then returned my gaze.

"It cannot be easy for you in these circumstances and surroundings," I suggested. "For your own sanity I would gladly see you return home and merely visit me here."

She placed a finger to my lips and dabbed her forehead with her handkerchief.

"No, no, I will not leave you. That is out of the question. You are going through very difficult and unpleasant times, which I am confident will end soon. I am here to bear your grief in any way I can." The fire burnt in Sophia's eyes. "I know, too, that your professional calling is inherent to your character. I also acknowledge that you are a caring and dutiful husband and father and that you are building the foundations of our personal lives which will give us the security of income so much needed for our family. Of that, I am sure."

She gently touched my cheek with the back of her hand. I was cheered by her words.

"You know you have my full support in all that you do. Despite my bias as your wife, I recognise the commitment and hard work that you put in each day that passes in order to have the best chance of success in your projects and inventions. And that we will all benefit from everything you do."

I smiled, but recognised her distress and fear.

"Then what can it be, Sophia?" We embraced again and this time she held me tightly for a few moments before softly whispering in my ear. "My problems have their roots in my time in France."

I gulped. My mouth became very dry. I eased myself out of her arms and leaned back, holding her hands tightly, listening intently to her every word.

"I'm afraid things went very badly for me for a time before I eventually returned to England from France. It is still frequently in my thoughts, which is only natural, perhaps. I have attempted to put the whole difficult episode behind me, which I thought I had succeeded in doing, but it seems I have unfortunately regressed."

"Would it be better for you if you told me more? Perhaps laying your soul bare to me may help you, which is what I would dearly like you to do, but not if it is going to make matters worse."

Sophia paused and looked downward to collect her thoughts.

"From the time you left and I was at the Carpentier's house in Rouen, the situation was precarious. The visit from the mob of revolutionaries was the start of the shackling of the educated and professional classes in France. The English were treated as spies and afforded no respect or standing in the new society. François and his family did their best to shield and protect me, but eventually, much to their horror, I was forcefully removed from their house and from a family that had been so kind and generous to me. It was very distressing. I wrote to you briefly about this, Marc, when I was finally set free from the long days of solitude and dread."

"Oh, my dear, I never received that letter, but François did tell me in one of his numerous missives that you were temporarily inconvenienced—no more—at that time. I can only think that either your letter was lost or that he did not wish to concern me with bad news or the depredations of your experiences when I was in America and powerless to do anything."

Backlit by candlelight and in a darkened, claustrophobic room, Sophia's solemn profile took on a new aspect: one I had not witnessed before, but which melted my heart and quickened my pulse in empathy and expectation. I was again about to tread the well-beaten path of guilt and soul-searching where the thorns of culpability and bracken of remorse would scratch and puncture my skin. This was as much a fight to make peace with myself as it was to understand my lover and life partner's grief. The deep guilt I felt on leaving Sophia behind on that fateful day over twenty-six years ago was carved into my very being. The regret lives on to this day and will stay with me until the end of my life.

The tears welled in her eyes (and mine), but she continued undaunted.

"I and others in similar predicaments were taken by open cart on a long and rough journey to a convent in Gravelines on the Normandy coast. When we arrived, we were offered as much comfort and reassurance as was possible by the resident nuns, but this was no longer a convent; more like a prison with peasant guards and other brutes in attendance everywhere you looked. We had little privacy in our daily lives. Any tokens of royalty and nobility in the convent had been defaced or damaged. Sacred vessels, vestments and ornaments had been removed and the church and sacristy were closed off.

"The new occupiers showed little respect for religion or belief. All 'prisoners' were continually harassed and ill-treated by visitors and minor officials of 'The Committee' who continued their oppression through threats and violence—particularly to the male prisoners who were often shackled. In winter, the only fuel available was from the cutting up of furniture and wainscoting."

I went to interject, but Sophia prevented me from saying anything by gripping my wrists even more firmly and looking at me intently, silently pleading that she should be allowed to finish; to suffer this ordeal of telling.

"We had very little to eat—only water and coarse black bread most of the time. François arranged for a servant to deliver, at great risk to himself, some milk and cheese through a small, barred window at a set time on certain days. I only heard afterwards when I was released that François himself was imprisoned for a while for harbouring a 'spy', and that the charges were dropped only after he had served some weeks behind bars."

"Yes. François did tell me about that in one of his letters to me."

The anguish inside me was tearing me apart. I was full of a combination of anger and desolation. And guilt, guilt, guilt. The bastards!

"But the worst of it—the very worst of it—was that every day I woke up from my hard straw and timber board bed, not knowing when this torment was going to end, and looked out onto the inner garden square to see the guillotine lying idly but threateningly in one corner. On three occasions, I was threatened that I would be next."

And at that she burst into floods of tears. I held her tight as we overbalanced and tumbled back onto the bed and first folded and then melted into each other's bodies, Sophia weeping uncontrollably, my tears flowing too: together in a union of love and empathy.

CHAPTER FIFTEEN

The Boar's Head, Southwark
May 1821

THE CRUMBS OF bread were swept off the arm of his woollen tweed tailcoat as he dabbed his mouth with his embroidered silk handkerchief, savouring the last mouthful. He ate well; his full stomach bore testament to that, lying, as it did, uncomfortably over the waistline of his pantaloons.

William Jones Esquire nodded in the direction of the bar; he knew the staff and landlord well, as he often imbibed here, and they too knew his tipple. Within moments, a replenished tankard of brown ale slid onto the table in front of him. The Boar's Head was a good place to meet his fellow prison wardens and staff who also liked a drink or two; being a public house in the immediate locality of the gaol that served both public and his penal institution well. As he gazed around the busy saloon, he recognised familiar faces in the throng—inmates who were granted temporary day leave on the payment of a small bond or security through the turnkeys as wardens of the prison.

He reached deep into his pockets in search of the necessary coinage to pay his due and thought of the welcome extra income from his cut of the levy imposed on the local hostelries and retailers who supplied his prison. His prison. His empire.

Earlier in the day Jones had taken a rare saunter through the prison grounds, exchanging pleasantries with his officers—deputy marshal, clerks and assistant clerks, turnkeys and watchmen alike—who also represented the many other sources of 'unofficial' revenue that Jones, and a few 'manipulators', enjoyed. He strutted around the building like a prize cockerel, safe in the knowledge that he had become a man of wealth and means.

Passing through the main gate, he momentarily broke step and gazed up at the coat of arms decorating the iron grillage. He was proud to have been appointed by the king himself to perform his duties as Marshal of the King's Bench Prison 'for so long a time as he shall behave himself well, and shall be resident within the walls or rules of the prison, and no longer'. Jones smiled to himself; he had 'behaved' himself well for nearly twenty years now.

He retained an air of confidence as he thumbed through the pages of the latest prison financial records in the isolation and security of his private office. The cost of salaries, the bills for the upkeep of the building and surrounds, taxes and law fees were all neatly accounted for and in good order; as were the inputs on the opposite margin of the balance sheet—amounting to fees for the rent of prison rooms and the coffee house, profits on the sale of porter, ale and wine and, toward the rear of another leather-bound file, the carbon copies of the 'chum tickets'—a ticket and signed receipts for the prison admission fee of 10s 2d received at the prison gate at time of arrival. He counted over 400 inmates on the prison registry spread in front of him; arrested for debt and confined to 200 rooms, distributed as he saw fit within his own doubtful, susceptible but legitimised moral compass.

"And how is our new inmate getting along?" he enquired of the equally portly, red-faced man who sat opposite him in the public house.

Thomas Brooshooft, the first clerk to the marshal, shuffled uneasily in his seat, chewing the grizzled beef that refused to dissolve in his dribbling mouth. "He has settled in well for a man of his obvious opulent background and education. I expect he is finding it difficult to swallow his medicine," he spat through his food.

"His detectable French accent is a little unsettling at first, but given the recent history between our countries I find his incarceration is, well, not exactly a form of compensation on behalf of the misdemeanours of his homeland, but may I say that it gives me a little more comfort in the realisation," Brooshooft sneered.

Jones sniffed away the sentiment like swatting a fly. He was not necessarily interested in the culture and background of the Frenchman, or indeed Brooshooft's prejudices, more his ability to pay.

"And is there likely to be any licence for us to take our share of any chummage or associated dues that might arise through him declining to share his room with a poorer inmate?"

Jones was interested now.

"Not in this case I am afraid, sir. He is of decent appearance and disposition together with the air of good circumstances, therefore disposed to having a separate room on the upper floor levels."

Jones snorted.

"I believe, too, that he occupies high station amongst the elite class, being an engineer and inventor of some repute. Indeed, I have it on authority that this is a man well respected in society, holding, amongst other titles, a Fellowship of the Royal Society here in Greenwich." Brooshooft continued, "He has even brought a large two-drawer table, a chair and a trestle bed to furnish his room, and his wife insists on being attendant to him for as long as he is incarcerated."

"Well, we must treat this 'gentleman' with the respect he deserves," Jones offered, with a touch of irony whilst leaning forward for emphasis.

Mr Brooshooft was Jones' private clerk and acted as keeper of the prison, directing and managing everything on Jones' behalf, despite the fact that he had no legal appointment and consequently was vested with no authority. Jones paid him well and gave sanction to many more means of his income not necessarily declared to the authorities. Besides, the marshal had interests elsewhere and better things to do with his time. He would visit the gaol only when necessary, just to oversee its running and intervene if he felt certain controls and methods were not being adhered to. This week, for instance, would probably be a good time to inspect.

"Tell me, has Lushington, in his capacity as Master of the Crown Office, made arrangements for a revisit since his last report? I feel it may be imminent."

"Not that I am aware, no, sir."

"Well, let it be your business to be more than aware. I expect the deputy marshal Boydell will assist him under the direct rules and orders of the Court. We don't want certain misgivings in our management techniques or shortcomings in our practices to be laid bare as they were last time. Mr Justice Dampier will be most displeased otherwise, and his displeasure may result in certain redundancies, official or otherwise, amongst the current prison staff, if you understand what I mean."

Brooshooft understood.

CHAPTER SIXTEEN

The King's Bench Prison, Southwark
May 1821

I WAS AT my desk again. But this time I had deferred my projects and plans to dedicate some time to writing to one of the many engineers and men of influence that I had had the pleasure of making the acquaintance of since my time in England. He would surely know, if he hadn't heard already, that I was being held at His Majesty's pleasure unreasonably and illegitimately in starkly unhealthy conditions. When would this distress and embarrassment end? My wife and I were going through such difficult times I was determined to do as much as I could to gain my release.

Samuel Bentham had the professional integrity and personal conscience to resign from his position of Inspector General of Naval Works under the tide of corruption seeping through the Navy Board at that time; not before influencing and approving my work in the mass production facility at Portsmouth...

* * *

Portsmouth Docks
November 1802

I was proud to be sitting at my bureau catching sight of the numerous dry docks that dominated the quay line and estuary with abundant ships of the line at temporary berth, their new copper-bottomed keels glistening in the sun. Everywhere was bristling with activity: tradesmen and dock labour interspersed with the clatter of transportation, banging of hammer and sizzling of saw. Chargehands and gangers were much in evidence, both as security and as supervision to the workforce. It was strange to consider that this relatively small but important harbour town sprang into life and was at its busiest in times of conflict and national restlessness.

Sophia and I, with the assistance of my confidant Mr Bentham, had managed to obtain an unassuming, two-storey dwelling in Britain Street, Portsea; not exactly a picturesque area of town but adequate and safe, I considered, and just a short walk from the dockyard. My morning journey on foot unfortunately could not avoid the narrow streets of a downtrodden district that housed small shops and tenements. I had to watch my step for fear of treading in the excrement that had been thrown indiscriminately on the cobbled thoroughfares. In wet weather, this dreadful mess was driven into the few drain gulleys present, or dispersed by passing horse-drawn traffic, all of which contributed to the chaos and stench. I was informed that in warm weather the windswept dust clouds from horse and human detritus made one's eyes water and one's throat burn.

Today was my first working day at my offices in this exciting and busy port. This would prove, I trusted, a memorable occasion marking the first day of my public service career here in England on a project of great importance to the Navy and, ironically, against my motherland.

France was no longer the country I had known. She was now in the hands of a Napoleon Bonaparte—a military tyrant who had returned from campaign failure in Egypt to a hero's welcome and dared to declare himself 'First Consul of France'. I had it on reliable sources from my friend and fellow émigré de Bacquancourt that the New Republic was effectively bankrupt and The Directory ineffective and unpopular. *Quelle surprise!* There was an uneasy peace between France and Britain through the *Treaty of Amiens,* with neither side really trusting the other, so the work of block-making and the larger industry of shipbuilding continued unabated. These were nervous times.

I was pleased to be here in Portsmouth to progress the block-making invention and finally see the fruits of my labour take form in the mass production of the timber components. However, my pleasure was countered by my wariness and agitation; not only because I was aware of the raised crime levels here, but also because I was blighted by my French accent.

There remained great suspicion of me amongst some of the ruling classes. I frequently noticed the sideways glances and nods from perfect strangers and an air of misgiving amongst even my own modest workforce of six labourers and two carpenters. I was not allowed to enter the dockyards without an official permit. I found this very disconcerting, but understandable perhaps. I could only place all these minor obstacles to one side and trust in my confidence and divine providence that matters would improve in time, perhaps when I was more openly accepted by English society.

Although I acknowledged, too, that this was unlikely to be realised until France and England ceased hostilities, which I did not think would come about very soon. Bizarrely, I had to dig deeply to find the Frenchman in me at times, although I had a rude awakening every time I reached into my waistcoat pocket and fingered the special permit which I was instructed to carry about my person ready for inspection at any time. Fortunately, I was buoyed by the fact that I had married into a well-respected English family, and associated with professional and meaningful members of English society, many of whom had become my friends and fellow collaborators.

My chair slid back easily on the stone-slabbed floor as I stood and stretched my aching body before making my way across the drawing-strewn room. My heavy timber office door provided an effective barrier to the noise and bustle of the machine floor, which was suddenly exposed to my senses as I entered the workshop beyond.

The recently replaced thirty-horsepower steam engine chugged and stuttered like a racehorse driving the overhead shafts, and spoked wrought-iron wheels fed the machines with power. Vast plumes of smoke ballooned into the air as the engine hissed and spitted its piston-thumping cycle.

I approached William Connelly and Thomas Smith, who were crouched over the first machine. Smith, I had personally trained to operate the machinery, Connelly to assist and attend to the machines' mechanisms and smooth running.

"Good day, Mr Brunel," they uttered almost in unison.

They were good men, reliable and steadfast, well paid for their services, but I always expected more. That was my nature. I had taken it upon myself to train and supervise the eight men employed by the works, and they were now producing the timber sheaves and shells as 'unskilled' labour at around ten times the rate of Taylor's 'skilled' men.

I had been successful in securing an initial reward for my endeavours so far, through Bentham, of a sum equivalent to the savings from one year's full-scale operation here, and an expense allowance of one guinea a day for being engaged on His Majesty's service. I also enjoyed a travelling allowance of ten shillings a day, and my coach expenses paid in full. Not a bad start, but this remuneration did not reflect the efforts and time I have spent during the intense design, experiment and developmental period of the past three years. I had written to the Lords of the Admiralty to this effect but had yet to receive any formal reply, despite the fact that Bentham had intervened on my behalf. I was assured that a positive response would be forthcoming.

I hoped very soon, for further installations of machinery to expand my manufacturing base rapidly and meet the Navy's targets for production, but it had become increasingly evident that labour resources were difficult to obtain. I particularly needed specialist skilled workers for the installation of any future machinery: these men were in even shorter supply. I would have to write to the Navy Board for assistance in this regard. I was sure they would be helpful, as it was in their interests that this production process ran to the optimum level of efficiency, and I was in no doubt that the flimsy peace treaty with France would not last and that the demands for more blocks would reach ever-higher levels.

CHAPTER SEVENTEEN

The King's Bench Prison, Southwark
May 1821

THERE WAS A strong and purposeful knock on our cell door. It was mid-afternoon and we were not expecting visitors. Sophia and I glanced at each other momentarily before I opened the door. "Mr Brunel, I believe."

I nodded. The stout, piggy-eyed man on the threshold seemed familiar. His intrusion was not exactly improved by a waft of pungent air emanating from his person.

"We have not met before. May I introduce myself? I am James Winstanley, the turnkey and watchman for this sector of the Establishment."

"Oh, yes?"

"Yes. Mr Brooshooft, clerk to the prison marshal and acting keeper, requested I make your acquaintance. Now, being an observant man, I note that you have been residing in this room for some days now."

I stood blank-faced.

"Now, I would like to help you, sir."

I was immediately intensely suspicious.

"Are you aware that, for a small 'negotiated' sum, I am able to grant you, officially of course, temporary freedom from the confinement of these walls? Within a certain jurisdiction, as you would expect, either as a Day Case or longer at your discretion, sir. But you would need to return here by six o'clock each day."

I was quite taken aback by his effrontery.

"Does, Mr Jones the prison marshal know you are here?" I enquired.

"Oh yes, of course, sir. It is with his blessings too that I have come here. He sends his regards to you and your wife."

I stared indignantly at this objectionable creature, before responding.

"Then you may tell him that I have no intention of moving from this penitentiary. I am here as a consequence of the British justice system. Although I consider I have been harshly treated, I am currently seeking early release by legitimate means, not that this is any business of yours, Mr Winstanley."

The man returned my stare with a smug smile.

"Please tell the marshal that I seek no assistance from him or his fellow officers in making my stay more 'comfortable', and certainly not from additional payments, whether legitimate or not."

It was then that I realised who this man resembled so closely. He even had the same Christian name…

* * *

En Route to Portsmouth from London
Summer 1804

James Burr jostled and shifted in his seat. He hated cramped conditions and even more so when he was sandwiched between sweaty bodies in a crowded and stifling carriage.

He was not a journeyman and despised being sent down to Portsmouth by the Admiralty to carry out duties that were not to his liking. The carriage had already stopped three times en route from London—Guildford, Godalming and Liphook—for refreshments and fresh air as a welcome break from the claustrophobic cab confines. One of these stops was away from the security of a coaching inn or gatehouse, which he did not think wise, even if his burly figure and confident air were enough to discourage any opportunistic thief or beggar that might be unwise enough to cross him.

In these times of conflict, the economy was bound to suffer, but the docks, and in particular Portsmouth, were enjoying a boom as war gave employment to many, albeit with an absence of long-term security. Ironically, if the country did eventually descend into peace, workers and managers alike in dockyards all over the country would be out of work and on the street. But these times also meant great expense to the Navy Board, hence Burr having to travel with the regular coach loaded with heavy coinage and accompanied by a company of dragoons, all to pay the dock workers their due.

The route was known to be frequented by highwaymen, and Burr was pleased that they had just passed the most dangerous point—the six-mile climb between Godalming and the Devil's Punchbowl—where the carriage was forced to slow down to walking pace.

He did his best to stretch his legs, by carefully placing both shins either side of the elderly bearded gentleman opposite, but only succeeded in accidentally kicking him on the ankle, provoking an annoyed look. He raised his thickened hand in acknowledgement and mouthed an apology, as to attempt to speak over the din of creaks, rattles and horse hooves was difficult. Anyway, he reasoned that the man was probably one of the overpaid members of the government treasury, a bank representative or an executive of the Board, and he had no time for any of them, particularly the ones in power.

Trying to relieve his battered buttocks and aching back, Burr leaned forward and peered through the moisture-covered glass of the carriage door. Fresh gibbets had been erected at the side of the road and supported the dangling corpses of convicted highwaymen as a warning to others of the penalty for robbery. Burr shrugged his shoulders and smirked at the visions; it would take more than that to dispel desperate and starving families at the expense of the upper classes.

Besides, he knew that there were better ways of gaining money illicitly, and his position as port manager gave him every opportunity and licence to do so. *'A position of privilege offers privileges not always accepted as salary but in the form of "payments in kind",'* he thought to himself. And when the higher echelons of the British Navy also willingly accepted that such misdemeanours were nothing but a way of life, there was an acceptability—a legitimacy even—that bribery and corruption were inherent in the national system to promote the official running of the country, Burr mused with a lop-sided smile.

Bentham would not last, he knew—he was too honest. A good and capable man, but far too professional to be open to bribery. Burr's appointment cut across him, and he was directly in the employ of the Admiralty now and so felt a renewed sense of purpose and importance. He loathed France and the garlic-breathed French, so an encounter with a Frenchman, one who had become accepted by the best in English society, would be interesting.

CHAPTER EIGHTEEN

Portsea
Winter 1804

IT HAD BEEN a long and wearisome day at the plant. I shrugged off my long leather boots and coat and sank into my favourite chair.

Sophia entered the dim, candlelit drawing room and positioned herself next to me on the arm.

"My love, you are home now and you can put the travails of the day behind you."

I had been away for three consecutive days, both at the dockyards and at a local sawmill where I was hatching an idea on more effective ways of bending timber; it seemed like an age.

"Thank you, my darling."

Just then little Sophie toddled in, hand-in-hand with Emilia the children's chaperone, smiling at my presence.

"Look who's come to see you!" Sophia exclaimed.

"Papa!"

I leaned forward and held out my arms as little Sophie tottered unsteadily towards me, giggling as she came. My gentle squeeze on her delicate young body was life-affirming and joyous. I felt enhanced and revitalised already.

"And where is baby Emma?"

"I'm afraid she couldn't wait for you any longer. She's fast asleep in her cot now."

"Ah yes, it is after eight, after all. I suppose even adorable baby girls need their beauty sleep."

We all laughed.

"Your dinner will be ready in half an hour, sir."

"Excellent. Well, I must retire to wash and freshen myself before eating," I rose whilst cradling Sophie in my arms and kissed her soft cheek. The brightly coloured deep pile rug yielded only slightly under her light footsteps as I put her down and she padded back to her nanny.

When Emilia had retired from the room, I took a deep breath.

"Sophia, I need to speak with you about certain matters relating to my working life and circumstances; nothing to unduly concern yourself about. It is only that I need your support and sympathetic ear as my loving wife and devoted friend. Underneath my confidence and capability, as with all men, there is a softness which benefits from feminine understanding and encouragement, and the unique support that only you can give."

"Oh, Marc." She took my hand and kissed my cheek. "Yes. Let us talk on in privacy over dinner, once little Sophie is in bed."

* * *

Sophia looked wide-eyed at me, her pupils reflecting the candlelight like mirrors, her head resting elegantly on cupped hands, her elbows balanced on the polished mahogany table. Her image was so childlike and lovely. The sight of her in this gentle light made for a romantic atmosphere; but romance was not in the air as I further illustrated my concerns, whilst picking at the roast before me.

"So, you see that the manufacturing plant has developed into quite an enterprise now, with forty-five machines now installed. These are very exciting times. The problem is that the payments I have received or have been promised do not match the cost or level of investment I have made, mainly from savings I brought over from America.

"Yes, I eventually recouped my initial outlay in the early days, but the Navy Board then chose to pay Maudslay directly. One would have considered that there was a contract of mutual benefit in place, as I am able to make good profit from my mass production of blocks, and the government have the plentiful supply they have demanded to feed their ships and war effort. Sadly, that is not the way. The Admiralty seems to want to hinder and obstruct me. God knows why. Is it because of my French background? Is it because I befriend Bentham, a good and honest man who is exposing the undercurrent of corruption at the highest levels in the hierarchy? Or are the gentlemen in charge just plainly uninformed and ignorant about the importance these blocks represent and have other more 'important' matters to address?"

Sophia made no comment. I continued.

"I have repeatedly written to the Board requesting more workmen, without even the courtesy of a response. I have employed only two more block makers in the last eighteen months and trained them myself, but no more. That, combined with acute problems in the timber, brass coaks and shivers supply, and quality issues, has led to the whole facility operating well under capacity with overheads not even being recovered. The Board themselves set us a target of producing seventy thousand blocks a year, and we are well short of that."

I paused to collect my thoughts.

"I can only imagine that the grievances that I determined to set in writing, and are endorsed by Bentham, may have inadvertently caused friction at the Admiralty. But I have acted in an honest and forthright manner, no more and no less than any man would have done in my position and circumstances."

My wife sighed. "Oh, Marc. This sounds quite awful. No wonder you needed to talk."

"Yes. I know I can confide in you fully, my darling, but there is more. The members of the Board, in their wisdom, have now decided to appoint a certain Mr Burr—an inexperienced and illiterate man by all accounts—to take over the management of my plant and my machines, effectively giving me only second say in its operation. I am outraged!"

Slowly, Sophia placed her arms on the table, before lifting her tearful eyes to me. "I think you have done all you can to mitigate matters, Marc. You are dealing with some difficult men here, and, if may I say so, some skulduggery. And at the highest levels. You are an honest and intelligent man, not only a foreigner to them in culture and tongue, but also in virtue and valiant enterprise. I am proud, even if they are not."

I smiled. "But why the deliberate obstacles and manipulation?"

Sophia's demeanour became one of concern and gravity.

"The disease of corruption infects many and knows no bounds, neither through class or circumstances. Greed in society is present at all levels. It seems to be intrinsic in humans, unfortunately. From what you describe, and from your previous discussions with me, I would not have thought it impossible that some Board members are in the pocket of rival enterprises."

Sophia paused and then placed her hand over my palm.

"I believe, too, that there may be people who are jealous of you and your capabilities, Marc, as you have made an immense impact here since your arrival. I know I say that as your wife, but I am also well-read, listen to the word on the street, and my brother and I discuss many topics, so I am well informed."

Sophia's insight was remarkable—her comments direct and accurate, but no more than I would have expected from this brilliant and dedicated woman.

"As for Burr, do not concern yourself too much with the likes of him. His remit may be to act as the controller and manager, but it will be your knowledge and influence that will win through against his rhetoric. Besides, he may not be the ogre that you are painting."

* * *

His face and gait were not what I was expecting. The stocky-figured man standing before me bore high cheekbones and a jutting jawline that made him almost wolf-like, while the thick mop of brown hair added to his feral edge. His slightly bent nose may have indicated he had been in a fight in the not-too-distant past, but he didn't seem the fighting type. He was neither handsome nor ugly.

"Mr Brunel. Very pleased to meet you."

I wished I could reciprocate his welcome, but I was still quietly seething that this was happening. My half-smile and diffident handshake probably gave away my true feelings.

"Allow me to show you around this facility, Mr Burr," I uttered, reluctantly.

CHAPTER NINETEEN

Portsmouth Docks
January 1805

IT WAS DISAPPOINTING, to say the least, that, after being absent from the plant for a fortnight on other business, I should hear it from Jackson, one of my leading hands and among the best of the semi-skilled machine operators I had.

I picked up the pile of papers on my desk and slammed them down as I felt my face redden and my blood boil. How dare he? My deepest concerns were realised.

There was only one thing to do—confront him immediately. To ignore it would be a dereliction of duty and a dilution of my morals, and I would be undermining my integrity as a gentleman, and my profession to boot. I did not enjoy confrontation, and if I could seek a solution through dialogue and conciliation then I would favour this path. But this was a serious enough matter to demand direct action, otherwise I would be creating a rod for my own back.

The bottle of my favourite cognac was in its usual place in the cabinet to the side of my desk. I took a warming tot and collected my thoughts, before opening the office door onto the factory floor. I spied him next to one of the machines, in conversation with one of the operators.

"Mr Burr! A word, please!" I shouted above the din of the machines and men.

Burr raised his head in my direction, acknowledging me with a look of surprise. The workers around him gaped, somewhat taken aback by the force of my fervour and words. They had never seen me like this, I was sure.

I stood and leaned over the back of the desk chair as Burr approached.

"Ah Mr Brunel, you have returned. I trust you had a pleasant journey and that your meetings were successful," Burr said.

"Never mind the platitudes, Burr. What has been going on here in my absence?"

"Mr Brunel, I am not sure I like your tone. May I remind you that I have been brought here by the Navy Board to assist your production line and to determine the most efficient manner to operate the plant for maximum productivity? That is exactly what I have been doing in your absence."

"And don't give me the official line about your purpose here. You know exactly what I am talking about."

Burr looked blankly at me. There was a false innocence in his gaze: an expression of being castigated for no reason, like a schoolboy reprimanded by a teacher for disturbing the class when he knows it was his friend seated at the next desk.

I was forced to continue.

"You have been admitting visitors from the general public to our block-making plant here, without my approval. Furthermore, you have been receiving payment for such services in the sum of one shilling per visitor without recourse to myself or the Board."

Burr's expression turned from bewilderment to realisation. "Oh that, Mr Brunel. Well, this plant has stirred the imagination and interest of everyone here in Portsmouth, and the public and influential people want to know more. If that publicity is bad for our business, I doubt very much. It can only do this facility, and your reputation, good in the long run."

The audacity of the man was plain.

"It is not the act of admission I am referring to, Burr, it is the fact that you did this with no authority, and that you are pocketing the money, illegally, to supplement your income."

"Mr Brunel. Everyone recognises that the paltry payments that the Government make for my wages, and for many more like me, need to be, shall we say, 'enhanced' somewhat to make up ground. I am merely adding some pocket money for my extra time and effort in running matters here in your best interests and those of the Board."

I was incredulous.

"Are you saying that this type of behaviour is the norm in England?"

"Let us just say that they are probably equally as corrupt, if not more so, in your revolutionary France, Mr Brunel."

I did well to control my mounting anger. I took a deep breath.

"Well, not here. I will be making arrangements to secure these premises and prevent this from happening again, Mr Burr."

"As you so choose, Mr Brunel, but please remember my duties and responsibilities are ultimately to the Board, sir."

Our eyes met in a fixed stare for a few seconds before Burr turned and stalked out of the room. I would either erect a fence around the wood mill or lock all doors and post a security man on the main door in future. Burr could do as he pleased, but he would not be allowed to enter the premises outside normal working hours.

* * *

482 Fontanka River Embankment
St Petersburg
Russia
14th February 1805

Dear Marc

Your letter finds me in the imperial capital. I trust this letter finds you in good spirits and health. I have heard much about you since my last visit to Portsmouth and am pleased for you and Sophia that the Brunel family is ever expanding on English shores.

As you may be aware, I have taken up the position of chief advisor and inspector of shipbuilding here where the British Navy has a strong presence. I thought the appointment somewhat strange, given the good work I considered I was undertaking in England in my capacity of Inspector General of Naval Works, but it may be that I ruffled a few feathers amongst the Board in my efforts to reduce corruption at home, although I am reliably informed that the plentiful supply of oak in this part of Russia was a major reason for the British Navy facility to base itself here.

I am naturally disappointed that you are considering resigning from the project of block-making in Portsmouth. Burr's appointment must have been an aberration for you, to say the least. I can say only that it is traditional for the Navy Board to act in this manner, since they want to be directly represented and pass authority through directly employed dockyard officers, so please do not take this action personally. The Board are known, however, to run a little rough-shod over people at times, and I am well acquainted with the fact that Taylor's long-term contract for block-making was recently terminated by the Admiralty with little notice, forcing Walter Taylor to commence proceedings against them.

I can understand your frustration, particularly as Burr has employed, without your knowledge or consent, a number of young boys to act as machine operators, resulting in losses of productivity compared with your tried and tested way of training a small number of dedicated, experienced men. I know that skilled labour is at a premium in England, and particularly in Portsmouth, at the moment, but that is no excuse for his underhand behaviour and insolent attitude towards you. You rightly deserve more respect.

In his defence, should I make so bold and consider myself so disposed to do so, he did work for me as a draughtsman in his formative years, and although I had certain reservations concerning his application and attitude to work, I found that his finished work was often worthy of praise. That is not to go against your opinions or credibility, Marc, which are undeniable. I am just attempting, in a perhaps clumsy way (as Burr has demonstrated admirably), to provide a more balanced picture.

I implore you not to resign. Burr will not be there forever, and I have entreated the Board on more than one occasion recently to support your endeavours in employing more capable labour and smoothing the supply lines of timber. It will not be long, I am sure, until the Board take you fully into their confidence and give you complete control. They know this is all in their best interests, particularly at this time of conflict. It has also been recognised that a born and bred Frenchman of your standing and endeavour who has openly decried Napoleon's new France is a major asset to the English cause. Your work ethic, imagination and engineering skills are the envy of many and are openly contributing, somewhat ironically, to the successes at sea that our navy is enjoying against both the French and Spanish fleets. I am confident that all your efforts will be recognised at the highest levels of government and that your wait for remuneration will soon be over.

Further, I have it on good authority that your influence has spread even to these distant shores and that Czar Alexander himself is planning a royal visit to Portsmouth to experience the mass production facility that I know is your pride and joy, at first hand.

So please do not despair, my dear Marc. Better times are on the horizon—I know it and can feel it as your friend and confidant.

I trust I will see you again soon—perhaps with the Czar himself!

Trust me in this, my dear Marc.

Yours in great truth

Samuel Bentham

* * *

Bentham's letter brought me some cheer and I was gladdened by his support, but the problems with the plant persisted. My report and accounts to the Board showing my losses to date fell upon stony ground; they now requested I provide an estimate of the savings made in one year's working of my block machines, but I was unclear as to what benchmark to use for comparison. All very frustrating, and merely delaying tactics to avoid paying me what was rightfully due.

On reflection, and after discussing the matter with Sophia, I decided to stay on for the time being, or at least until the new, larger capacity steam engine being manufactured by Maudslay, and drawn up from my designs by his capable draughtsman Joshua Field, was installed and commissioned. This would offer even greater productivity, but the labour problem still remained.

It was ironic, but Samuel was also strangely accurate in his statement that 'better times are on the horizon'—but most certainly not in the way that he perhaps intended, or that I envisaged.

CHAPTER TWENTY

The King's Bench Prison, Southwark
May 1821

I SHUT THE cell room door firmly and returned to my work.

"To whom were you speaking?" Sophia enquired, after a time, looking up from darning my socks.

I paused at my document-strewn desk to collect my thoughts. I was still extremely vexed and distracted by my small encounter. I was also a little reluctant to let Sophia know all of what was said for fear that she may persuade me to allow her family or friends to raise the money to allow us, at least temporarily, to leave these squalid surroundings. I would be standing firm. Any easing of my situation would detract from my entitlement to justice and dilute my cause. Of that, I was sure.

"Just one of the prison's so-called officials trying to draw me into a bribe in return for certain privileges. I am, of course, having none of it."

"Oh, my dear Marc. Please come and sit by me for a few moments before you return to your work."

We sat together on the edge of the trestle bed.

"What is more, the man reminded me of that awful Mr Burr."

"Oh Marc, I am sorry that your state of mind is being affected by such past matters. I remember that Burr was a thorn in your side at Portsmouth for some time, and that you came close to resigning from the Block Mill Works as a consequence. But let me help you reflect on better times."

Sophia held my hand.

"Do you remember, not long after Mr Burr appeared on the scene, when we attended the gay and vibrant regatta on the Thames? Mr Farthing and his wife were excellent company too. I was pregnant with Isambard at the time..."

Battersea
September 1805

The billowing canvasses of the flotilla of catboats provided a colourful guard of honour to the main event as the leading racing craft came into view on the river. Battersea was enlivened with the hustle and bustle of a multitude of onlookers and supporters of the annual Cumberland Society Regatta, where many were cheering on the participants of the race in progress.

Almost everywhere one looked there was a collection of social classes enjoying the day out—from the luminaries perched at vantage points on the verandas and balconies of the riverside dwellings and company grain warehouses, to street urchins at the quay edge, dangling their feet in the cool grey water. All heads suddenly turned upstream as a broad line of four-man skulled wherries steadily came into view through the misty autumnal air; their oars rhythmically striking and foaming the water as they made steady progress towards the finish line.

Men, women and children alike started to raise their hats and wave their fists in the air, cheering on their favourite crew. For this was the peoples' race. An annual event where the proprietors of businesses fronting this silent highway would bestow the river vessels to be crewed by their own young apprentices—a chance for glory and to be watermen for the day for the adolescent men, an opportunity for the employers to boast their successes through the efforts, attitudes and fitness of their employees. The Challenge Cup was in full flow.

On a suitably decorated sloop, bedecked with bunting and moored some distance from the landing steps, stood a throng of tall-hatted dignitaries, amongst them a Mr J. H. Farthing, whom I hoped to meet today. From a distance, I spotted his tall, slender frame immediately. As Chairman of the Cumberland Society he had the honour of wielding the finishing flag, which he held aloft and unfurled, poised for the moment when the first boat would pass the line.

My travels always seem to lead back to London, and in particular to the Thames. Was I escaping or merely following the leads and opportunities that were placed before me, either through fate or as a consequence of invention and indulging my engineer's mind? It mattered not.

It had been a while since I met Farthing. I had licensed my polygraphic machine under patent to him a couple of years ago, and since then his business had grown with a vigour that reflected the character of the man. Eminently likeable but a shrewd businessman, he had improved upon and added other such devices to my invention with a manufacturing process that was the envy of the mechanical copying and writing world.

Sophia held tightly onto my arm as the crowd roared their approval and the hats and caps spun dizzily into the air. I was careful to protect her and the small swelling, now beginning to show, from the bustle of the crowd and uneven cobbles forming the walkway at the quayside.

The winning crew held their oars aloft. Farthing caught my gaze and tipped his hat in my direction. I reciprocated with a broad smile and a touch of my top hat.

* * *

The celebrations and dinner in the tall-ceilinged annexe to County Hall were almost as joyous as the day's festival that preceded it. Farthing had generously invited the wives and families of the apprentices and managers that made up his workforce. The air of festivity and merriment was clearly evident amongst all present—a tribute to a man who also possessed the worthy attitude of involving and encouraging his employees.

The wives and elder daughters were in full conversation at the table when the men retired for cigars and brandy in the oak-panelled drawing room.

The soft leather chair eased its way around the contours of my body as I sat back and took in the events of the day, whilst puffing with satisfaction the rich tobacco smoke into the space above the heads of all six assembled gentlemen.

"What a fine day, and a memorable occasion!" Farthing announced. "Worthy of the cast and all who contributed to its success, as usual."

This brought smiles and murmurs of agreement all round.

"Thank you, gentlemen, for your support and attendance today. The apprentices of all companies have benefitted from the experience and we can look forward to even better times, I'm sure. Men such as we represent the backbone of English industry and invention which is currently enjoying a renaissance, despite the fact that we are officially at war with our cousins across the water."

I smiled nervously, but decided against speaking.

"Now, a man that I am very keen for you all to be acquainted with, although I am sure you have already had informal discussions with him over the day and at dinner—Marc Brunel." I continued smiling and raised my glass in acknowledgement.

"Marc and I will be working on a new project concerning a new sawmill and timber treatment works here in Battersea. He will be concerned with the engineering aspects where, I am pleased to say, that his latest innovations in saw design and timber treatment will be used to great effect."

I certainly hoped so.

* * *

The old, discoloured sawdust swirled around the exposed corners of the derelict building, driven by sudden draughts from old, ill-fitting doors. The machines and pulley systems had long been silent. The only sounds echoing through the solid floors and brick walls were the banging of an open window or the scurrying of mice or rats.

"Well, this is it, Marc. The venue of our new enterprise. It doesn't look much now, I admit, but in a few months, and with your ingenuity and my finance, we can get this to work, I'm sure. Your two patents for the circular saw and the cutting of veneers will be at the forefront of this new manufacturing business, and with the new steam-driven engines powering the mass production process we can look forward to giving this place the lifeblood it needs and resurrect its past anew."

I had spent some time observing the activities of the wharf at Battersea and the inordinate amount of time it took to offload the raw timber, transport it for treatment and then cut and process at different plants and sawmills before the finished components could be brought back to the dockside for distribution. One plant, able do all this and situated on the quayside, would have efficiency and cost benefits far in excess of the present clumsy and time-consuming arrangement.

Farthing was expansive concerning the prospects at this juncture. Taking the best elements of the Portsmouth plant and transporting those ideas here without being hamstrung by the government's shortcomings on labour and raw timber supply, whilst introducing my new inventions, was a tantalising prospect for me also.

I stood in silence for some time and scanned the open aspect of the now redundant building, my mind alive with the possibilities. I visualised the new segmental 'V'-shaped circular saws of up to five feet in diameter whizzing their way through logs thrust forward on sliding carriages; I almost caught the familiar smell of singed wood and machine grease; heard the reassuring drone of activity where machine and man become one; saw the cut timbers being transported to the steam room to be softened and moulded into finished timber to any requisite contour or shape, all without being removed from the whole operation.

"Marc?" Farthing interrupted my daydreaming.

"Do you think the East India Company will invest in this project?" I enquired.

"They are proceeding to discuss this at Board level, as we speak. The various pulley blocks and thin cut timbers fit with the planned expansion of their fleet, and the fact that we can produce our goods more plentifully, and at less cost than all our competitors, speaks for itself."

* * *

On this day, 9th April 1806, at five minutes before one o'clock in the morning, my dear Sophia was brought to bed of a boy. I was overjoyed, and I gave thanks to God.

CHAPTER TWENTY-ONE

Chelsea, London
Autumn 1809

THE UPSTAIRS CASEMENT window of the grand premises of Lindsay House that sat on the north embankment was an ideal location to view this stretch of the Thames. On the upstream side, the water stretched and curled away beyond sight; to the east, the impressive stacked timber piers and deck of Battersea Bridge broke the view downstream.

The bridge was particularly busy this morning, but Sophia was still able to spy the figure of a tall-hatted man resplendent in coat and cane striding purposefully in the direction of the south bank and another day at the sawmill. She was as in love with Marc as the first time she had set eyes on him. He had lost none of the qualities that had so impressed her when they met, and she had also discovered a sweet innocence, almost a boyishness, about him, that seemed to manifest itself only in the most intimate moments that they shared together.

Marc was honest and forthright with a redoubtable spirit and indefatigable zest for life, and Sophia, like many who made his acquaintance, was often swept up by the tide of his emotions and his infectious character. They were invaluable to each other. She was his rock; he was her champion.

But she had noted recently the strain on her husband's face. His eyes had lost a little of their sparkle and his forehead appeared more furrowed than usual. She had advised him of her concerns about his long hours and the strain on his health. Although he had listened to her intently, he just shrugged and went about his way as usual. He had confided in her that money and payments from the Navy Board were still a worry to him, but that he was confident matters would be resolved soon. She did not dig any deeper: it was not her place to do so unless specifically requested.

* * *

I looked back at Lindsey Row and the familiar shape at the upstairs window, and gave a wave and smile. It had been very satisfying to spend the last couple of days with my mind at rest, in the bosom of my ever-growing family. Albeit this represented a temporary respite from my busy schedule and working life, where seventeen-hour working days and frequent sojourns away from home were the norm.

Money, or lack of it, was a constant source of anxiety to me. In my opinion, the Admiralty Board had been deliberately withholding monies from me while inventing spurious excuses for non-payment of my dues. I knew that Sophia had noticed the strain that I was under, but I had refrained from discussing this sorry state of affairs with her so as not to unduly worry her.

The truth was that the Admiralty had only just approved a payment on account of a paltry one thousand pounds—a drop in the ocean compared to the amount I was legitimately owed. There had been experiments, designs, drawings, models that had taken up all of my time during the six years that I had been dedicated to Portsmouth in the service of the government. As a consequence, I had turned down the opportunity of involvement in interesting and challenging projects elsewhere through my now (seemingly misplaced) honour and commitment.

I knew that the plant at Portsmouth was now regularly producing over one hundred thousand blocks of every size, using many species of wood in a year—more than was previously produced at Portsmouth, Plymouth, Chatham, Deptford and Woolwich combined. All the machinery to drive it was fully commissioned and working well. After much persuasion and pressure from Bentham and his ilk, the Board had recently relented on Burr and given me back overall control; this I delegated to Jackson as Operations Manager. Everything was as it should be to do exactly as the Admiralty and the Board decreed! What more could I do?

I reached the steps to the main plant room door and halted for breath, mopping my brow with my handkerchief.

My meeting was firstly with Borthwick, who had travelled down from Edinburgh yesterday, then, later, dinner with Colonel Uppage. I had met both of these gentlemen only recently and both of them wished to discuss plans for the expansion and improvements to the sawmills at Leith Docks and the Royal Arsenal, Woolwich.

Mechanisation was catching on fast in the industrial world, and the news of my mass production methods at Portsmouth and Battersea was now spreading to eminent and influential individuals in society, representing both private and public enterprise. They wanted to see the facility at Battersea and experience at first hand the unique vertical saws and production line at work in a demanding industrial unit environment.

After the day's meetings, I felt compelled to return to my home and family and rest somewhat, perhaps even take to my bed, as I felt the onset of nervous fever taking a grip on my body and soul. This was not like me at all.

CHAPTER TWENTY-TWO

Woolwich, London
Autumn 1809

VICTOR BOUCHER KNEW Marc Brunel. Not personally—only by sight, but that was enough for him.

The hulk gently rocked on the water, not from any particular disturbance in the tidal flow or even from a passing ship's wake, but from the sheer mass of nearly five hundred mobile, sweat-laden men who were packed into the five cramped decks.

Victor had been a model convict, and had been promoted to the penultimate deck which meant he was away from the stifling, stinking, semi-dark hold of the hulk and could at last breathe deeply the fresh air permeating through the portholes that punctuated the cabin space. He might even receive some food that was not filled with maggots or weevils, and he would be able to urinate and defecate off the side of the ship rather than into overspilling pots and bowls.

His right leg was bruised, and it ached from the shackle that he had to wear at all times, but that was nothing compared to the ordeal he had suffered since being at sea with the French Navy.

From the frayed tally stick which he carried in the side pocket of his ripped and stained pantaloons, he estimated that it had been over a year since he first embarked on this Godforsaken vessel; captured as a prisoner of war after the bloody and fearsome French and Spanish naval engagement with the English some six miles out from the Spanish port of Cadiz.

The English sailors and crew were like wild animals in combat. Fuelled on rum and ale, they would cut you to pieces as soon as look at you. Victor shifted his bony backside on the rough timber bench, closed his eyes and reluctantly cast his mind back to the rain of flying shot ripping through the upper decks and captain's quarters at the stern of Le Redoutable from the broadside fired from the imposing British flagship manoeuvring on the starboard side.

He almost cried aloud at the stark imagery of the killed, injured and bleeding, many of them friends and comrades that he had got to know so well, their bodies strewn across the deck where flying lead and splintered oak shrapnel had ripped them apart. He remembered the screams and panic; the locking of the masts of the two ships in the heat of the battle, and the melee that ensued with hand-to-hand fighting, cutlass and dagger slicing and fizzing through air and flesh; dismembered limbs and pools of blood.

He shook his head, but did not weep. He had done with weeping. How he had survived he would never know. Moreover, why he should be amongst the 'fortuitous' number taken prisoner on that fateful day—it must have been upwards of ten thousand men or more—he was not at all sure, but here he was; alive and kicking and living in hope that one day, one day the war would end and he would see the fields and vineyards of his beloved France again and be united with his friends and family...

But the momentary comfort of escapism was soon jolted away by a sharp kick in the shins from a burly guard.

"Time to get yourself moving and walk the gangplank to your daily taxi, sir."

Victor was not stupid. The guards always referred to the inmates as 'sir', mocking convicts and prisoners of war alike in an attempt to bolster their own feelings of self-importance.

Along with at least twenty other inmates, he was locked through his shackle into the large rowing boat as it cast off from the imposing dark outline of the hulk's hull; the morning light was rising over the London sky to the east, signposting the start of another day for this, and a dozen other boatloads of men being transported to work at the dockyards.

The sprawling naval expanse of Woolwich drew nearer as the four prisoner oarsmen guided the boat through the stinking, brown-grey water, under supervision of the tall, uniformed guards.

It was not too long a trudge from the quay steps to the dock promenade and on to the carriage works sawmill, but you were immediately aware that the atmosphere and smell did not improve; the air was tainted and stale from the stagnant water in the open ditches and swamps of the surrounding marshes.

Victor sighed deeply as he made his way to join the other men on a new work shift. He noticed that the attitude of the employed English labour force contributed towards a constant atmosphere of unrest and revolt, as there were regular complaints about late or poor pay and conditions. He knew, too, that there was widespread pilfering of the company stores, encouraged by the managers, as they were also the owners of their own small yards fronting the river. *'But at least they are free,'* he thought to himself.

As usual, Victor was stationed for work in one of the main steam engine rooms adjoining the main manufacturing facility where production of the many carriage types, primarily for military use, was in full swing. It was his job, along with two English labourers and a supervising charge hand who also doubled as a security guard, to fetch and carry the water butts and oil barrels to refill the water supply sump and to ensure the machinery was sufficiently lubricated to run smoothly. On most days, he would also stoke the boiler and carry the waste timber in barrows to the fire grate. He was on pain of death to comply with all instructions issued to him. It was slow, laborious work, but he was still young and strong enough to endure it.

The machine room was a mass of steaming valves, slowly dripping pipes and high humidity—a welcoming warmth in the midst of winter but an oppressive hothouse in the height of summer.

The factory bell rang promptly at midday, marking the start of 'Watering Time'.

Victor sat and chewed on the bread husks and cheese and drank deeply of the ale brought in from one of the many local public houses—a chance for half an hour's respite from work; a chance to close his eyes in thought and contemplate his few options. He had a plan, and it was just a matter of how to implement it successfully; the preparation work had been done. He had time and patience on his side and considered that, with a little good fortune, he would make Marc Brunel regret leaving France to work for the English enemy.

He remembered seeing Brunel's smug face through the tall wrought-iron bars of Chateau Carpentier all those years ago in Rouen when he was young, impressionable and proud to be amongst the rebels that were transforming France. Brunel had got away then, but he would not now. The ale refreshed Victor's body and mind and boosted his sense of purpose and confidence.

Today was Monday, the day when Brunel usually visited the sawmill of the Royal Coachworks to inspect his machines and facility and talk with the management. But it wasn't until that afternoon that the unmistakable man with distinguished high forehead and bright enquiring eyes visited the machines, escorted by the plant room manager.

Brunel still seemed as young in gait and appearance as the day Victor last spied him, and he was almost unbearably cheery in behaviour.

The machines and pulleys lay silent as the inspection took place—a break from the unrelenting noise and clatter of mechanical apparatus and steam hissing and belching. Victor knew that this would happen, and he became aware of the ringing in his ears as the room dropped to silence.

He looked on as Brunel shook hands with everyone but him. He knew that, as a prisoner of war, he had no place here, and no invitation to welcome this educated and high-positioned man, but the act of ignorance still angered him—particularly from this despised traitor. He waited until his target was close enough to the main machine: where the worn rubberised leather steam ducts bent around the external corner of the wall; the place where he had implemented his plan when no one was watching. He willed the figure in tail coat and baggy trousers to get nearer and nearer…

After a short interval which seemed a lifetime, at a signal from the attendant manager, the twenty-horsepower mechanical Hercules coughed and snorted back into operation.

Without warning there was a whizz and a sound like flood waters bursting through a broken dam as an explosion of scalding steam engulfed the end of the room where Brunel was standing. Vision was impossible through the hot cloud, but a man's piercing screams could be heard penetrating the air. A noisy fumbling and jostling of men immediately followed as everyone scrambled to work out what had happened.

Victor smiled.

"For God's sake, give the man space and fetch a doctor immediately."

* * *

4 Lindsey Row, Chelsea
The Same day

I awoke to the stifling heat and high humidity of an unseasonably hot autumnal day. A wet towel rested on my brow as I shifted carefully between the sweat-soaked sheets. The bedroom window was open, but that offered little respite from the incessant heat. The day was still, and bright sunshine dominated the London skyline. I could hear the sound of the children playing in a distant room.

"I am so relieved that you are awake, my darling. You have been drifting in and out of sleep now for three days. We have been quite concerned." The soothing voice of Sophia cut through my fever. I attempted to rise from my bed, but she gently placed a hand on my shoulder.

"You are no doubt keen to rise and recommence your working duties, of which I know there are many, but the doctor has advised that you take more rest until the nervous exhaustion and high temperature have passed. I might add that the household finances have been running smoothly in your absence, so there is no need to concern yourself."

To involve one's wife in financial affairs was exceedingly rare in Regency society, but Sophia was different. She was intelligent, dedicated and capable, and I had no qualms in letting her take the reins temporarily. Many men of my age, standing and position would not approve, but I loved her and respected her in equal measure.

* * *

The pavement was damp from the overnight rain, but the cloudy sky and the strong westerly breeze did nothing to dampen my spirits. I felt revived and agile of mind and body again. After my short walk over Battersea Bridge and visit to the developing and industrialised area of the south bank where the sawmill and other fledgling works hugged the Thames, I took a ferry boat to Woolwich and the Arsenal.

I was greeted at the wharf by a very concerned-looking Major General Uppage, as he now was.

"Ah, Marc. I am glad you have come today. I have some bad news, I'm afraid. We have had an unfortunate accident in the main engine room, the circumstances of which are currently under investigation—we suspect sabotage."

"Oh my God, sabotage! Are you sure? What happened?"

"Yes. You know the promising young plant manager, Brisley? He of high forehead who, by your own admission, closely resembles your good self?"

"Yes, of course."

"He has been taken to hospital with severe burns as a result of suddenly becoming engulfed in scalding water when one of the cast iron beam and water cistern engine steam pipes exploded under pressure."

CHAPTER TWENTY-THREE

The King's Bench Prison
June 1821

THIS DECAYING PLACE was taking its toll on me. My depression was deepening and my twilight walks became more commonplace, but nonetheless eventful. The dimly lit, confining environs continued to challenge strength of mind, but the exercise and the transitory break away from our cell room was at least a small means of liberation for me. During the day, I was happy to escort Sophia; but as night drew in, I did not want to expose her to the prison clamour, sickening odours and threatening atmosphere that festered all day and came to life at night.

I quickly passed along the passageway, just as a man was exiting a room in the near distance.

Drawing near, I could make out a figure in a heavy greatcoat. He was familiar to me, I had made his acquaintance and had early dialogue with him in this Godforsaken place. I was looking at Burns, the surgeon.

"Mr Brooner, what are you doing around this building at such a late hour?" Burns inquired in his Scottish brogue.

I no longer corrected him on this mis-pronunciation of my name. I had attempted it at the second and third time of asking but gave up. Besides, I almost preferred to remain at least partially anonymous whilst in this gaol, as my incarceration continued to cast a shadow of shame on me.

"I was about to ask you the same," I replied, both thankful to see a familiar face and a little disconcerted to have my solitary walk interrupted.

I had discerned through our previous brief encounters that he had been a prisoner for eight months. He spent a large proportion of his time attending to the sick and infirm, as many of the prisoners lived in squalor with no proper sanitation. In the overcrowded conditions, disease was rife. Burns had occasionally used his own money to purchase the necessary tinctures and remedies for these unfortunate wretches. How could such a gracious and charitable man be locked up for financial misdeeds?

"The usual things, I am afraid, my friend. Attending to the sick and applying my skills and knowledge when I am able, anything from rheumatic gout to serious illness, mainly typhus. Some are unfortunately beyond my help." His tired face took on a resigned look. "I discovered a man lying dead in his bed in one crowded room. God knows how long he had been lying there; no notice of him had been taken at all. The smell was so offensive that frankincense and myrrh were burning in an attempt to remove it."

It was beyond belief.

"Now you must excuse me," the keen-eyed surgeon concluded in a rush. "I have to continue my round."

"Yes, yes. I would hate to stand in your way, but please protect yourself, as you too are exposed to disease and infection."

"Thank you. Perhaps we can meet and have a more civilised discussion during the day in the front courtyard or even outside the prison walls if you have applied for day release and paid the fee due to the turnkeys."

I called to mind the brief encounter only a couple of weeks ago, when I was confronted by the turnkey at our door.

"I shall not be doing any such thing, I am afraid. I am neither going to feed the corrupt and unjust system any more that should be required for my beleaguered stay, nor be seen to accept a more comfortable position as a result of privileges given to me as a result of my status when so many are suffering. I believe too that any such action would dilute the pleas I have put forward for release and payment of my debts in the eyes of my friends and supporters. There is a real risk that my incarceration could be extended indefinitely, which would be unbearable for me."

Burns was taken aback.

"I am sorry, Brooner. It was just a suggestion."

"Your work here will not go unnoticed: I will personally see to it. When I eventually leave these confining premises, I will make known your charitable works. I pray God to relieve you—us all—soon of this burden. What is your situation now? Is your release imminent?"

Burns shrugged his shoulders. "I am reliably informed that my bankers are about to receive a substantial sum owed to me by the former Government War Office for medical attendances and operations I carried out in the local infirmary on servicemen injured and disabled in the recent conflicts."

Clearly, I was far from being the only person ill-treated by the government. I was both reassured at the realisation and disconcerted that Burns' debt was also unresolved.

"Now I must be on my way."

I touched his shoulder as he gathered up his worn leather shoulder bag and disappeared into the gloom of the corridor.

I was left on my own. I stood and reflected on the moment, absorbing the prison's unique discomforting and claustrophobic mood, punctuated with the all too familiar distant wails and groans.

My mind strayed back to when I had witnessed those poor war-wearied and blood-stained wretches, disembarking at the quay and the origin of the Boot Factory...

* * *

Portsmouth Docks
Winter 1809

Bentham looked on incredulously. William Kingdom's face, too, was full of disappointment and concern. It was not supposed to be like this. War was a paradox; both the just and the unjust simultaneously won and lost. Whether God was on your side and whether your endeavours were led by the flag of righteousness and for the greater good, was a matter of opinion. All England would argue that this war was merely a right of defence in the face of invasion and domination; France would counter that the hostilities were a clear sign that she was making a stand for her long-downtrodden people—a nation now emerging from political and social backwaters. Liberty, Equality, Fraternity.

The mood amongst the three of us had changed radically in the space of only a few hours. This morning, at the block production facility, the Czar and his ensemble were notably impressed with the works; and we were more than happy to be in the company of such a powerful political figure. He was a robust and portly gentleman, with a keen mind and inquisitive manner. Russia was clearly benefitting from this well-travelled and seasoned stately figure and British ally.

Now, the sight of men-at-arms struggling down the ship's gang-planks as they returned from foreign fields dismayed us. Disabled and disillusioned, they populated the quayside landscape as each slowly made their way to the safe haven of a family's arms or boarded a cart to the central hospital for medical treatment.

Many of the men wore bloodstained bandages and rags with leaking sores and malignant wounds, particularly on their tired feet; dirty toes poking through split leather on pitiful boots.

Bentham approached a gangly officer in a muddied red tunic standing, arms folded, to one side of the gangplank; his red hair like a beacon and his white freckled skin sunburnt and peeling from his time in hot foreign climes. I knew this soldier from the description provided to me by Bentham prior to our visit to the Portsmouth quayside—it was Colonel Anderson, one of the officers close to Sir John Moore, the remnants of whose army were now solemnly setting foot back on British shores.

"Colonel Anderson, a sad day for us all." Bentham stretched out a hand, firmly shaken by one of the few ratings that were left from the depleted army of men.

"Sir, we have returned an exhausted and dishevelled force of men, but our spirits and dignity remain high. Many people here in England hold the view that ours was a retreat from the field of battle at Corunna after defeat, but that could not be further from the truth. We are a proud band of comrades who stood firm and successfully defended the town against Napoleon's troops. The loss of Sir John was hard to take, though, sir."

"Yes. That must have been very hard on you and the men."

Anderson's blue eyes stared blankly into space for a few moments, his bulging Adam's apple sliding uncomfortably in his sun-wrinkled neck.

"Yes, sir. I was at his side when he was hit in the shoulder by cannon shot. His ribs and shoulder bone were shattered by the impact, his flesh and lungs lacerated and bleeding.

"Despite his obvious life-threatening injuries, he still barked out important orders and we won the day for him." Anderson had become too battle-hardened to break down, but his expression gave away the pain and grief he felt inside.

"I served with him for a long time, sir. He became a man I respected and felt close to. Most of the men felt the same."

"Yes, I understand," Bentham acknowledged.

After some more polite introductions and words of condolence and understanding, we all took our leave, walking reflectively back to the block works.

"Not good times," William uttered, perhaps compelled to say something just to break the uneasy silence, even though his words were not exactly chosen very well.

"No," Bentham replied.

I ventured to add my observations of the scene we had witnessed, and the awful condition of the soldiers embarking at the quay.

"I could not help noticing the poor quality of their uniforms—particularly their boots."

"Yes, standard Army issue, I'm afraid. Perhaps not as robust and as durable as they should be."

This minor and brief discourse set my mind racing. It would not be beyond the realms of possibility that the mass production line I had designed and implemented for ships' blocks could be applied to most other items where there is repetition of the product involved. Boots and shoes certainly fell into this category. However, I was disinclined to have the government defence department as my clients; they had been demonstrably less than fair in my dealings at Portsmouth and with my remunerations to date. I therefore believed that, should this venture progress, it should be as a private business enterprise, retailing the boots to the general public at a reasonable and affordable price.

I was excited by the whole concept. As soon as I returned to my office in my home in Chelsea, I would go about designing the necessary machinery, and employ Maudslay to manufacture the equipment and locate this enterprise close to the sawmill in Battersea. I knew just the place.

Patents would be needed. One for the boot and shoe making machinery itself, the other for adding the necessary durability to leather.

My deliberations were cut short by Bentham.

"Marc, by the way, I would very much like your presence at Chatham Dockyard. We have a few problems with the efficiencies and logistics of the sawmill and log handling affairs that I would like you to examine and offer your considered advice and opinions."

"Yes, of course."

I nodded and smiled. I would have many irons in the fire now; but as always, I welcomed the challenges and personal involvement, and the opportunity of maintaining the momentum of projects with like-minded and influential figures in English society. I was no business-man, but my engineering knowledge and the support of professional colleagues would see me through, I was certain.

* * *

Chatham Docks
July 1812

It was not just a simple matter of designing and installing a sawmill. The regime at Chatham was expensive and labour-intensive, built on years of tradition and lazy habits. Logs were dragged from the wharf by men and horses and there was double- and even treble-handling of raw timber before any seasoning, treatment and cutting. The logs were ingrained with the gravel and sand dragged along the ground, and there was a considerable amount of effort expended merely in transportation and storage.

To my disappointment, I was escorted by one of the senior officers of the dockyard, John Smithe, throughout my visit. I had felt I had emerged as a professional and capable engineer commanding some respect and had become naturalised and accepted by people who mattered in English society, so to be reminded again that I was regarded as a Frenchman was a thorn in my side. I had little choice but to reluctantly accept this fact and go about my work. Besides, Mr Smithe proved to be an admirable escort and advisor. He answered without hesitation most of my enquiries concerning the current management and finances of Chatham.

From my vantage point on the lower slopes of the hill flanking the docks, I counted in excess of one hundred sawyers positioned in pairs in pre-formed rectangular brick pits; the man at the top aligning and securing the timber before and during cutting, the man in the pit using a two-handed saw to cut the timber, engulfed in sawdust as a reward for his labours. The man above, or 'top dog' as he was appropriately named by his fellow tradesmen, was, to my surprise, more highly paid. From enquiry with Smithe, over 200 feet of timber could be expected to be sawn in one working day with the earnings around fifty shillings a week. Such a laborious, outmoded and expensive process.

Woolwich also needed some improvements to the quay areas, with new or remediated mass masonry river walls, widening of concourses and cobbled dock roads, and new timber jetties projecting into the river to maximise the available areas to land goods. The Thames was always very congested, with fully laden ships of all types often having to wait some days at anchor, inviting robbery and organised crime, frequently aided by the ships' captains accepting bribes.

I was therefore pleased, albeit guardedly, to be engaged by the Navy Board for the improvements required here, including the construction of housing in the vicinity for the many civilian workers, particularly at the Royal Arsenal and Sawmill.

But Chatham, although similar in some respects as the whole dockside revolved around the sawmill, was a different kettle of fish.

"Have you seen enough, Mr Brunel?" enquired Smithe.

"Yes, I think so, Smithe. Thank you for accompanying me and answering the many questions I had. I will await my survey colleagues and liaise with them before taking my leave."

I turned to proceed down the hill and then stopped short.

"Tell me. Who owns this hillside land? Do you know?"

"That I do not, sir. It is quite an encumbrance to the potential of expansion here, sir, is it not?"

"No. The hill must be bought, Smithe."

"Oh yes, Government has been so recommended; but the cost of the removal of so great a mass of earth has deterred them."

"Remove? Take away that noble hill? The most valuable bit of ground in the yard?"

Smithe looked at me, dumbstruck.

"No, no. But buy it—buy it as quickly as possible!"

My vision of the new Chatham Dockyard was taking shape in my head. I could not wait to return to my home and office room in Chelsea—and my drawing board.

* * *

Meanwhile, at Battersea, production of the boots was now in full swing. My patents for the machinery and durability of leather were granted. The previous manufacturers had got away with layering clay between the thin outer and inner soles, to give the appearance of a heavy, substantial boot. Considering that this practice seriously jeopardised the ability of England's own brave fighting men to carry out their duties on behalf of king and crown in foreign fields, where they were prepared to make the ultimate sacrifice, it was inexcusable. Beyond negligence, it was criminal.

No wonder that our facility had eventually met with the attention of the Army, who I knew had already made some tentative purchases of our products. Hypocrites!

Now I had received news that Lord Castlereagh, the Foreign Secretary, had been prompted by his Army Board dignitaries to issue an official order to supply sufficient boots to meet all of the Army's requirements. This would mean a considerable increase in production—to four hundred pairs a day; an amplification in overheads would result, which, I was assured, could be financed.

Whilst I was moderately pleased to be recognised in this manner, and welcomed the order and income that I might receive as a consequence, I would seek to gain assurances that payment for our products would be forthcoming, and not laden with the encumbrances and shortfalls that the Navy Board had all too readily employed.

I had a dedicated wife and a growing family to support, who would, no doubt, become more demanding over the passage of time. Consequently, I could not afford to take undue risks with my life, or theirs.

* * *

The King's Bench Prison
June 1821

I made my way down the stairs and out into the courtyard and fresher air. The high brick walls confronted me as I exchanged nods with the warden on the main gate. It was a warm evening, and I was content to be able to stretch my legs.

There were a few dishevelled prisoners in the yard; some sitting cross-legged or splayed on the ground, others leaning against the perimeter walls of the prison, either asleep or staring blankly into open space; no doubt affected by the alcohol which was their only escape.

A couple in ragged clothing were embracing by a return in the wall. They turned to me as I passed, and muttered something which I was glad not to hear as their tone was unfriendly.

I discovered a small wrought-iron bench tucked around the corner of the main building, and sat in isolation to gather my thoughts. The King's Bench Prison is the grim setting representing a great reverse in my fortunes. Just to think I escaped certain death as a young man in revolution-ravaged France, only to be faced with this!

But, despite my low mood, I knew that I had full support from my family and friends. My daughter Sophie's regular visits and constant support and encouragement sustained me through these dark times. What was the day? Friday, I reminded myself. I was beginning to lose all track of time. I could not allow myself to slip further into the mire. I must be strong. I was not alone. I was sure assistance was on its way.

CHAPTER TWENTY-FOUR

The King's Bench Prison
June 1821

HOW COULD I have been so naïve? My finances had already started to suffer badly by then. Just as it was of benefit to me in prison to use my designs and innovative ideas as a gratifying distraction to my and Sophia's woes, I had also reached the unpalatable conclusion that I had an inherent tendency to behave in exactly the same way outside these walls. That was the reality. My strength in engineering was undermined by a weakness in commercial affairs. Putting the fire at Battersea and the ensuing problems in my financial affairs behind me was almost too easy. With the benefit of hindsight and a greater application to money matters, would the circumstance have been different?

I made a conscious effort to stop berating myself, as the tension across my furrowed brow eased. My attention was happily redirected to steam power and the further development of my plans for engine efficiency. Now, if I contained the excess of steam that should be captured by the insertion of a safety valve in the waste pipe, the excess entering into the condensers... An easy modification for the capable Mr Henry Maudslay, I considered.

I cast my mind back to the running of this prototype. Maudslay and I were pleased with our efforts concerning the paddle steamer, Regent, on the London to Margate trip, despite the poor reception we received from the townspeople—well, one person in particular...

* * *

Thames Estuary
Summer 1814

My party on board The Regent were full of smiles and infectious excitement; amongst the mingling throng of dignitaries, it was easy to spot my dearest Sophia looking radiant in her azure dress. Waving goodbye to our young family hand-in-hand with Emilia, our family nursemaid, as we had set sail from the pier below London Bridge but a few hours ago, had set my heart racing, and my gratification was unbounded. The paddle steamer, newly equipped and powered by my double-acting steam engine, chugged and hissed its way along the Thames Estuary, as though the ship had a life of its own, with each piston cycle like a breathing, panting animal.

"She's running very well, Brunel," Maudslay commented as I turned from my view of the clay cliff shores of the Isle of Sheppey on the starboard side.

"I never doubted it, Maudslay. You've never let me down yet."

* * *

The hotel held an enviable position on the raised ground of the town's main thoroughfare, with largely uninterrupted views of the sea and harbour only a stone's throw away.

Margate was at the height of Regency gaiety and holiday life, as a mix of classes from London and beyond enjoyed the welcoming sandy beaches and lively public houses.

John Hyde did not consider himself a difficult man. Obstinate and opinionated, yes, but that was part and parcel of being a Yorkshireman; traits that separated him and his like from softer southerners. His life and adventures in the catering and leisure business, and marriage to Florence, a Kentish lass (or was it a lass of Kent?), had brought him to Margate. Naming the large guest house that occupied a prime position on the seafront 'The York Hotel' brought a certain inner smug satisfaction—as though he were imparting his own personal heritage and social culture on this corner of England as some sort of crusade.

'The army of well-wishers stretching across the quay with waving arms and festooned in vivid colours are delusional,' John thought. Their loud cheering and animated enthusiasm prompted by the

newness of it all—the notoriety, elegance and power of steam. It was as though the ship were humanised, as the steam cycle resonated like an old uncle breathing heavily under strain. John was not taken in. He would not admit to being impressed at the sight of this ship cutting elegantly through the harbour waters on its approach to the quay— pragmatic and sensible, his head would rule any feelings of romance.

The packet steamer The Regent represented a new era in ships. Whisps of vapour and puffs of smoke issued from its stout chimney as the rays of the setting sun bounced off her paddle wheel. It was the future. But not for John. It was going to be the start of the decline of the Margate Riviera, and of his livelihood. Sailing boats would be no more; fast, powerful, manoeuvrable steamships such as these would deny him, and the rest of Margate, valuable business from visiting Londoners; there was no doubt. They would degenerate into day trippers who would no longer need to stay.

There was one such man on board that ship today; a dignitary and engineer of noble esteem and French background, judging by the information John had heard and read in advance of his arrival. Esteem. *Est steam!* He chortled under his breath at the apt pun he had thought up on the spot.

And to think that this was all in the name of scientific progress, he mused.

From his vantage point leaning out of an upper bedroom window, John continued to watch the scene unfold before him, as the ship's passengers slowly disembarked onto the quay.

Women in gay dresses and flamboyant bonnets, men in grey-blue suits and top hats—apart from one man who wore a burgundy jacket and white cravat. This man seemed to be the centre of attention as he shook hands with all the suited bigwigs that lined up for his arrival, nodding and chatting as he went. '*That must be him,*' he thought.

He had had enough of taking in this scene. There were tables to prepare and lay and the chef to consult over the menu for this evening's dinner, and umpteen other things that this man and his wife needed to do as part of the routine management of his small but proud empire. He made his way down the wrought-iron balustraded staircase to the reception area.

"He's arrived, Flo."

His wife looked up from the bookings register and gave John a knowledgeable nod and forced smile. She accepted her husband's view on things, and had reluctantly accepted his decision. *'It was not wise to turn business away on principle,'* she thought, particularly when that business would likely lead to others of the uppermost level of society visiting their quaint abode and spending lavishly. They were busy, yes, but busy with guests who were out most of the day and spent their money in the many bars and public houses of Margate. Would steam ships ultimately destroy their way of life and affect their income? She doubted it very much, but her opinion counted for nothing. John was in charge of this business, and largely of their lives together.

To John, this notable man was the very personification of a threat to the livelihood of the hoteliers and other businesses in this quaint and busy harbour town. His feelings were further compounded by the fact that he was essentially French; repatriated yes, but still French. France—a nation that had been held to ransom by its own people and that had inflicted fear and loathing throughout Europe; governed by a tyrant who had placed all England in fear of invasion for many a year as his armies ran amok on the other side of the channel. John's close friend's son had lost his life at Waterloo, as had many brave young men of this country, and he was not the forgiving type.

The official announcement of this man's arrival had been received by the hotel some days ago, as an advanced booking for his stay. John had not replied. He felt, with tongue in cheek and an element of spite, that his humble and sparsely furnished hotel would surely be inadequate and insufficiently presented for a man of such notoriety. He deserved better!

Just then, three gentlemen and a well-attired lady entered the hotel lobby and stepped forward into the reception area—with porters carrying trunks and bags of various sizes, chattering and gazing around as they went.

The imposing gentleman he had earlier remarked upon lifted his head with a smile.

"Good evening, sir, madam. You have rooms here for us tonight, we believe."

The accent was undeniably Gallic. The gait and air of the man exuded confidence.

"No, I am sorry, sirs, there must be some mistake. We are full tonight," John replied with a smug, self-satisfied grin.

CHAPTER TWENTY-FIVE

The King's Bench Prison
June 1821

I DETERMINED TO work on my projects into the night, principally as a diversion from the reality of my confines and an escape from my ever-deepening depression. To stay focused on my work as an engineer left no room for selfish reflections of my decline. Sophia was very tolerant and understanding of my habit, and she lay asleep despite the glow of a candle from my work table.

The designs were set, and my pencil coursed sketches of my ideas and representations. As the thoughts and proposals became a coherent reality, and I applied the mathematical analysis to prove it, the ink would flow. This venture would mark a new era in mass production, and efficient processes were needed to produce goods plentifully and of good quality. I glanced up momentarily for inspiration; as I was wont to do.

I called to mind similar considerations in the economic management of timber and the hill overlooking the docks which would be the centre point of the new improved mechanised facility at Chatham. The hill was taken by all but me to be an encumbrance to the expansion and improvement of the dock facilities. To me, it was a distinct advantage.

I had designed a twin-walled elliptical shaft which was sunk into the hillside, rising some thirty-eight feet above high-water level and some sixty feet overall into the underlying chalk. From the bottom of this shaft, a tunnel was driven through the mast pond to the River Medway; the bottom of this shaft becoming a reservoir for timber floated from the river; clean timber—free of sand and gravel.

Close by, the sawmill, replete with new steam engines, was placed, served by a crane running on rails on a raised iron gantry with a flatbed carriage in tow. The carriage was winched up a gentle incline and delivered to the sawmill floor, where one of the single saw frames with seven sawblades attached to a high-level gantry spun at high speed, powered by the thirty-two-horsepower steam engine situated adjacent to the boiler house, with a cast-iron water tank in its roof.

Once the logs had been cut into laths, they would again be loaded onto the flat carriage and returned to the travelling crane, which would hoist them onto a rail truck, travelling some 800 feet to a shed for seasoning. Timber stacking areas would be available either side of the track. A tall chimney adorned the engine house and sawmill.

The design of the hydraulic apparatus necessary for raising the timber from the shaft reservoir consisted of a drum and pulley chain-driven elevator suspended in the shaft and counterpoised by water from a separate holding tank. When a balk timber had to be raised, the elevator was allowed to descend, at the same time raising the water level in the counterpoise sufficient to overcome the weight of the timber and float the timber to the surface of the shaft. I knew that my instinct was good and was confident my plan would work, but I remember at the time that I just needed a period to resolve a few issues...

"What is that, darling?" Sophia's voice permeated the stuffy stale air like a gentle, scented breeze.

I turned to touch her arm and gaze into her alert blue eyes.

"I am just musing over the old plans and proposals I did for Chatham dockyard and the new sawmill facility."

"Yes, but it is after one in the morning, my love. Cannot this wait until the morning, when perhaps you will have a clearer mind and a freshened body?"

She was right, as always.

Her hand felt comforting in mine as we made our way in silence to our bed. But my mind had been aroused by my project and reflections of Chatham, Ellacombe, and onward to my father's burial, and then a maelstrom of recollections—the Boot Factory finances... the fire at Battersea! I tossed and turned as images came and went. Sophia did not stir.

* * *

CHAPTER TWENTY-SIX

Chatham Docks
Autumn 1815

I DID NOT anticipate as many problems as those that occurred during the construction phase of the works at Chatham. These were rarely practical problems or ones concerning engineering design or specification, but rather with politics and people. To my utter dismay, I was not given sole charge of my project. As building progressed, my deliberate exclusion from matters directly affecting my design, and *de facto* building methods, inevitably manifested results in the overall low-quality standards achieved generally, but more specifically in certain structures.

I became concerned in particular about the structural integrity of the one-hundred-and-twenty-foot-high chimney serving the mill building. I noted that it was founded partly on clay and partly on chalk, which may have resulted in uneven settlement at foundation level. I wrote to Mr Edward Holl, the architect to the Navy Board, expressing my unease, whilst I halted the works on site for a time, which I considered prudent. I was overruled by those I considered unqualified to present a viable opinion—the Master and Assistant Shipwright, endorsed by Sir Robert Barlow of the Navy Board. To my disbelief, the work was restarted without any acknowledgement of my observations.

Six months later, following completion of the brickwork of this structure, I noted that cracks were appearing, and the chimney was bulging out. Mr Vinall, the works officer, was aware of it, and proposed to prop it by means of buttresses, but I recommended that, in addition, some wrought-iron ties be buried into the brickwork to reinforce the walls against the tensile stresses present as a result of the movement. No further displacements occurred.

My tunnel design, too, suffered a similar fate. Without my knowledge, my detail was altered from my elliptical inclined profile to a vertical segment section; presumably to simplify construction of the brickwork. It had disastrous results. In my absence, and as a consequence of the poor workmanship of the bricklayers (who often comprised unskilled labour or prisoners of war under little or no supervision), a collapse occurred, killing one man and injuring ten others. I was powerless to prevent this occurrence, and aware, too, that even had I had the opportunity to offer them, my advice and opinions would have probably gone unheeded, and matters would still have proceeded apace.

Whilst my conscience was clear, my moral duty and professional contractual obligation were left tarnished and devalued.

I had unfortunately encountered similar problems with the employment of suitably experienced and capable gentlemen both to manage the operations of the completed sawmill and to act as resident engineer. I considered that to leave such major considerations to the dockyard officials themselves (given the shortcomings admirably demonstrated during construction) would be folly. I therefore put forward the names of Mr Bacon and Mr Ellicombe to act in these capacities. Both were well-known to me: Bacon through his superintendence, mechanical skill, undoubted integrity and successes in the erection and commissioning of Borthwick's mills in Scotland, and of similar installations at the Woolwich Arsenal; Ellicombe as a friend and God-fearing man of immense practical knowledge and boundless enthusiasm.

My application for Bacon was rejected out of hand. The Navy Board wanted their own man in charge of operations again. Fearful of a repetition of the Burr saga that I had experienced at Portsmouth, I wrote directly to the Navy Board, pointing out that before untried combinations could be brought to act in unison and harmony, nothing should be left to chance. My words struck the intended chord and Bacon was reinstated 'until it shall be brought to that state that it may without risk be left to the management of others'. Bastards. They always wanted the last say, but I was prepared to acquiesce on this occasion, to keep the peace—both externally and in my head.

* * *

Hacqueville, France
Winter 1815

The sodden earth eased under my feet. Drizzle and murky skies fitted the mood amongst the mourners as I stood with my arm around the youngest of my siblings, partly for mutual comfort, partly for a show of unity. The raindrops dripping from my hat and running down my cheeks gave an appearance of grief, but I was not tearful; respect and resignation gave way to sorrow.

Father Bourget had intoned the required words, and we had all joined in silent prayer with hands clasped. The slightly bowed figure with walking stick that was now the elderly and frail François Carpentier looked solemnly on; glancing occasionally in my direction with a show of empathy for my feelings on this solemn day.

I had seldom felt close to my father. There were times, instances in my formative years, where his warmth shone through and I enjoyed his presence and his dedication to me; when he would carry me on his shoulders, introduce me to farm life, read me stories, carry me to bed after I had fallen asleep by the log fire—his cheeks close to mine; the sweet scent of wine on his breath. His influence, ironically, fuelled my sense of adventure and natural inquisitiveness. But my self-realisation, my growing independence and resourcefulness, put me in conflict with him and his determination to follow French culture and custom in committing me to priesthood against my will. In many ways, I was like him; determined and with a strong will. It was probably the similarities in character that paradoxically set us apart.

I wiped my eyes with my coat sleeve. Was that now a tear coursing down my cheek? Or just the path of another raindrop? Licking the top of my lip, I tasted the salt.

* * *

Chatham docks
Spring 1816

"It is good to see you back amongst us again, Mr Brunel."

"Thank you, Ellicombe."

Ellicombe was keen to demonstrate the efficiency and power of the counterpoise chamber for the raising of the balk timbers and their onward transportation through the mill. As we watched from above, the water level sloshed and rose from tunnel invert to just under chamber crest level, sweeping large and small logs in its vertical wake. I timed thirty seconds on my pocket watch for this occurrence.

"It was somewhat quicker than that, sir, but the timbers were flying up out of the chamber with such velocity that I had to introduce a braking system through the elevator, and counterpoise chains through balanced weight on the drum and base anchorage." Ellicombe ventured.

"Very good, Mr Ellicombe," I responded with a smile. "I appreciate your advice, and shall modify the design of this apparatus accordingly."

"Thank you, sir." He broke off. "But there are matters I beg to draw to your attention regarding my continued employment in the capacity of resident engineer. These have transpired since your departure and return from France."

This was unexpected.

"There is a letter on my desk addressed to you, Mr Brunel, in this respect. Although matters have evolved a little more in your absence, through my personal intervention on your behalf, I am afraid to say that I feel that my continued commitment to this project is compromised somewhat as a result."

* * *

Mr Brunel

I have to inform you that we have desired Commissioner Sir Robert Barlow to signify to Mr Ellicombe that his services are no longer required at Chatham to superintend the works connected with the sawmills.

We are your affectionate friends,
R Sapping
H Legge
Riley Middleton

* * *

I was deeply disappointed, and felt betrayed. Affectionate friends? I have had more affectionate enemies.

"Sir, I took it upon myself to respond directly in the manner of agent to your good self that I could not conscientiously abandon the trust you have committed to me in your absence, and certainly not without your authority," Ellicombe explained.

"Excellent."

"I subsequently received a response from the Naval commissioners to the effect that they acknowledge my letter and the sentiments expressed therein, but maintained that my salary will not be continued longer than the second day of next month."

I clenched my fists.

"I will remonstrate with the Navy Board forthwith, Mr Ellicombe. This cannot be. Your presence here is critical to the present and future success of Chatham, where I continue to place my trust and confidence in you. Those qualities I see in you, and my appreciation of your application of mind, have not in any way waned with the passage of time. I shall cite your superior education, liberal connections and your uncommon acquirements as qualities that are fitted to this role in every respect."

Ellicombe looked at me with wide eyes. I had a feeling that the sensibilities of this man of honour had been shaken, and that his confidence had been inexorably undermined. He knew in his head that I would write with all haste. I knew in my heart that he had given up, and that he would return to serving the Church.

* * *

Josiah Field and I pored over my drawings and sketches for the double-action steam engine I had in mind for the packet boat The Regent. Maudslay's capable draughtsman and technician would soon transform my ideas into detailed fabrication drawings to set the production of this beast into action.

The Chatham Mill office door flew open.

"Marc, I have some grave news for you," Bacon gasped. "Your mill at Battersea has been engulfed by fire."

I swallowed hard.

Bacon continued, "I understand that at the time another fire was raging in the city, so fire engines were delayed, and with the low water levels of the Thames very little could be used to extinguish the flames."

"My God, was anyone hurt?"

"There are no reports of any casualties, and all exertions were made to preserve the stock of wood and veneers. But all but the steam engine and one wing of the main building were, sadly, destroyed."

This was dreadful news. Over six years of work, expense and ingenuity had gone into this project, but I had to remain positive; I had no choice.

"That is a setback, but at least I can make better machinery now." I tried to sound sanguine.

Bacon looked a little perplexed, but Josiah smiled politely.

I knew that this misfortune would not be without its consolation, and I should now have the opportunity of carrying out the many improvements which I had often contemplated. The implications on the finances would have to wait. Insurances were in place.

CHAPTER TWENTY-SEVEN

The King's Bench Prison
June 1821

WE WATCHED FROM the small casement window as the summer shower ran down the windows and listened to the sound reverberating through the rafters. Our isolation was made all the more real as the raindrops resembled our tears, the drumming on the roof representative of our heavy hearts. Sophia and I were keeping our heads above water, but it was difficult for us not to sink beneath the waves occasionally. I continued to write to friends and colleagues for assistance in my case for release through payment of my debts from the Navy Board, but nothing had yet succeeded.

The room remained grey and damp. The downpour persisted. Sophia put her arm round me, and we stood in silence for some minutes. Words were not needed. Our silence spoke volumes.

The rain and wind called to mind our return from France through a storm and tempestuous seas. If I had not taken control of our vessel to steer an alternative course into Deal Harbour, further up the east coast of Kent, we may all have perished.

* * *

Northern France
Spring 1817

We were all returning through France after embarking on our first visit *en famille*. I had not been in my mother country since my father's funeral two years ago, when the country was still under Napoleonic rule. Out of necessity, I had taken a calculated risk coming then; but no such threat represented itself this time.

The revolution was now over. Napoleon was exiled and the displaced supporters of the monarchy had returned to France in their droves to support the brother of the executed king. Louis XVIII was now in power through the newly restored Bourbon dynasty; the *Ancien régime* was consigned to the past, and a constitutional monarchy under reformation reigned. Some civil unrest and disturbances were occurring, but in my country, now enjoying a reverse in politics, that was always likely to be the case. The revolution had pushed the population to the extremes of rebellion and discord, but even I could see that some good had come of it, as an element of democracy and compassion now took hold. I say 'my country', but it no longer feels that way. Yes, it is the country of my birth and my early upbringing, but that part of my existence now seems as if it was another life. I have married an Englishwoman and have children who are growing up in England; these realities, and the fact that England became my solace, my harbour and shelter from the storm raging on the other side of *La Manche,* made me feel almost an Englishman myself.

Paris, under the control of Napoleon in the dark days of revolution and beyond, had forgotten about the importance of life's necessities—too troubled and diverted by matters of rebellion and fighting to notice that food and water were needed too. Hence the reason for my return. The English company employing me were tendering for a formidable project which had the blessing of the king—to supply the capital with clean fresh water—and I was employed as their ambassador. Whether the scheme would proceed or not I was not sure, as the city was already served by numerous water porters whose livelihood depended on their continued employ.

Sophia's profile, silhouetted against the early morning sun radiating through the coach window, made me smile and eased my troubled mind. Emma's small hand held Sophia's tight as the coach bumped and swayed. To her left, and nestled snugly against me, Sophie grasped my arm with one hand; she was rapidly growing into a fine woman and was the apple of her mother's eye.

It was bright in the east, but threatening dark clouds were moving fast across the sky in the west; a prophecy, perhaps, on my life? So many things were happening that it was sometimes difficult to keep track, but paradoxically I preferred it that way. Life was like a fast-moving stream where you had to keep the boat upright and sail in the right direction—sometimes deviating where necessary, occasionally tacking with the wind, but never effectively changing course. My work and profession drove me on; my family would benefit from my endeavours and live in the style and comfort that befitted their position in society. I was determined this should be the case, and would do everything in my power to make it so.

The fields and avenues of France danced by as we made our way to Calais; the tall trees wrestling with the wind, the long wheat-fields rippling in swathes with every gust as the light changed from sunlight to shade with the passing of each cloud. It was safe to travel in France now, and I was thankful not to be in fear for our lives.

The rain advanced across the horizon, driven by the strengthening winds from the west. We boarded the French schooner as the sails were being set by the crew members, their strength tested by the sheer force of the gale facing them.

Once we had cast off and left the shelter of the harbour, the sea and vicious wind took over. White-topped waves soon unfurled and crashed against our bow as we plummeted into La Manche and rolled our way across the short stretch of sea to Dover. I had experienced similar circumstances many times before in my travels as a cadet and since, but my young family clearly had not; the wide-eyed expressions and grey complexions told their own story, as did those of the handful of other passengers making the difficult journey.

Most were reluctant to go below deck as the continuous rocking and rolling of the ship would exacerbate their *mal de mer*, so instead they sought cover from the rain in the outside cabins near the wheel-house, watching the oppressive swell and breakers from a position of relative safety.

Captain Chevalier gave the appearance of a competent seafaring man at first sight; a man with weather-beaten face and fixed stern expression. But as the short voyage progressed and we gradually lost sight of Calais harbour, his confidence seemed to evaporate. You could see it in his eyes; fear has no hiding place. He was making straight for Dover, defying the onslaught south-westerly whipping around the ship and driving the waves into towering rolling peaks: the frail vessel was being forced further east. Chevalier's attempts to tack and compel the craft back on course were admirable, but eminently futile, as the sails shook and the rigging rattled.

A huge breaker, having raised the ship up momentarily, came crashing down, rendering the foredeck awash with a foaming lake of salt water.

It was at this juncture I became convinced that the captain's navigation of this vessel was less than capable. It appeared I was not the only one. The fear on the faces of the crew, and the manner in which they were issuing orders to each other, revealed that faith in the captain was wearing thin. The terror of the passengers, my family among them, compelled me to confront Captain Chevalier myself.

I staggered across the slippery wet deck and entered the small bridgehouse where the captain struggled to control the ship's wheel.

"S'il vous plaît, puis je vous offrir mon aide, mon capitaine? It is my opinion that we should be running with the wind, sir."

Chevalier gave me a look like thunder. *"Je peux vous assurer, monsieur, je sais ce que je fais."*

"I respect you, sir, as a seafaring man of standing and experience, but as one who has myself experienced similar situations whilst I was with the French Navy, I implore you to change course."

"The crew members and passengers are my responsibility, Monsieur."

The scent of alcohol on his breath told me that a little Dutch courage was fuelling this man's determination and bloody-mindedness. I shook my head. It was hopeless. Unless something was done soon, the ship was in grave danger of floundering on rocks or being swept onto the notorious shallow bank of Goodwin Sands. We were at the peril of a foolish and foolhardy captain acting independently from his crew, who were now refusing to obey orders.

Just then, Monsieur Becancourt, an eminent fellow whom I had met briefly at the harbour docks passenger waiting area, joined us in the sea-swept bridge house.

"Monsieur Chevalier! The passengers are in fear of their lives, and it is obvious we are all in grave danger. Even this experienced and capable seafaring man at your side can see it. On behalf of all the people here present on this ship, I beseech you to defer from your current course, and hand over command to Mr Brunel here." A small wad of bank notes was suddenly thrust into the captain's face.

Chevalier's determination changed to reluctant acceptance. No doubt, the money helped. He left the wheel house and trudged slowly below deck to the shelter of his cabin, but not before turning to us and muttering.

"J'espère que vous sachiez ce que vous faites, monsieur." And with that, he stumbled and just managed to prevent himself from falling down the last few steps to the lower deck by grabbing the short length of timber balustrade, wrenching his arm in the process. "*Mon Dieu*!" A burly crew member staggered to his aid, and escorted him below deck. I immediately took hold of the ship's wheel.

"Monsieur Brunel, the whole crew is with you, and will respond to your orders! The second in command of this ship knows you from your navy days and has full confidence in your ability," Becancourt cried.

I wasted no time, changing course to favour the prevailing south-westerlies. My heart was beating fast; my head a mélange of excitement and caution. We would head further east along the Kent coast away from Dover and seek haven at an alternative port.

CHAPTER TWENTY-EIGHT

The King's Bench Prison
June 1821

TODAY I RECEIVED a letter from my friend Louis Breguet, prominent horologist in Paris, extolling the virtues and capability of young Isambard as potential apprentice to the makers of fine chronometers, clocks and scientific instruments. I was naturally extremely pleased that he was continuing to make good impressions and progress, following on from the college in Caen and the Lycée Henri-Quatre in Paris. As I had planned, a sound academic foundation through mathematics and science was being supplemented with practical knowledge; mirroring my formative years and passion for mechanics on the *ferme Brunel* in Normandy all those years ago.

This news was a sliver of light in our dreary, soul-destroying gloom. I would continue to protect Isambard from the knowledge that we were here; it would do him no good to learn of our serious decline of fortune. News of his progress delighted and emboldened us. We missed him very much.

Isambard was gaining independence and knowledge speedily. He left the family bosom as a schoolboy and would return as a young man. But naturally it was the evocative image of him as a young boy that stayed with me during these dark, foreboding days.

* * *

4 Lindsay Row, Chelsea
Summer 1817

I was happy to be back at my office in Lindsay House, to spend some time on my designs and be alone for a period of reflection. It was paradoxical, I mused, that I found some solace and peace away from the rush and clamour of London and business life by retreating here and immersing myself in my drawings and calculations. There were occasions when I barely had time to draw breath. This was different.

I sometimes found it difficult to accept that Isambard was fast becoming a man. I remembered the first time he sat on my high stool, giving him an advantage, as my drawing board was in a raised position and too high for a child. His legs swung back and forth and youthful eyes gleamed as he took in the sight before him. His enthusiasm for drawing and sketching was exceptional, and his readiness to immerse himself in mathematics brought a warm feeling of satisfaction to my heart. He had already absorbed the fundamentals of Euclidean geometry from my teachings. Notes and diagrams peppered with equations, numerical and Greek symbols gave way to beige parchments showing details of the bridge I was working on with its main and navigation spans; all were absorbed by his willing spirit and inquiring, exploring gaze.

"Is this a bridge that will be built, Father?"

"Yes, I certainly hope so, my son."

From the age when he uttered his first words Isambard was inquisitive, almost as though he were in a hurry to open the door to the world and rush in, feeding his desire for adventure. The fact that this adventure took the form of engineering drawings and calculations enthralled me. My first child, Sophie, had the same insight and intelligence, but the opportunities to make the most of them in this profession were not open to her. Engineering was for stout-hearted gentlemen; a messy industrial environment not at all suited to the gentler sex and a professional landscape that would neither tolerate nor be accepting of women.

It doesn't seem so long ago that I was cradled in similar fashion by my father. He undoubtedly was an influence on my life, but without the connection that exists between my son and me. I felt this strongly from Isambard's early age. It could be argued that a combination of my nurturing and the expectations of society have contributed to my son's character, but I have seen that this young man was born with natural ability, too. Early signs are that he can at least emulate my professional success as an engineer. A pipe-dream? A father's desire for his son to achieve meaning and focus in his future life and reach his full potential? A strong protective arm around a slender and innocent boy's narrow shoulders? Yes. All of these reasons and more.

I would naturally take it upon myself to ensure Isambard would have the very best education and guidance—not only academically but in manners and breeding necessary to be in the best possible position to enjoy life through a work ethic and drive to succeed. Much of his early academic tutoring and guidance came from myself, supplemented by schooling by Dr Morrell in Hove, where he studied the classics. I had dedicated the time and effort in his home life through my influence and fathering. Isambard spent long spells in my office, and I presented him with testing and extensive homework in mathematics, French and English to give him a foundation for a successful professional livelihood—hopefully in engineering like myself. I will do everything in my power to make this so.

With Isambard now safely ensconced at boarding school in Hove, I felt satisfied that his education was proceeding on strong lines.

* * *

The bridge over the River Neva in St Petersburg was proving to be quite a challenge for me as I began to re-examine the drawings and designs that I had begun all those years ago. His Imperial Majesty Alexander I, Czar of Russia, had sent word through his ambassador here in London requesting my services on this project. I naturally felt privileged. I had met the Imperial family when they paid a visit to our factory at Portsmouth, and I had obviously made a favourable impression. I looked again at the diamond ring on the little finger of my right hand as I briefly reflected on that event, and on this unexpected gift 'in recognition of my worth and high regard'. There were a number of difficulties to overcome with this bridge's structure—the span in excess of eight hundred feet and the harsh winter climate, to name but two.

I gazed upward to the corniced ceiling and thought of the many times I placed my son gently to the floor, embracing his warm young body, pressing my face onto his smooth cheek. I closed my eyes momentarily and was filled with satisfaction and comfort.

Sophia appeared at the door just in that instant.

"Marc. It is after midnight. Time for you to retire to bed. You need your sleep."

I smiled and kissed her waiting cheek. "Just a few moments more, my dear."

It had not been a good time for Sophia. Baby Harriet had lived but a year before being taken from us without warning one dreadful night. I put all thoughts of what might have been to the back of my mind as much as I could, but it was difficult. I had to tell myself that, if God had decreed it was not to be, it would be for the good of all.

I returned to my calculations and preliminary drawings scattered over the drawing board. I had already spent some months on this bridge project with no remuneration to date, as the vast majority of the work I had already carried out was on feasibility studies only. I visited many alternative approaches until they either met a natural end through problems of scale or proportion, or by adopting the recognised properties of each of the construction materials used and their allowable stresses through mathematical analysis.

My first inclination was to take an innovative approach and study a suspended bridge option, but this floundered early in my considerations, as the proportions were huge and the deck would need to be elevated well above the masts of passing ships at high tide in the river below.

My experience of tunnelling design and construction at Chatham gave me the impetus to consider a similar crossing here, but, as I discovered late in the process, unlike at Chatham the geology in and around the Neva was predominantly weak clay and soft alluvium as opposed to stable chalk rock.

I sat back and scanned all in front of me. The drawings had a symmetry and purpose that encouraged me to develop this exciting venture more. The central arched timber truss section would be hinged so it could be raised for ships and lowered for road traffic. This had not been attempted before, but was entirely achievable. I would engage upon a memorandum to the Russian Ambassador here in London, giving more details of my proposals. Fir timber, I considered, was best adapted to the construction of an arch of such dimensions.

I envisaged that this massive structure would be constructed in some convenient locality, sheltered from frost, and, when completed, and the river free of ice, floated into place.

Yes! Four massive pontoons would form the platform; the abutments and piers would rest on the heads of a number of timber piles designed not only to support the weight but also to take into account any lateral pressure…

My mind began to race; my enthusiasm buoyed. All thoughts of sleep departed. I could hardly put my ideas down on paper quickly enough.

CHAPTER TWENTY-NINE

Pall Mall, London
Autumn 1817

HENRY SANSOM TWISTED the ends of his long moustache and pondered over the sets of figures in front of him. His high-ceilinged office in the annexe of private chambers in Pall Mall was testament to his position as a man of proven banking experience. A friend of the Kingdoms, and a man whose acquaintance I had made in private functions, I trusted his opinion. I knew he would speak his mind and provide good advice.

I sat in silence and expectation at the other side of his impressive oak desk, occasionally glancing at the view of the busy street outside through the arched windows. The muted sounds of hooves on cobble and men's voices were punctuated by the shuffling of the pages between Samson's fingers. My mood was circumspect, as a result of the official letter I had received not three days ago from the Czar, confirming that, regrettably, the Neva Bridge project would not be proceeding in the near future due to a lack of finance. Although the missive expressed some hope that the project would be resurrected in the future, when more prosperous times were expected, this was of little consolation to me as I had devoted considerable time and effort to this scheme to no avail, and, more importantly, no income. I had even constructed scale models of the bridge ready to take to St Petersburg and present to the Russian authorities and dignitaries as a precursor to finalising my design and commencing construction on site.

My thoughts were interrupted by Sansom as he rested the papers on the desk before him and peered over his narrow-rimmed spectacles:

"Marc, may I ask you a few questions?"

"Yes, of course."

"I have here the accounts and bank records for the sawmill at Battersea and the boot factory, together with an inventory of your personal transactions over the period. It is disturbing, to be frank."

I was under no delusion that my current financial position was anything other than challenging—after all, that is exactly what initially prompted me to attend Mr Sansom's establishment—but I did not necessarily expect such an austere approach from him. I decided to break the silence.

"I am acquainted with the actuality that profits from the boot factory are disappointingly low. Most of the holding stock had to be sold on only slightly above cost due to the withdrawal of the order from the Government following the cessation of hostilities with France. I have pleaded my position to the highest standing I am able to—namely the Chancellor of the Exchequer himself—in order that such monies that I am due are settled fairly and amicably. I may add that I also have approached the Prussian government and am expecting to enter negotiations with them quite soon for the supply of similar shoemaking machinery for their regiments.

"As for the sawmill, it is still recovering, with the help of insurance money, from the unfortunate fire that almost destroyed the whole works a year past. It is now back in production and making good headway. I expect a full recovery in due course as the products that this facility produces remain in high demand."

Sansom listened intently, with a half-smile on his face.

"Yes, and I know too, Marc, that the boot factory provided necessary employment to those British war veterans invalided out from the recent conflicts. Your generosity of spirit and presence of mind deserve the utmost recognition and credit."

"Thank you, Henry. You are most kind."

"The problem that exists across this horizon of endeavour and fortitude that you have most ably demonstrated is that, notwithstanding the ill-fortune and bad treatment you have received at the hands of others, the successes you have enjoyed are unfortunately not reflected in your bank balance."

I could sense that he was fighting within himself; on the one hand showing the empathy of a personal and understanding friend, on the other a gentleman of sound standing and impeccable business habits who would have to state plainly and robustly the way things were. I respected that.

I continued.

"Money is still owing to me from the Admiralty regarding the Portsmouth Sawmill, and design work I have undertaken at Chatham and elsewhere under the auspices of the Navy Board. I am pressing them for payment. I also embarked upon a bridge design and tunnel feasibility study for the Czar of Russia on the promise of a commission, which was unfortunately not forthcoming."

"Yes, I see." Sansom acquiesced. "However, you unfortunately allowed the shoe operations to become financially intertwined with the saw establishment in a most confusing way. The balance sheet and profit and loss record for each company demonstrate disparities almost beyond the regular understanding of normal accountancy methods."

I felt a little embarrassed, but also considered there were mitigating circumstances that he, or indeed most others, would not know about or appreciate.

Sansom broke off for a moment to collect his thoughts. The timber floorboards creaked in response to the rise and fall of his tall frame as he fidgeted for position and stance.

"The more I investigate, the more I feel it necessary that for your safety you should sift to the bottom of every cash transaction. It was a most extraordinary jumble, which you have certainly not understood, and I should have wondered if you had. I could hardly have been more surprised had one of your saws walked to town."

I could not help but blurt out a laugh, much to my and my host's temporary embarrassment, quickly followed by a feeling of admonishment like a schoolboy who had misbehaved in class. But I pressed on.

"I can accept that things are not exactly as I would like to find them at the moment, but I have many other irons in the fire, including very firm interests in the printing industry. I am convinced that the cylinder press represents the future of mass printing for wider circulation newspapers. I have patented improvements in making stereotype plates with engineering firm Taylor and Martineau of Whitecross Street here in London. The proprietor of *The Times*, John Walter, is keenly interested. A pocket copying press is also in the throes of manufacture and supported by my former business partner Mr Farthing, with whom I believe you are well acquainted."

I felt I had Sansom's full attention now. I had no doubt that, despite his misgivings regarding my bank account, my prospects could only improve.

"I may add that I have also filed a patent for 'A New Species of Tin Foil' which will decorate many a gift in a most effective way and is already proving popular. The capital investment in this venture is modest. I am confident that, apart from any other of my ventures, a strong upturn in my finances will result from this very quickly."

Sansom removed his spectacles and rose from his desk. He took some deliberate strides toward the window and then stood in silence with his back to me for what seemed some considerable time but which was probably only seconds.

"This is all very encouraging, but the fact still remains that, as we stand today, your present state of finance does not match your obvious confidence and innovative engineering achievements."

He turned to face me:

"In short, one cannot bank promises. It may take you some time to recover from your present position. It is, as you so rightly say, just a matter of time. But how much time?"

Sansom continued, "You came here today to seek my independent opinion on your position, which I am happy to do. Your enterprises all offer huge potential, as would be warranted of a man of your professional standing. But I would say that you now cannot afford to commence any more business ventures on the back of the many that you have already embarked upon. Your energy, enthusiasm and capacity for launching multiple business enterprises are all qualities to be admired, Marc, but you must tread more carefully from now on if you want to avoid over-commitment and undermining the basic resources that your household needs to survive. I say this as both your friend and your banker.

"I will present a full report to you in due course once I have undertaken legal advice."

The realisation of the poor state of my financial affairs, whilst not entirely unexpected, alarmed me.

* * *

4 Lindsay Row, Chelsea
Winter 1817

"If you have ever been ill in your life, and have depended upon medical advice, fall down on your knees and bless God that you have fewer doctors than you have had lawyers about you. If that had not been the case, you might have been making sawmills on the other side of the Styx, or inventing a steam boat for old Charon."

Sophia turned to me and smiled. "My goodness, I didn't realise that Mr Sansom had the ability to look on the lighter side of life through adversity."

I had passed the letter from Sansom to my wife for her perusal. It was frank and helpful, but through the veil of humour there was a dark undercurrent. I was prepared as always to share my burdens with my wife, not necessarily in a quest for answers but more in the sharing of the pressures of everyday life. She was generally little acquainted with my professional working life; but I deliberately took the time to involve her from time to time, particularly in monetary affairs, as I considered it her right to know how matters stood, and the potential effect on our family. She asked very few questions of me regarding my professional work and finances. It was I who sought out her valued opinion on these occasions, in order to seek comfort. I was not afraid of admitting that to myself.

Sophia read on.

"Your conduct from the commencement of our treaty has been in the highest degree honourable, liberal and convivial; and, although I am very anxious for my friend, I can sometimes hardly help regretting that I could not myself embark with you. Your business at Battersea, I can very clearly see, is to be made a very lucrative one, and if I were your partner, I would answer for showing you a very different balance sheet for the year 1818."

"Yes, the letter is sympathetic and friendly, Sophia. Sansom is a good man who talks with integrity and vigour, and not without some wit, as you note, my darling."

Sophia moved closer to me on the sofa, held my hand and looked into my eyes.

"I know things are difficult for you at present, Marc, but I want you to know that I will always remain at your side to provide the succour you desire."

CHAPTER THIRTY

Battersea
Spring 1819

THE IMPRESSION ONE gained after visiting the Battersea Factory depended entirely on which section of the plant had been seen and experienced. One area was clearly marked with industry of purpose and noise as workers, busy about their tasks, performed their duties with dedication and determination. This was the tin foil manufacturing sector, where men and machine worked in harmony in the process of first melting thin sheets of foil on iron plates, running them out smoothly and excluding all air pockets before applying additional heat to produce fusion through gas flames creating crystallisation before being placed in acid baths and then varnished. The colours and hues were magnificent and would go on to adorn many a decorative box, lamp column or all manner of household ornaments.

Only a few paces away, in a separate division of the plant, saws buzzed and workers were animated as production continued apace, albeit now on a reduced capacity and modest scale since the need for ships' blocks had waned.

The drone of activity from these two areas of the facility contrasted starkly with the now silent and empty factory space that had, until recently, been occupied by the disabled and compromised servicemen who had worked so dedicatedly on the production of leather footwear. Only their spirit and the eddying breeze through half-open doors remained.

Samuel Shaw paced across the sawdust-strewn floor, taking time to stop and make individual comments to operatives and labourers alike as he saw fit. He also paused occasionally to reflect on a bygone era; the high, uneven stacks of unsold boots in the store adjacent to the now ghostly section of Battersea told their own story. It was his habit to retreat to this part of the plant to collect his thoughts and gain some peace of mind away from the hurly-burly and noise of men and machines, and to set about the task of reconciling the business orders, requisitions and invoicing.

His tall, sinewy body slumped into the upright wooden chair; his mood reflective. Shaw was a man of principle. An educated gentlemen of good stock with a supportive family, he had become a friend and business partner to Marc Brunel through like-minded London businessmen. Although initially a little distracted by Marc's French accent, unlike some of his friends in English society, he had no axe to grind with the French nation. After all, the Paris orders for foil were plentiful; but now he harboured reservations. Not concerning nationality or the fact that he and Marc had become partners in this business, but ones surrounding the present management and financing of this facility. These reservations were counterbalanced with the respect and understanding he had for Marc—a man of proven engineering ability. But Shaw had a mind of his own, and the present facility, particularly vulnerable to foreign copycat imports of similar tin foil products, was at the nub of his worries. They were encroaching upon the very patent Marc and he had spent so much time over. They had to start protecting their rights. Shaw would have to write to him to make these opinions known.

He shuffled the paperwork strewn across his desk as he reached for his quill and ink.

I am so sick and tired of the vexatious occurrences and disappointments at Battersea, that I should be glad to get rid of the whole concern altogether. Others are making fine profits by the invention applied to tubes alone, of which, as I told you, 500 were supplied by one man.

As to going out to the works, I must give up. The walk is too much for me, and, upon my honour, I cannot afford 12s for the ride. I feel no inclination to incur fresh expenses by going to law; indeed, the uncertainties of the whole concern do not appear to me to justify it.

Further, I have nothing to recommend for the extension of this business as you propose, but an active traveller to exhibit specimens of the works.

Shaw lifted his slight frame and fixed his eyes on the words he had just written. He was aware of the brusque nature of his missive, but the continuing pain and discomfort from his legs had soured his mood considerably.

* * *

I was disappointed, albeit not entirely surprised, to receive the latest missive from Samuel Shaw. Does he not realise that I have always considered that exact plan, and have pressed for its execution for a long time as the only way to ensure the success of this, or any business? The most valuable time is now wasting away. Many of those who have manifested a wish to have the product have heard nothing of us since. If Mr Shaw would have come only once a week, he would have then directly seen how matters went on. It is obviously impossible to trust everything to correspondence with this man. I kept only the colours in order to prepare the product as it is required. Others can sell plates, whereas the Battersea concern is left to itself! How can this man expect any satisfactory result from such mode of proceeding?

It is six months, if not more, since this man set foot on the premises of a concern in which he was so deeply interested.

In saying that, the books are in good order; the manufacturing part is, I think, complete; but the main point appears left to chance.

Now is the time to consider putting in place an individual of trust and integrity who will act as the link between myself and Mr Shaw. We then would see Mr Shaw in the City as frequently as it needs to progress matters with greater efficiency and purpose than is being exhibited now.

In the present state, I would rather do as he proposes. Wind up the business in a way that will protect it against those claims that are upon it. I would rather sacrifice the whole at once than suffer things to go on the present way.

Time now to place these exact sentiments in writing to Shaw before taking the time out from my other commitments to meet up with him at the plant.

CHAPTERTHIRTY-ONE

The King's Bench Prison
June 1821

YESTERDAY I WAS visited, here in my cell room, by my old friend Dr Woolaston of the Navy, who brought along his colleague the Admiral Sir Edward Codrington. Their presence and intelligent discourse raised my spirits for a time, which sadly diminished again on the realisation of my predicament. My sanity was being maintained; firstly by diversion as I plunged into examining improvements in marine steam engines for which I hoped to file a patent as soon as I escaped the clutches of the accursed law, and secondly through Sophia's dedication. She has never left my side and gives me undying comfort and reassurance. Even as I sit at my desk, drawings, calculations and letters spilling out before me, she sits on the bed mending my stockings. I try to keep my anxieties to myself for her sake and that of the family, but I know that she understands my real mood. She smiles as our eyes meet.

"Marc, you know that your good friend Lord Spencer is conducting a campaign for your debts to be paid by the Government and hasten your release? He is supported in this quest by the Duke of Wellington and other dignitaries who are leading negotiations on your behalf. These influential men are concerned that you might be inclined to take your engineering knowledge and experience out of our country, as well you could."

"Yes, I am aware, my darling. Whether anything will come of it to change this government's entrenched obstinacy, I doubt. Also, our Sophie tells me that her new husband is campaigning on my behalf."

It was ironic that Sophia should interrupt my scribbling to invoke Lord Spencer's intervention just as I was considering putting ink to paper in a letter to this very gentleman.

She was right in her observations, of course. A thought suddenly occurred to me. The only figure on an international stage who would be able to assist me in my plight and take on my employment in future would be my acquaintance and mutually respectful ally Alexander I, the Czar of Russia. I should contact him immediately through the Russian Consul here in London. And what jealousy might that stir up from the upper circles of England as a result! It smacks of desperation, perhaps, but these are desperate times. Might it be possible that my favoured project, the Neva Bridge, could be resurrected and that the Russian Treasury would now be prepared to sanction this wonderful project that I had spent so much time on?

I sat back in my chair and stared, unseeing, at the grey stone wall in front of me. My spirit was elevated simply by contemplating this remarkable possibility. I could quite easily declare myself and family ready to leave for St Petersburg, take Russian nationality and work under the protection of the Czar. In my meetings with him, he had certainly appeared more enlightened, liberal and honest than this callous British government.

I scratched my nose with my quill in excited expectation. Yes....

CHAPTER THIRTY-TWO

Government House
Rotten Row
City of London
18th June 1821

Mr Benjamin Hawes esq
Barge House
Lambeth

My dear Sir

Mr Arbuthnot has told me that it is the intention of the Government to do something immediately with a view to relieve Mr Brunel from his present difficulties. He added that a report was current, that Mr Brunel would, on being released, go to Russia, and that, if such were to be the case, the Government would not relieve him; for the step they now take is more in liberality than absolute justice, and they have a right to hope for the benefit of his future services. I answered that I had, in the first instance, made it my business to come to a distinct understanding on this point with Mr Brunel, who had told me that it was not his intention to go to Russia if he could get employment here; that upon his relief from his difficulties, he should apply to the Government for employment.

If they would not give an immediate answer, he should wait, and if in the meantime a distinct offer came from Russia, he should then go to the Government, and say: I applied to you for employment—you gave no answer—here is an offer from Russia. I must starve, or get employment here, or go to Russia. You cannot expect me to starve; will you give me employment, or shall I go to Russia? And then only should he, upon further declining to give him employment here, go to Russia.

Yours

John Bandinel

On behalf of The Foreign Office

* * *

Benjamin Hawes, with my daughter Sophie at his side, presented the letter to me. Sophie—my ever-present hope in heart and mind. My darling daughter whom I loved so dearly, looking as radiant and beautiful as the day of her wedding just last year...

* * *

Lambeth, London
Summer 1820

She was the light of my life and the mirror image of her mother; I would be more than a little grieved to see her leave the immediate family, but this was inevitable. I could not hold onto my dearest first-born forever. She had her own life to lead, and what better consort and husband than the eldest son of my dear friend and confidant, Benjamin Hawes?

Sophie looked absolutely beautiful today in her full satin dress with her dark hair piled up in curls. She was so happy that she sparkled like the precious jewel she had become. It didn't seem a day since I first held her in my arms. I had high hopes for her. Although society decreed that, as a woman, however capable, Sophie would never be able to pursue the professional career for which she was eminently suited she would, I was sure, be fulfilled by the choices she made in life.

I sat hand in hand with Sophia, a broad smile on my face as I surveyed all before me. The elaborate chalked patterns on the polished timber floor were slowly being eroded by the steps of many dancers as they glided effortlessly around the gaily bedecked ball-room. The new waltz had arrived on these shores from the continent and, despite the misgivings of some of the more staid Englishmen and women, our guests seemed to have taken to it with enthusiasm. The gentlemen in their silks, satins and white ruffled shirts were almost as resplendent as the colourfully adorned ladies, all swirling happily to the music of the enchanting string quartet.

I myself was more adept at dancing the French cotillion, though I was not as young or agile as I used to be. The occasion, and fuelled no doubt by a small excess of wine, gave me the courage to take my turn at the dance. I could not be happier. That was not exactly true. My son, Isambard, was unable to attend, obliged to remain in Caen to continue his studies. I missed him greatly.

"Ah Marc, what splendid proceedings!"

My former business partner Farthing, with his charming wife on his arm, approached us as we left the dance floor.

"Naturally, I am overjoyed." I beamed.

"By the way, your pocket copying press currently being manufactured by Messrs Taylor and Martineau is an immediate success."

"That is good news, on more good news!" I responded heartily, but in a manner brief and blunt enough for Farthing to realise that I had no intention of discussing business with him today.

Our grand and glorious occasion was drawing to a close. Sophie and her new husband would soon be leaving the gathering to take up residence here in Lambeth at the home of the Hawes family. The guests, tired and happy, were saying their reluctant goodbyes and strolling slowly towards the carriages awaiting them at the door. No one, least of all myself, wanted this magical celebration to end.

* * *

The King's Bench Prison
June 1821

My dear wife looked over my shoulder and we read the letter from Bandinel at Government House together. I was relieved more than joyous, but Sophia embraced me delightedly.

"Marc, at last this is good news!"

"The letter comes with a grant of £5,000 on the understanding that you will abandon any thoughts of going to Russia," Benjamin added.

I reflected on this. I had been forsaken and then abandoned by this government numerous times before, but it appeared that, in this instance, my plea was at last being heard.

"No doubt this appears, on the face of it, to be welcome news, but it will all take time. The cogs in the machine of politics and justice in this country move very slowly."

CHAPTER THIRTY-THREE

The King's Bench Prison
July 1821

I WAS PENNING a communication to my friend Dr Wollaston in utter consternation. Time was dragging on with no further word despite my having given assurances that I was prepared to devote my future services and talents for the benefit of my country. I was still entombed in this stinking den, along with my resolute but now weary wife, and entirely depressed and disconsolate:

> *...If I had been guilty of any crime against the State, I could not be treated with more severity, not to say cruelty, than I am. After the most unequivocal assurance of relief with profession of liberality, nine successive Board days have gone by without producing the least effect. Good God, when will this end! Day after day without any favourable issue. My worthy friend Bandinel is ill. I am indeed wretched, much beyond I was in the first fortnight of this confinement, when my whole property was, as it were, gone from me. I then, feeling confidence in my own exertions, had made up my mind for the future. I am at present so completely overcome as to be at times alarmed as to the state of my nerves.*

* * *

I returned to the letter I was inscribing privately to Lord Spencer:

> *...but I feel now, as the months have dragged on, that my affectionate wife and I are sinking under it. We have neither rest by day nor night. Were our enemies at work to effect the ruin of my mind and body, they could not do so more effectually. It is now ten weeks that I am in this cruel position. I have called to my aid all the forces of my soul, but I feel I cannot longer support that which may compromise my name in the eyes of the world.*

CHAPTER THIRTY-FOUR

The King's Bench Prison
10 August 1821

AT LAST, I was released from the dreaded King's Bench Prison.

There was little rejoicing in me; only a sense of due justice and relief, as if a great weight had been removed from my shoulders, head and heart.

It would take many weeks to reconcile ourselves to the fact that this dreadful experience was at an end, but my emergence from it would breathe new life, and enable me to start afresh.

CHAPTER THIRTY-FIVE

Lindsay House, Chelsea
17th August 1821

THERE HAD BEEN no real cause for celebration, but I had nevertheless been very pleased to enjoy centre stage at a modest gathering of friends and family; all arranged and hosted beautifully by my wonderful wife. I was pleasantly surprised at the abundance of food and music. I had indulged a little reluctantly at first, until the effects of wine and song took hold and my reflections on the unpleasant and hugely depressing recent times slowly melted into the past. It had been eighty days of incarceration that seemed like a lifetime. Justice had eventually been served with the assistance of my family, closest friends and business and professional allies, and I should never be able to thank them all.

My thoughts came to rest on one influential figure in particular—his Grace the Duke of Wellington. I had had the honour of meeting him only briefly on a few occasions when on public duties and engagements. Yet his support and friendship had proved a significant factor in my release. Brushing aside my reverie, I continued to pen my gratitude for his encouragement and interventions.

My Lord Duke,

I was very much disappointed at being deprived, through your Grace's absence from England, of the opportunity of returning in person the thanks I owe to your Grace, for the favour shown to me by the British Government in the adjustment of my affairs, and the consequent liberation from my confinement.

Sensible as I may be at the happy termination, I cannot find expressions to say how much I feel at the peculiarly fortunate circumstances of having been deemed worthy of the notice and patronage of the most distinguished character of the age—a circumstance not only most flattering and most honourable, but which has materially contributed to softening of the gloom which so distressing a reverse would otherwise have left on my mind.

The only way by which I could make a suitable acknowledgement to your Grace was in employing my time preparing plans for the service of the British Government.

***

From my desk in my newly formed office in Poultry, Cheapside, I gazed out at the worn, cobbled street and passers-by, and reflected more kindly on recent times. The time, the generosity and genuine warmth extended to me by many during my period in prison made me feel valued and secure and filled me with renewed energy and vigour. I would now throw myself into my professional work—there was much time to make up!

The crowning glory of my homecoming was the return of my precious son after three years' education in France. We had embraced as only father and son can do—openly and fondly, the rest of the family looking on. This episode will linger long in my memory.

Through the reassuring muddle of drawings, sketches and calculations, I looked at Isambard as he examined the information at hand. He was so like me in many ways, I mused; not only in his innate talent for accurate sketching and numeracy, but also in how he had so positively taken on the values and benefits of formal education through my nurturing and encouragement. His determination and studious presence of mind, combined with his naturally inquisitive nature, left me in no doubt that he was ready to take up the mantle of responsibility working alongside me in my many projects.

It was disappointing that he was not able to go on from Caen University and *Lycée Henry IV* in Paris to further his academic studies at engineering school at the *École polytechnique* in Paris (and how ironic, too, that entry was denied to him as he was considered a 'foreigner'!) but I knew that, with my guidance, he was ready, even though he was approaching only seventeen years of age.

I could still recall the kind words of the notable chronologist and my dear friend, Louis Breguet, on Isambard's leaving his tutelage in his final year in France. 'I think it is very important to cultivate with him the happy inventive tendencies which he owes to nature or to education and which it would be a pity to see wasted.' I had no intention of neglecting this advice.

Isambard, feeling my stare, lifted his eyes from the drawing board and smiled.

"Father, may I seek your advice over the detail of the anchorages for the suspension chains of the Serpentine suspension bridge? I have determined the applied forces and reconciled the stresses in the wrought iron, but have doubts about the strength of the ground behind the abutments."

"Yes Isambard, I will be with you shortly. I am just concluding this letter."

I had given him responsibility for elements of the design of this structure, a swing footbridge for Liverpool Docks, plans for a cannon boring mill for the Dutch government and designs for paddle-tugs on the Rhine; I was confident that he was more than capable to undertake these tasks. And anyway, it was a matter of necessity, as I had projects abroad too—recently completing plans for a sawmill on Trinidad in the West Indies for the British Government with suspension bridges for the Île Bourbon in the Indian Ocean for the French Government.

Naturally, given the hardships that I had faced, his mother was concerned that our son would follow a similar professional engineering life as I, but I considered he could and should be relied upon to assist me directly and responsibly in this business. I needed him; he needed me. Engineering was one thing—business quite another.

"Ah yes, I too am concerned about the foundation soil shear capacities in these locations. The geological survey and report points to sandstone, but I have my doubts as the borehole information is distant from these locations. It may be prudent to instigate additional intrusive site investigation to more accurately determine the ground conditions at depth here."

"Yes, Father. I will write to Brown and Company and order more work here through our client."

"Very good."

"May I suggest that I visit the site when this occurs, to give some guidance and oversee matters?"

"Yes. That would be beneficial for your understanding, and provide first-hand information, but do not forget that I am away from this office a large proportion of the time. I have had no shortage of approaches for work since my incarceration, and these often require me to travel around the country investigating them and acting as an expert witness in patent actions. Your presence here is therefore invaluable to me. The experience you have rapidly gained and the responsibility I place upon you is to your credit. You will mature very quickly with my guidance and help. You already carry the weight of expectation well on your young shoulders."

"Thank you, Father." Isambard's eyes narrowed. "May I ask how matters are progressing with the other suspension road bridges on the Île Bourbon?"

"You may, my son."

I retrieved the parchment drawings from the tall cabinet and unfurled them on the plan chest, moving the brass paperweights to each corner as I illustrated my work to him.

"Suffice to say that the design has proven to be a little challenging, each structure having to withstand one hundred miles per hour winds, one with two 131ft 9in spans. Additional bracing chains are required to sufficiently carry the huge lateral forces into the bridge decks and thence to iron towers sighted on massive stone masonry piers. The project has progressed to fabrication stage now. I am due to visit the Milton Ironworks in Sheffield again this week to monitor and review the trial erection before they are shipped via London to the Indian Ocean. I have employed a trustworthy man, one Thomas Mathews, to supervise proceedings throughout the process. Needless to say, there have been troubles, but fortunately not insurmountable ones.

"But come now, it is time to break off and eat. Even aspiring and impressionable engineers cannot live merely on their wits! There is a pleasant hostelry quite close that offers a very good selection of wines—French, of course."

* * *

A brisk north easterly wind cut through the East India Wharf, swirling around the grand warehouses and flapping the sails of the myriad of moored ships; a rare and welcoming breeze amidst the August heat. Men and carriages hurried back and forth with crates and wooden packaging of all sizes and shapes, jostling for position to be amongst the first to unload and transport their goods to the quayside where gangplanks and ramps were awaiting their arrival.

We made our way through the busy scene to No 5 goods shed—the temporary store for the iron components of the dismantled bridges bound for Île Bourbon.

"I told 'em. Of all the jobs I have ever been at, I never saw such goings on as these."

I had never seen Mathews so distraught. We continued apace, matching strides.

"Yes, I understand, Thomas. That is the single most important reason I have found it necessary to visit the works in Sheffield so often in the past two years. My suspicions still linger regarding the integrity of the staff and the precision and control of the processes. That is why I have insisted on being here today."

My confidence in Milton Ironworks was at a low following the numerous inspections leading up to the problematic erection at the premises in Yorkshire, made doubly embarrassing by the presence of Monsieur Sganzin of the French government. Mathews' resulting reports did not reflect well on Milton's factory, where it seemed that every effort was being made to cover up work and elude his watchful eye.

Mathews continued. "I know full well that the weighing of the ironwork was mainly carried out at night. It was only on my insistence the following day that paint was removed and it was discovered that holes from the poor casting had been filled with clay."

"And do you know, Thomas, the contractors had the temerity to demand an extra payment of £500 for 'additional unforeseen work' which has had me embroiled in unnecessary protracted correspondence and the involvement of solicitors? My time is certainly better served in other, more useful directions."

Mathews shook his head in disbelief.

We stopped briefly before entering the storage building, and removed from our leather bags the fabrication drawings and inventory of the bridge's wrought-iron components for the requisition we were about to inspect.

"Before we go in, sir, I have instructed the dock labourers and hoist operator to shift selected items of our timber-crated cargo to one side for opening up and inspection before being transported to the wharf side for final loading onto the waiting ship."

"Very good, Thomas. Let us proceed."

The clanking and hissing of machine met the reverberating shouts of men as the familiar sounds of a busy storage and transportation facility were amplified as soon as we entered the building.

Josh Beloved, senior manager of Milton Ironworks, and two other men whom I recognised as erstwhile members of his company's senior management stood next to the huge packing cases; our concerns and the unwelcome atmosphere surrounding this meeting temporarily masked by cordial handshakes and politeness of demeanour.

"Ah Mr Brunel, Mr Mathews. Very pleased to meet you again; albeit, and with all due respect, I consider both the occasion and our meeting not necessarily warranted."

It was a poor start to proceedings. I did not react, but deferred to brevity; I was becoming more English than I would necessarily admit to.

"We shall see, Mr Beloved, we shall see."

The timber splintered and cracked as the crowbars went to work opening the elongated timber packing case containing the first of the bridge under-chains. The wrought iron links appeared in good condition; their smooth rouge-painted surface giving some confidence that all was well underneath; first impressions therefore were encouraging.

The inspection was thorough and time-consuming. Some twelve or so cases and packages were opened, much to the chagrin of Mr Beloved and his entourage, who continued to huff and shrug their shoulders throughout.

"Mr Beloved, we have now completed our inspection. I am pleased that this has been conducted in my presence today, in order that I have been able to survey, at first-hand, the readiness of this consignment to be transported to its destination on a remote island of the Indian Ocean. As we have discussed and agreed during the course of our inspections, there are many minor indiscretions which do not necessarily add up to anything significant, but I am afraid that the gross negligence associated with the under chains being a total of 800 feet shorter than required and the omission of over 200 of the flat links cannot be ignored."

The gathered Milton Men were red-faced and truculent, like scolded children.

"I therefore have no choice but to postpone this consignment from ongoing transit until I am personally satisfied that your company can demonstrably produce exactly what it is being contracted and paid for, sir. Good day to you."

CHAPTER THIRTY-SIX

Althorp, Northamptonshire
March 1823

I HAD BEEN invited, together with my wife, to spend a few days in the company of my friend Lord Spencer at his ancestral home, Althorp. This I managed to accommodate on my return journey to London from yet another visit to Sheffield.

"In my view, Spencer, the mode of heating the library and other rooms in the house is inadequate. On my return to London, I shall contact Mr Silvester, who has a thorough knowledge of heating systems, and one in particular that can convey heated air through horizontal flues. I can survey the existing stoves and flues here and provide him with plans in order that he will have an appreciation of the scale of the matter in hand."

I spoke directly as I wanted to assist this man who had become a dear friend, who always afforded me a most cordial welcome. It was a bitterly cold day in January; leaving my coat on was the only indication needed that something should be done.

George John Spencer stirred in his high-backed leather chair. He remained a fine-looking gentleman, defying the onset of years, as he brushed his thick grey locks away from his face and smiled.

"Brunel, is there not a moment of the day when you don't think of work?"

"Now, that, I must admit, is very rare. My mind is always alive with possibilities and prospects, and the opportunity of doing my good friend a small favour such as this is irresistible to me. Your support was invaluable to me during the dark days of my internment. I shall never forget that."

Spencer laughed and waved his hand as if to disdain my statement, although I knew him and his manner well enough not to be offended. In fact, I was warmed by it. His gesticulation clearly implied that he would have done the same for any valued and close friend. I was honoured to have received his help, and to be in the presence of this erudite man in the library of his lavish home. I was surrounded by his special collection, comprising thousands of books and periodicals. As an avid collector, he had acquired many of the rare books and manuscripts from a Benedictine monk, following the secularisation of religious houses in South Germany by Napoleon.

Anyone unacquainted with this gentleman could be forgiven for thinking him strangely aloof: but I have always found him to be a man of immense sociability. My colleague was President of the Royal Institution and a former Whig MP and Home Secretary. I was pleased to be the companion of this person of standing and influence in English society.

"And have you been able to place your financial affairs in order now?" my host enquired.

I was a little surprised at his enquiry, for I was still uncomfortable with the experience of being labelled a criminal debtor.

"Time is a great healer, my friend; and the eventual payment from the government was a long period in the realisation, but no more than I was owed. Things have improved, yes. I have benefitted from forthright and professional assistance from Sansom, my banking advisor and ally.

"I have also altered business arrangements at two of my concerns; the inefficient Mr Shaw at the Battersea sawmill has been replaced by the Hollingsworth brothers and a Mr Mudge, who is related to Sophia through the marriage of her sister Elizabeth to Thomas Mudge junior. I have dispensed with the tin foil and boot-making businesses and retain only a half share now of the sawmill, the other half being in the ownership of the Hollingsworths and Mudge."

"That should make them more responsible to the business, as they now have a vested interest in the future success of the venture. Wise decision, Brunel."

He puffed on his cigar.

"And how did you find York?"

"Well, I was impressed by the grand style and colossal feat of the Minster architecture, as expected. The work that the masons put in over many years demonstrates both their craftsmanship and their belief and dedication to the power of God. I couldn't help noticing, though, that the flying buttresses on the south side seemed largely structurally redundant, as they were only supporting the roof, not the massive masonry arches adjacent."

"Ah, an engineer to the last!"

"I must admit I felt the cathedral did not compare favourably with those I am acquainted with at Amiens and Rouen."

"Showing your Gallic bias there, I think."

"Well, be that as it may. The service I attended was a worthy one, but unfortunately attended by only one person, which was a great shame."

Spencer chuckled. "The next time I will join you, and we can then treble the congregation!"

I smiled and swirled the last dregs of my brandy around in my glass. It had been a fine day and luncheon in the presence of the Spencer family—son John and spouse Esther, with George and his wife Lady Lavinia. We had been treated as royalty at Althorp and even given a guided tour of this splendid house with its many works of art adorning the rooms.

I caught sight of Lavinia now, arm in arm with Sophia, as they approached the house from the vast grounds of the estate. Sophia had needed a respite from home life. It was rare that she would travel with me on business, but her presence gave me immense pleasure and I considered it quite a novelty; she was intelligent enough both to know her place when it came to my business commitments and to offer her opinion on personal matters when requested.

"George, I would very much like to give you a gift to thank you for your valued friendship and generosity during what have been very difficult times for myself and my family."

"Now Marc, you well know that this is not necessary."

"Necessary? No. But I do desire it."

Again, Spencer waved away my offer.

"Please, George—hear me out. Walking the grounds of your wonderful estate, I was reminded of my time in Rouen, when I was of impressionable age and resided with my family's good friends and mentors the Carpentiers. The spreading lawns and long sweeping driveway here call to mind the landscape and setting of their house. I have happy recollections of my time there—a place where I first met my future wife and fell in love. Amongst my fondest memories was walking hand in hand with Sophia around the ornamental lake and feeding the beautiful ducks that resided there.

"The Rouen breed of duck is a large bird with notable plumage and striking patterns of colour—quite sought after here, I believe. I would very much like to bring some of these ducks here, for Lady Spencer's lake. I am sure that she will look on them with as much admiration and delight as my dear wife and I did in the Rouen countryside, and perhaps think of us when doing so."

George smiled broadly, but not directly at me—over my shoulder. I felt a soft delicate hand on my lapel which I held momentarily before turning to see my Sophia. She beamed at me and a tear slowly rolled down her cheek.

CHAPTER THIRTY-SEVEN

Poultry, Cheapside
Summer 1826

THE DOOR TO the office slammed shut with more force than I intended, and the two new employees, a draughtsman and a technician, looked up from their boards. Removing my coat and hat, I was all fingers and thumbs, and even the familiar coat stand became an enemy against my cause. It had been a long and arduous journey from Liverpool, but that alone was not the reason for my frustration. Isambard stood up in welcome amongst a sea of plans and paperwork strewn over working tables and desks. We embraced fondly, but he could sense my inner turmoil and see signs of strain on my face.

"Good day, Father. I am pleased you have returned safely, albeit not in the best of moods, I surmise."

"No. I am afraid not, my son." I shook my head. "It may be best to retire to the meeting room, where I can tell you more."

The mixed scents of polished mahogany and new leather met us as we eased into wide soft chairs at the head of the long table.

"How have things been here in my absence?"

"Oh, very busy, and challenging as always. I have developed the drawings and design for the suspension bridge at Kingston as far as I might but will require a little assistance with my structural analysis. The Bermondsey cargo docks design is nearing completion to preliminary stage, ready for you to discuss with the group of financiers. The Government is pleased with the final design for the sawmill in British Guyana—a letter from the Home Office is on your desk, Father. I have also progressed a plan of the proposed route, and Joseph is currently drawing up cross sectional details for the extensive brickwork arched culvert to convey fresh water from Hammersmith to Hampstead. Oh, and the Grand Surrey Canal Company has written to us requesting a design for their new coal docks."

Isambard was performing admirably and obviously taking the pressure in his stride.

"May I ask what occurred in Liverpool, Father?"

"The Liverpool Dock Management, in their infinite wisdom, kept me waiting a long while for our meeting, about which I was most displeased. Not a good start to proceedings.

"When we eventually convened, I was met by a sea of unfamiliar faces. The newly appointed surveyor, who is also the chairman, informed me that they have undergone a radical change in personnel now through reorganisation and a new department has been fashioned under his control. They advised that the finance committee had declined funding for the project for now, so we will have to wait again before matters move forward."

"Not necessarily bad news then, Father? Is this the swinging footbridge design for which we constructed a model and which I demonstrated to the Dock Committee many months ago?"

"Yes, the very same, Isambard. The fact that this project has been postponed comes as no surprise, as this ensues quite often. No, my concern is that I sense there is a real risk that all the design work will be developed from our template for others to benefit from when the work eventually does proceed. I feel let down by these people who should act with more integrity and professionalism; after all, they invited me to carry out this detailed and complex work. I, of course, met all their requirements."

"I appreciate your distress, Father. Will you call upon legal advice now?"

"I have considered it, but as control of this project has already passed through many hands, our case would inevitably be diluted and probably result in a protracted and difficult legal process. Besides, I have little faith in the British justice system after my, shall we say, recent experiences."

"So be it. But we have many other projects in hand at the moment. We should accept that this setback is merely ill fortune."

I smiled and made no attempt to expand further on my frustrations.

"I did visit Huddersfield Canal Company on my travels, by the way, in response to their request for two suspension bridges of modest span. Two more perhaps for you, but I am conscious that your experience is being somewhat restricted to this type of structure at the moment."

"That's no matter, Father. Each one calls for a different approach. Besides, I am well aware that due to the importance that society is now giving to infrastructure and engineering, there will be little cause for complaint against diversity of form and function in the future."

Isambard's capability, both in theory and practice, was remarkable for one so young. I was indeed fortunate to have such a fine son.

* * *

There was something about the banks of the Thames in this part of London, particularly at this time of year, that pleased me. Summer in England was always agreeable, but to retreat from urban life, just for a couple of hours, and stroll along the tree-lined river embankment was as near as I would get to an escape. The Thames was not as blue as the Seine, it must be said, but the gentle rush of water and soft breeze liberated me.

The delicate hand in mine was an added delight.

I smiled down at my dear wife. We paused and kissed briefly before seating ourselves on a bench in the dappled shade of a weeping willow.

"Marc. Your spirits are raised today. I notice your change of mood, particularly when you have been away from home for some time. Although your work often takes you away from us, I am very pleased for you, and the family are recognising your example—particularly Isambard. But I do miss you when you are absent."

"That is kind of you, my love. Yes, our son is doing even better than I imagined. He is growing into a fine, responsible man. I am confident that together we can achieve much. Also, it must be said that I find myself in a better financial situation, but sadly there are still those who, through greed and malpractice, have sought to profit illegally from my hard work."

"Oh Marc, I know that you are doing everything possible to protect your business interests, and I understand that you face many difficulties. But perhaps through your generosity of spirit, certain selfish individuals feel they can take advantage of you. What or whom in particular is on your mind?"

"I'm afraid this is a little close to home, my dear." I cleared my throat. "There are clear signs that the Hollingsworth brothers at Battersea are pocketing considerable sums of cash not declared as sales through the books. The accountants have carried out an audit and things do not add up—missing receipts and the like. And I'm afraid your cousin's husband, Mudge, has not exactly proved himself an effective manager either; he is often absent from the works on other business and appears reluctant to make decisions, to say the least."

Sophia took her eyes from mine to gaze upon the boating scene.

"Marc, I want you to know that you will always have me to confide in. Although I cannot always provide advice or solutions, as it is not my place to do so, I will always support your endeavours. Your work is at the very heart of our family."

* * *

"Father, you are a little late for your meeting with representatives from Portsmouth City waterway committee. They await you in the conference room. We have served them tea."

"Thank you, my son."

I picked up the prepared agenda from my desk: 'A discussion on the feasibility of constructing a ship canal from Portsmouth to London'. I shook my head and made my way in.

* * *

"A disappointing outcome, I think you will agree, Mr Brunel. But common sense shall prevail, nonetheless."

"Indeed, Mr Grimshaw, indeed."

Isambard and his assistants were in conference over the detailing of one of our many projects, when I eventually shook the hands of the not-so-learned gentlemen as they donned their coats and hats and left.

"What transpired at the meeting, Father? I know you were not optimistic concerning their proposal."

"No, I am afraid that this particular project will not come to fruition. I was prepared to listen to what these men had to say, of course, out of politeness and in gratitude for the fact they chose me to examine this assignment, but it was apparent to me some time ago that such an undertaking would not be financially feasible."

Perhaps I should be a little more discerning when it came to examining schemes instead of being so damned polite and accommodating to everyone. It was the same with the proposal put to me to install locomotive steam engines into carriages for use on common roads. The turnpikes, with their potholes and rough surfaces, were bad enough, as I had experienced at first hand on many a journey up and down the country—and these highways had only to support the rigours of horse-drawn stagecoaches, never mind heavy steam engines! Roads needed to be improved and realigned and bridges strengthened before higher speeds could be achieved with confidence and without risk of accident.

But some good had come of the meeting; the rekindling of an initiative I had back in Chatham docks all those years ago. If I could make this idea work in practice, it would probably consume all my energies as never before. My heart began to race at this exciting prospect. And all because of a little worm!

CHAPTER THIRTY-EIGHT

Bishopsgate, London
February 1824

THE OPULENT DINING room of the City of London Tavern was a popular venue for public and private meetings held to rally support for various political, charitable and commercial ventures. The building stood tall and imposing—testament to its importance and status amongst the professional classes who travelled from far and wide to enjoy its congenial atmosphere.

The prospective shareholders of the newly formed Thames Tunnel Company shuffled and murmured in anticipation as I made my entrance through the Corinthian-columned hallway, where I was greeted by the president and chairman, William Smith.

"Good afternoon, Mr Brunel. Welcome."

He introduced me to many other gentlemen of influence and standing, as I made my way around the room, shaking hands and warmly greeting the smiling faces. The stout, moustachioed Smith, member of parliament for Norwich, and the Woolastons I knew by sight from previous connections, but others were strangers to my eye, though not necessarily to my pen. The network of prominent people in English society that I had corresponded with in order to stimulate interest in my vision was many and varied—Dukes, Duchesses, Lords, Ladies, MPs, cabinet ministers, fellow engineers, architects. I had cast my net wide and was very pleased with the number of large fish that I had landed.

I had been encouraged previously, as my presentation of my plans for the tunnel had aroused great enthusiasm amongst my peers at the Institution of Civil Engineers in Westminster. Now it was the turn of the investors.

After the initial introductions and formalities, we made our way into the long dining room, where the highly polished mahogany table was already set for luncheon.

* * *

"Gentlemen, welcome to this, the first meeting of those who have expressed an interest in the prospect of forming a tunnel under the Thames from Rotherhithe to Wapping. This vast and bold feat of engineering, which will, no doubt, excite and astonish public and investor alike, will be the first of its kind in the world."

Smith stood proud and upright, the last remnants of his food dabbed away from his lower lip by a convenient napkin in his left hand, his notes firmly in his right.

"I'm sure that those present here today need no reminding that currently the only means of crossing the Thames close to the East and West India London and St Katherine Docks at Wapping for the transportation of cargo to the factories, mills, and warehouses, is over London Toll Bridge. This crossing is three miles distant. Blackfriars offers some relief, but that bridge is even further away. When the numerous horses, carts, drays and wagons are mixed with foot traffic, the congestion that arises is momentous and is slowly grinding the machine of business in our proud city to a halt. Pedestrians are choosing to use the wherry more and more often now, which is resulting in higher crossing fees, and many are becoming irritated and even angry at these circumstances.

"There is a constant backlog of merchant ships, which are compelled to anchor midstream and await offloading, sometimes for weeks on end, resulting in the pilfering of goods and other criminal activity on these vessels.

"Constructing another bridge further downstream from London Bridge was ruled out some time ago as the elevation of such a structure would have to be sufficient to allow tall ships' masts to pass under, dictating that approach roads would also need to be at high level and extended by some distance into existing neighbouring suburbs.

"The idea of a tunnel crossing is not new, however. Mr Dodd's endeavour between Tilbury and Gravesend late last century fell at the first hurdle, as the expected capable chalk layer was not found at depth. No actual horizontal boring was attempted.

"Some of you may remember also that, as recently as nineteen years ago, Robert Vasie and Richard Trevithick, both from Cornish mining backgrounds, joined forces to commit to a modest shorter tunnel between Rotherhithe and Limehouse under the auspices of the Thames Archway Company. However, this tunnel was more in the mode of a 'driftway'—a small-diameter tunnel for experimental and drainage purposes prior to the main tunnel being excavated. Only one man could work the excavated tunnel face at any one time. Unexpected ground conditions, including running sand and persistent water ingress, thwarted their efforts and led to the abandonment of this project when Trevithick himself almost drowned."

I noted that the respectful silence of the invited guests turned to one of apprehension. *'Smith's summary, although accurate, might have been tempered a little more,'* I thought.

"So much for history. Where all this differs from the approach taken by Mr Brunel lies in the design and investigation process necessary to determine ground conditions before construction commences, and in a unique construction method. Mr Brunel, in short, has been thorough in his research. We can be confident in his approach and methods in advance, as exemplified by a new, innovative and unique tunnel boring method, which I am sure he will want to explain to you presently. All this is nothing more than I would expect from a figure respected and celebrated the length and breadth of England, a member of the Royal Society and a man renowned for his engineering prowess, integrity and determined application; fresh from a meeting he had only yesterday with fellow engineers in Westminster, where his plans have met with the approval of a Royal Chartered body of professional engineers."

Muted applause followed.

"So, without further ado, may I introduce Mr Marc Brunel."

The ovation as I stood both pleased and surprised me. The attendance was swelled by latecomers and others not present at the luncheon, some standing, some seated around the perimeter walls. There must have been upwards of a hundred people in front of me now.

"Thank you, William." I cleared my throat.

"My Lords and Gentlemen. It is with great and sincere pleasure that I find myself in your exalted company today. It has been a long journey for me to arrive at this juncture, as it has taken months of my most diligent of efforts to cajole and persuade many of similar disposition, authority and presence here to join me in this momentous and literally ground-breaking venture.

"I am therefore naturally very pleased to see so many in attendance who are willing to support this worthwhile venture as potential shareholders in this, the inaugural meeting of the Thames Tunnel

Company. I wish to assure you that any investment that you may make will be a wise one; you may rest secure in the knowledge that this project is driven by need and commercial success.

"But before I give more particulars of the plan and execution of the works, and details of the unique and innovative specialist piece of equipment I have invented and patented for this very challenging task, let me recount to you a little story which inspired me to progress on this venture.

"At a time, not so long ago, when a Mr Hawkins was proposing a method for sinking shafts on each bank of the Thames as a precursor to rekindling thoughts on this tunnel project, my natural interest was aroused. I was, at this time, employed at Chatham Docks undertaking designs of dock facilities and improvements, including a short length of shallow tunnel in chalk ground. One day, as I was passing through the main quay area, my attention was drawn to a piece of perforated ship timber. When I examined this exhibit close up, it became apparent that worms were living inside and boring through the wood. *Teredo navalis* is the infamous ship worm—responsible for the early watery grave of many a seagoing vessel. When I examined this small creature at close quarters and researched it further, I discovered that its proboscis, protected by a hard shell, eats its way into the wood and digests it, then excretes the residue as a paste to line the bore it has produced behind, which in turn hardens and protects the worm as it progresses. Now if I were to invent a machine that would be able to function in a similar manner, that would be quite something! So I set about this task with great enthusiasm and purpose. The result is what you see today. I have since taken out a patent for its application and use."

I turned and pointed to the detailed, large-scale drawing on display, which only yesterday I had presented to the Institution of Civil Engineers.

"I call it my tunnelling shield."

A polite, attentive silence prevailed.

"The shield is made up of twelve wrought-iron frames, each with individual compartments on three levels, where a total of thirty-six men can stand and dig away by hand at the tunnel face at any one time. The exposed earth is then supported by poling boards connected to threaded bars on the frame's columns. When all miners in any one frame have dug a similar distance, the whole frame is advanced using powerful screwjacks that push against the previously built brickwork tunnel lining following on behind. This allows a continuous construction process whilst also minimising the exposure of the unsupported ground, since progress is gradual, deliberate and controlled.

"My prototype was for a cylindrical shield where miners would remain protected throughout the excavation work, but I quickly discovered that to provide sufficient force to overcome the frictional resistance of the ground this design would require more horsepower than even the most powerful of steam engines that we have today could provide. I have, therefore, temporarily abandoned this idea. I am, however, also very active on steam engine improvement and development..."

A collective murmur of laughter eased the atmosphere. The audience's attention was now fully focused on the design and construction process. I would be ready to field the myriad questions which would now come my way.

* * *

"A successful day, it seems, Smith," I ventured, deliberately understating the accomplishment of the event. The venue was now virtually deserted save for Smith, the Woolastons and the new shareholders Messrs Gray and Richie.

"Indeed, Mr Brunel. Quite an impact, judging by the fact that we have initial subscriptions that number approximately 2,128, at £50 each with the promise of more when the word is passed around to a larger circulation."

Little did Smith know that the 'larger net of circulation' would include the biggest fish yet to be caught on my line.

"We shall of course immediately contact the city surveyor, Mr Montague, who will be responsible for the ground survey and valuation of the properties currently occupying the site on both the Rotherhithe and Wapping banks," Smith continued.

"May I recommend the firm of Joliffe and Banks to plan and implement the geological survey and carry out ground boreholes in order that the best longitudinal transition for the tunnel is chosen in advance of the works proceeding?"

"Yes, of course. It is projected that we move forward as a fully-fledged business enterprise and approach the government for a bill to receive royal assent. It is intended too, naturally, that we will retain your services and employ you as our engineer, sir. I shall write to you in due course with a formal letter of appointment."

Thus, the Thames Tunnel Company was born.

CHAPTER THIRTY-NINE

Poultry, Cheapside
Winter 1825

"PLEASE KEEP EACH project's plans and drawings together."

I was pleased that Isambard called attention to the need for the men to preserve the unique filing system that he and I had so meticulously assembled through the years of our tenure at these offices. Now was the right time to establish a base closer to the project that was taking up nearly all my time and energies. Vast, hanging drawing cabinets, plan chests and drawer files were being hauled onto waiting wagons as I made my way through vacant rooms, checking that no piece of paper, letter, parchment or drawing was left. To mislay or, worse still, lose critical design details at this stage would be disastrous.

This past week, prior to the move, had been even more hectic than usual. Bridge Street was quite a contrast to the lavish surroundings to which we were accustomed. I felt a little guilty moving Sophia, Emilia and the family entourage and, although they made no complaint, it was obvious that they were reluctant. I could see no alternative. This project demanded I be on location—at its very heart—as lead designer, project manager and engineer. The tunnel represented the single most bold and important civil engineering feat I had ever undertaken, commanding my undivided attention. I had continuing support from friends and family alike. I had financial backing from men of courage and fortitude. I had reserves of energy and the confidence of a man of half my age. In short, all the ingredients for a successful outcome.

I continued to look for remnants of drawings or any files that may have been inadvertently left behind in the bustle. Dust and cobwebs hung in corners and on skirting previously masked by furniture; the relic of Isambard's desk was now just a dim outline against the far wall. In my mind's eye, I can still see us there.

Barely six weeks had passed since The Thames Tunnel Company was inaugurated and I was instructed to commence detailed design.

"In compliance with instructions from the subscribers at the original meeting, your directors have made arrangements with Mr Brunel for the use of his patent, for which they have agreed to pay him 5,000l, when the body of the tunnel shall be securely effected and carried sixty feet beyond each embankment of the river, and a further and final sum of 5,000l when the first public toll under the Act of Parliament shall have been received for the use of the proprietors.

To effect the work Mr Brunel has received the appointment of engineer to the Company, with the salary of 1,000l per annum for a period of three years, the utmost limit which the directors contemplate as necessary for the execution of the work; the whole of which sum the directors have agreed to give him in case the work should be accomplished to their satisfaction at an earlier period."

I confided more and more in my son as the days went by; his thoroughness and determination were very pleasing; his capability in structural analysis and appreciation of the construction sequence a joy to behold. He took the young, newly employed draughtsman, Pinchbeck, in hand to continue his fine work on the tunnel project and in particular the drawings of the Great Shield itself. He and Isambard were dovetailing well.

"Let us examine the ground investigation report, Isambard. Ideally, the longitudinal alignment will need to remain within the stiff blue clay layer of soil under the Thames wherever possible."

"Yes, Father." He broke off from discussions with Pinchbeck and sat at the side of my desk. "I see that the bores go to a level of up to 60 feet."

"Yes, the new data in my possession shows me that a slowly descending tunnel will be needed, with the lowest point at the centre of the Thames, giving necessary clearance from potential disturbances to the river bed by ships' anchors. But it will be tight"

"We will be ready to issue the drawings for fabrication of the shield by the end of this week I think, Father."

"That's good news. You may know that Maudslay has recently been awarded the contract for the manufacture of the shield. I am naturally very pleased at this outcome, as there is a great understanding and trust between us, having worked so well together on many previous projects."

"I am very pleased, Father. Oh, on other matters, Professor Gay-Lussac is planning a visit here in the spring to continue your collaboration on the process for the refining of tallow for candles."

"Ah yes, I am aware. It will be good to see Joseph Louis again. I will need to keep this project simmering!"

Isambard smiled.

"But my experiments and preliminary designs for rope-hauled railways both here and in France, and feasibility plans for the canal from Fowey to Padstow in Cornwall may have to play second fiddle to the tunnel mission now; as will my diving bell crane project for the search of sunken Spanish treasure in the Bay of Vigo."

"That is understandable, Father. Oh, we have also received a very kind letter of invitation from the Duchess of Somerset regarding a design for a bridge over the River Dart in Totnes. I have it here."

"Thank you, son."

I read on out loud past the formal introduction:

You are always so obliging, that in the midst of your important business I venture to trouble you upon a concern in which I would ask your advice, well knowing that upon the subject in question no opinion is more valuable; indeed, were you not so deeply involved underground, I should propose your putting yourself into one of the coaches and coming to us in Berry.

"This noble woman flatters me with both wit and a persuasive tone! I feel personally obliged to return her invitation with an outline design in due course."

* * * *

I now turned my attention to the design and method of construction of the huge shaft that would be required firstly on the Rotherhithe side of the river to provide access to the tunnel works—temporary and permanent. As I worked, the ground on this side of the Thames was being cleared in readiness. I was already formulating a new idea for this method in the form of sequence sketches, which would be both pioneering in design and quite spectacular in execution. I was excited at the prospect!

Experienced personnel would also be needed—a dependable Resident Engineer, Clerk of Works, bricklaying and carpenter craftsmen and miners. I needed to consult with the directors over these appointments sooner rather than later.

It was now 16th February 1825—only three weeks away from the planned ceremony of the laying of the first brick. Two hundred or so guests had been invited to attend the feast and celebration. I would prepare my speech accordingly.

No one was going to usurp me!

CHAPTER FORTY

The Thames Tunnel, Rotherhithe Shaft
22nd April 1825

"MY LORD DUKE. Please take care when descending. Follow me." I was delighted that the Duke of Wellington himself, assisted by Lord Somerset and General Ponsonby, was the first amongst many dignitaries to visit 'the extraordinary sinking tower', as it was now hailed by the enthusiastic public and ebullient English press. The Duke and Duchess of Cambridge, the Duke of Gloucester, Prince Leopold, the Duke of Northumberland and Mr Robert Peel were amongst the eminent people now set to come; personages whose inquisitiveness and sense of adventure fuelled the fire of national interest. They were invaluable in spreading the word amongst the higher sections of influence in society, and thus, hopefully, expanding the Thames Tunnel Company's ever-increasing register of shareholders.

However, I had to admit to myself that I would prefer that the Company Directors would not take it upon themselves to invite so many people. The effect on the workforce was to cause interruption and frustration.

At the foot of the narrow, winding staircase, our entourage was met with the crunching of gravel on iron and the grinding and creaking of the colossal tower as it gradually descended into the ground, inch by inch. Like the minute hands of a clock, the settlement of the 42ft-high, 50ft-diameter vertical cylinder was barely discernible to the human eye as the 40inch-high massive iron curb slowly chiselled its way into the ground under the weight of over 900 tons of brickwork and massive internal wrought iron bolts and ties.

After a suitable pause, upwards of a hundred men, armed with an array of picks and shovels, resumed the practice of loosening the gravel around the perimeter of the shaft and barrowing the spoil to the centre where buckets and windlasses raised it to the surface.

The whole structure was on the move. The tower of today would be the shaft of tomorrow.

"I am very impressed, Brunel." The Duke beamed.

"Thank you, sir. You may observe that we are introducing water where we can in order to overcome the effects of the binding of the gravel with the surface of the curb, and therefore ease the descent of the tower into the ground. The rate of sinking is being controlled and measured as works progress now that the timber wedges and temporary piles have been removed."

"Ah. How are you controlling the groundwater infiltration, then?"

"We have also sunk a contiguous well, both to act as a drain and also to reveal the nature of the ground, and therefore predict any possible complications that may arise in advance of the sinking of the shaft. As you can see, there are many men dedicated to the task of removing the water by hand pumps on day and night shifts."

"Very good."

"Do you intend to continue with this manual method of excavation? Is there no possibility of mechanising the excavation process to improve progress and perhaps save the men's arms?" Ponsonby intervened.

"Yes, indeed, General. I have already designed and requisitioned such a powerful steam-powered machine. It is currently being manufactured under the auspices of my good friend Maudslay. We are awaiting imminent delivery."

I did not wish to mention my extreme frustrations regarding the delays with the bringing to site of this machine. I had only recently remonstrated over this issue with Mr Field, Maudslay's partner, face-to-face at his works; but I knew if I pushed too hard, I would risk undermining our well-established friendship. We had a solid mutual appreciation of each other's skills and strivings for perfection. I had no choice but to be patient and wait for the problems he had encountered during the manufacture to be resolved. It would, regrettably, be necessary just to soldier on for now.

* * *

John Armstrong looked on from his vantage point atop the enormous structure, Isambard at his side; the pulsating exhaust of the hissing steam engine combining with the shouts of many men. The flywheel whirled and eased the vertical conveyor belt of buckets of excavated earth up on to the waiting shute, for dispersal on the adjacent spoil heap. The tower reverberated with activity; men and machine working in harmony on a production line of controlled excavation, brickwork and iron staples as the walls were brought up in unison. It had been seven months since the first brick was laid, and now each bricklayer was laying one thousand bricks a day.

"Time to measure the settlements around the perimeter again, Isambard," Armstrong informed the attentive nineteen-year-old after consulting his pocket watch. "We don't want to risk potential for differential settlement again, as we experienced recently where the gravel stratum was found not to be uniform. The tower descended three inches more on the east side than the west due to soft ground."

"I will have the level instrumentation set up on the established survey points right away, sir."

Armstrong was proud to have been given the role of Resident Engineer at a modest salary which included his accommodation and allowance for coals and candles whilst he was away from his residence in the west country. A Northumbrian by birth, Bristol was his home now. He had become an engineer through apprenticeship and the accumulation of knowledge and practical experience, as opposed to any formal academic tutelage or training. He regretted not receiving the schooling necessary to complement his established skills, but he also knew that he was not necessarily a man who could cope with applied mathematics and the ability in science needed to meet such requirements.

Word and reputation spread fast in this industry and it was not long before this capable man's stature and achievements came to the knowledge of Marc Brunel, who had no hesitation in employing him in this key role. Armstrong felt both privileged and proud to be chosen by a man of such respect and standing in society and to be on a project that was now receiving national status and importance.

He was pleased to be recognised, though not altogether happy being away from home. But, as a determined and positive character, he avoided dwelling on his circumstances for too long, preferring to deal with the task in hand and look forward to returning to his family. After all, he had been given carte blanche authority to employ Mr Litchfield, whom he already knew well, as Clerk of Works, as well as the chief bricklayer and other key craftsmen who made up a workforce now approaching some one hundred in number. That endorsement, and the confidence that Marc Brunel had placed in him, exemplified by putting young Isambard under his wing, spoke volumes.

Isambard had returned.

"Sir, the instrumentation shows that the shaft has not sunk any more today. That is five days now that we have had little or no penetration, despite the fact that the ground has been cleared beneath the curb in readiness. The blue clay layer is holding the structure fast."

Armstrong already had already discussed this possibility with Marc Brunel. A contingency plan was in place for such an occurrence.

"We will have to order more bricks and raise the height of the walls to such a level as to increase the weight of the shaft and at the same time stop the pumps to allow the internal groundwater level to rise and soften the soil."

Armstrong had been informed that The Great Shield was now ready to be delivered to site. Underpinning the shaft with well-grouted rubble stone work, the sinking of a central drainage sump and finally removing the wrought iron curbs were to take place with all haste.

Time was of the essence.

CHAPTER FORTY-ONE

Bridge Street, Blackfriars, London
Early November 1825

"FIFTY THOUSAND EXTRA bricks it took in the end to sink the shaft."

"The steam engine is not up to the task."

"Repairs will be needed."

"But we will then have to cease operations, and the works will flood."

"So be it."

"The ground is now giving way; gravel and running sand."

"We will use sheet piles with iron walings, and push stiff clay into the cavity."

"Underpinning is now completed, and the reservoir formed."

"I am pleased. Turn on the new pumps."

"Marc, please rest, my darling. Do not be concerned. All is well with the tunnel in your absence." Sophia mopped my brow with the thick cotton cloth, avoiding the leeches that the doctor had earlier administered.

30 Bridge Street had been transformed by Sophia from a rather threadbare house to an elegant, warm and comforting home. I felt at ease in familiar surroundings and comfortable in my bed, despite my raised pulse and drifting in and out of consciousness.

"How long have I been here?" I enquired.

"Four days now. You are ill through exhaustion. The doctor insists you need time to recover. You have very competent people around you that you must lean on. Armstrong and Litchfield, to name but two."

This thought made me feel stronger, invigorated almost. I would soon be back at the tunnel...

* * *

The Thames Tunnel, Rotherhithe to Wapping
Late November 1825

"What do you mean, 'the directors objected'?"

The cast iron drainage pipes spewed forth into the waiting drainage channel; the water flowing past our feet and on to the large diameter vertical pipe set into the reservoir. This was certainly not the heading I had designed and allowed for to permanently drain the face of the excavation as the shield progressed.

"They said it would be too costly, sir," Armstrong maintained.

I hoped that this intervention from directors who knew nothing of engineering design, structural form and method would be the last. Money was one thing—proper purpose of work, good established practice and the act of minimising the potential for collapse were something else altogether. As it stood, the pumps were working well in transferring the water to the surface—for now. But this fact did not dilute my anger. This drain was critical to the success of the scheme.

"I fear that this system will not cope with the increased water flows once excavation of the main tunnel bore commences, and when the face in front of the shield opens up."

Our voices echoed in the gloom. The sounds of man and machine became more amplified as we trudged our way back into the damp and confined space that was now the enormous main shaft.

The man-made cavern continued to be the hub of activity, with men, pumps and tools all creating a clamour, and the breath and body steam emanating from their exertions, despite the cold dank air. The huge task of completing the last stages of forming the drift under the shaft and removing the cast iron curb in sections, building the stonework underpinning and introducing previously excavated clay to plug any voids between, continued apace.

"Ah, Litchfield. Good morning. How are things progressing?"

"Good morning, sir. We have had some difficulties holding back the water where the sand has infiltrated and clogged the pumps, but we have now overcome that and progress is being made ready for the shield. The ground beneath the clay layer is now standing exceedingly well."

"Excellent. Although we have encountered many types of ground other than the stiff blue clay that was expected."

"Yes. The clay appeared only in the top third of the excavation for the shaft. We have had to contend with silt, sands and gravels below that, which, when combined with the ground water influx, made the task more difficult and has taken more time and resources than expected. The men have taken many of the uncovered small colourful bivalve shells home as mementoes."

This made us both smile.

"We have also received from Maudslay delivery of the first of twelve shield frames. Each of the three fabricated compartments, and bolt and roller components, are standing by to be lowered, transported and assembled at the tunnel face. A local smith by the name of Redman is now making the numerous screw jacks, which should be ready imminently," Armstrong added.

"Thank you, men. I will visit his workshop and view his progress at first hand at my earliest convenience."

After the obligatory handshakes and nods to the workmen I passed on the shaft's winding stair, I made my way up into the London morning light and gazed down upon the hectic scene below me.

It would not be long before the Great Shield—my pride and joy—would be ready to advance towards Wapping shore. The bottle of vintage red wine that we had deliberately kept back from the First Brick Laying celebration awaited us.

My eyes glazed over, not just from the waft of moist stale air. I felt genuine excitement; but it combined with a disquieting sense of foreboding. The surveyors' report, announced by the directors, was troubling me:

> *'a stratum of strong blue clay of sufficient depth to ensure the safety of the intended tunnel…'*

I had proceeded boldly with the design of my shield, as this report painted a favourable picture of the expected ground conditions. It did not now seem that this was the case.

I make no excuses. It was in my nature to be innovative in my approach. The weight of support I had had for my design and method could not be ignored. The shield was more than adequate to resist the forces on it which I expected. Each element of the frames making up the overall structure could be dismantled, removed or replaced without affecting the stability of the whole. Miners would be able to work with impunity in the knowledge that they were contained and protected within each individual cell.

There was no going back now.

CHAPTER FORTY-TWO

The Thames Tunnel, Rotherhithe to Wapping
March 1826

HIS GNARLED AND dirt-encrusted hands gripped the pick as he struck the soil face with renewed vigour. Despite the biting cold air, sweat continued to fall from Goodwin's brow as he shovelled the clay and gravel arisings into the barrows at his feet. It had been a long and arduous shift under the diffused light of the sparsely spaced gas lamps. Not that he was unused to it. As a proud Cornishman coming from a long line of miners, his lineage and his family roots dictated that he would be set for this type of work. His resilience and stamina were testament to the hardships he suffered as a youth, brought up in a poor village among people who were restricted to manual labour for their livelihoods.

Safe in his three-feet-wide by seven-feet-tall cell, he was one of three miners operating in this frame; each in his own cell, all digging away, nine inches at a time from top to bottom, then supporting the excavated face with pole boards as they went, strutting them off the adjacent frame with the screw jacks.

He knew the score now; as did all the men on the shift. His three-man wrought iron frame was number 11 of 12. He glanced along the line of men through the rectangular openings to his left and right. Twelve miners were hard at work on the adjacent upper levels along the staggered line, digging, placing boards and replacing the screw jacks in an orderly, sequential routine that had to be strictly adhered to, to avoid risk of collapse.

Behind Goodwin, the bricklayers toiled, their hands a blur as they trowelled the quick-setting mortar to form the arch soffit, guided and supported in turn by a pre-former of timber, working around the circumference steadily and efficiently.

The barrowed spoil was trundled on to one side of the wheeled wooden staging, ready to be taken down the ramp and along the length of completed tunnel; on the other flank, bricks and mortar were being fed to the bricklayers in a criss-cross, organised maelstrom of activity.

Water oozed through the tiny horizontal gaps in the poling boards, staining the already browned timber. The stale air took on a new smell as work progressed; an occasional waft of a pungent odour that made Goodwin's eyes dry up, so strong was it. At first, he thought it was the recurring flatulence of the men, but when the stink persisted he realised that it was probably something more than that. He pressed his nose as far as he could into the exposed earth—it was coming through the water seepage.

Still, at least the works appeared to be being contained properly now. Not like when, in the early stages with only some 14 feet of tunnel bricked up, the water came gushing in. The tunnel floor flooded quickly as the pumps could not cope, he recalled. The incident had frightened the men, who had refused to work on without further assurance.

Repairs were necessary at the head staves of numbers 1 and 2 frames, and lead pipe drains were added. Goodwin and the others had greater confidence now following direct assurances from the Brunels, and soon settled back into an improved routine. Goodwin knew he had no choice; he owed it to his family to keep going and work as hard as possible despite the obvious dangers. His father had been a miner, and his father before him. Three shillings a day was a reasonable sum to receive for his labours. After paying for his food and keep, he was able to send at least one shilling back home to assist in the keep of his wife and baby daughter.

He leant his aching body against the frame side for a brief rest before receiving the signal. He was often the first miner to complete his section. Soon, the familiar sound of shovel on iron came as Brown and Grimshaw rapped hard on the roofs of their cells beneath him.

"Number eleven frame ready!" Goodwin shouted. They were the first frame to announce.

"Number three frame ready!"

The call was repeated from all the odd-numbered frames, reverberating through the dimly lit tunnel.

"Start the move forward." Clerk of Works Litchfield gave the instruction from his vantage point on the rear of the timber staging, Armstrong flanking him; Isambard Brunel observing and making notes.

The large-diameter propelling screws abutting the soffit and base of the brickwork arch were slowly cranked in unison by broad-shouldered miners. The top staves crunched as the side friction rollers between each frame gently whined into action; taking up the lateral pressure as each individual frame slowly jacked its way onward; inch by inch.

The works were now mostly dry, apart from the occasional small, confined discharges of groundwater. The shield was entering into ground that no known tunnelling system on earth had penetrated before.

And no man had suffered any injury so far.

CHAPTER FORTY-THREE

The Thames Tunnel, Rotherhithe to Wapping
April 1826

INTERFERENCE TAKES MANY forms. There is the gentle prying into one's personal affairs that those close at heart may do, usually with good intent. There is the intellectual intrusion when others question one's motives and aims, without proper knowledge of background events that have led to a particular decision, which is not to their liking.

Then there is the downright cold meddling and prying into analytically proven design, well-thought-out systems and sequences underpinned by demonstrable good practice. This policy leads to others taking the high ground in matters on which they are woefully under-qualified and misinformed; drawing ignorant and erroneous conclusions, often for financial reasons alone.

The directors of the Thames Tunnel Company were guilty as charged of the latter.

I found it particularly hard to fathom the change in William Smith. The warmth and courtesy he extended to me were plain for all to see at the company's inauguration. I trusted in him and his fellow directors just as much as he seemed to place his faith in me. But it appeared his attitude had turned. He had now laughingly criticised the Shield as an expensive luxury, and the method of brickwork lining 'false' in principle. I had heard strong rumours, too, that he no longer considered my decisions infallible, and deemed my designs inappropriate. In short, my position as Chief Engineer appeared to be under threat and one of his directors, of very limited engineering knowledge or experience, was waiting to fill my shoes at a moment's notice.

I should have sensed that all was not well at an early juncture, when Smith continually undermined my efforts to obtain government support for my scheme. Private investment alone was clearly not going to be enough to win the approbation of the official high quarters of society in England, let alone the general public. Without the support of MPs, the Tunnel Act would not have been passed and this project would never have got off the drawing board. Had he forgotten that?

"And on what basis does Smith consider that the works need to be abandoned?"

Isambard looked on, wide-eyed; awkwardly shifting his frame from one side of the completed side arch to the other. The men watched. They could see from our respective stances that all was not well.

"I don't think he said 'abandoned' exactly, Father. Rather 'modified' to his plan; which is, of course entirely unworkable. I know Armstrong was not entirely comfortable with it."

"Does he actually have a plan, then?"

"He wants to use contract labour and simpler methods. There is talk of bringing Irish workers in and dispensing with the more costly miners."

"Ridiculous. These men we see before us are strong, experienced miners. They represent good value for money. Without them, the tunnel progress would slow, and men could be at greater risk of injury, through complacency or just plain incompetency. Look at the recent experiences we have had with sudden water ingress into the works, the partial collapse of the upper section of a frame and the way the men have applied themselves to the task of stemming the flows through unexpected sodden ground. It has taken us some time to get these men on our side. We should not forget that!"

"Yes, Father, I agree. But the decision may still be taken out of our hands."

That was a disquieting but realistic thought.

"Is our resident engineer recovering well from his malady?"

"Mr Armstrong has not taken the stress of the whole situation well, no. I am of the opinion that he may be seriously reconsidering his position here."

I was not entirely surprised. Armstrong was showing signs of strain; but to resign? This construction was problematic on many levels; it was also taking its toll on me. I had once again been confined to bed for a week at the same time as Armstrong; and for similar reasons, too.

"Isambard, despite the interference and attempts to alter the direction of operations here by those unprincipled individuals, I have observed that the shield is actually performing very well. The workforce is performing equally well under difficult circumstances in a hostile environment. We have now completed a substantial first section of tunnel bore. This pleases me, and I can therefore bear the criticism and misdirected behaviour of the senior members of the Company as long as things continue in the way they are. I can be as thick-skinned as many an Englishman and am able to contend with a lot."

I placed a hand on his shoulder.

"I know you are still young, my son, but your diligence and speed of thought show experience and capability beyond your years. You are the most efficient inspector we have. Your vigilance and dedication to this project are shown through your willingness to work both day and night in supervising the work and ensuring it is correct. You seem unaffected by the stress shown in others around you.

"I think you are now ready to move on and take responsibility for directing the works. All is going according to plan, but I feel a young, energetic management team would provide a new impetus to the project, and may even pacify those troublesome directors. You will need support from assistant engineers, of course. We will make a joint decision on whom these individuals will be."

Isambard smiled and shook my hand.

"I place my trust in you, my son."

CHAPTERFORTY-FOUR

The Thames Tunnel, Rotherhithe to Wapping
June 1826

IT TOOK ME some time and effort to convince the directors that the supervision levels would have to be raised, and even though Smith was against such investment, the day was carried by the rest of the members of the board. Isambard had been working continuous shifts of up to 18 hours each, often sleeping on the timber staging above water level and remaining at the workface for 36 hours at a time. I could not allow myself to expose my son to such pressure, even though he shrugged off the strain and took on the responsibility willingly and without complaint. Mr Gravatt, son of Colonel Gravatt of the Royal Engineers and a civil engineer of practical experience himself, was to be employed, as well as a Mr Riley, also experienced in works of this nature.

The directors, in their misguided wisdom, and much to my continued annoyance, had placed the bricklayers on piecework now, and had instructed that excavation needed to continue at twice the rate originally planned—an increase in forward movement of 18 inches or two brick lengths at a time. More ground would be exposed between the rear of the upper staves and the brick arch as work progressed. This was against my better judgment and left the work open to greater risk of collapse; but I reluctantly acquiesced. This, combined with the omission of a drain heading under the tunnel invert, was making the whole process more hazardous and much more difficult to manage than originally intended.

In order to mitigate the new risks from increased excavated ground exposure, I instructed Redman to fabricate longer poling screws. In parallel, Isambard deployed the most muscular of the labourers to crank up the additional large diameter screw jacks, which would generate the extra effort to drive the shield forward the increased distance.

Despite more interference, and the even greater challenges forced upon me, the shield would continue unimpeded.

* * *

The Thames Tunnel, Rotherhithe to Wapping
8th September 1826

"The water is in!"

A fantasy of fumbling. A mayhem of men, shifting this way and that. At first sight, it would seem to the outsider that a blind panic had taken hold as a cacophony of sound met the ears; raised voices, the clatter of shovel on plate, the trundling of barrow on timber trestle, desperate pumping and retreating bricklayers. But nothing was further from the truth. The miners were wet with sweat and water but brave and standing firm amidst testing conditions under the firm and competent guidance and direction of Isambard and his young assistants Beamish, Gravatt and Riley. I remained in the tunnel through the day to instil morale, give advice and active guidance, but it was largely Isambard's intuition, steady hand and speed of thought that were driving the work.

The ground had changed again to silts and running sand. The work face normally oozed water, it was true; but seepage could often change into a flow, which in turn could become a gush. The risk of ground failure was ever-present. We were therefore conditioned to expect the unexpected. Being prepared was the key.

The pump handlers toiled diligently, their arms in rhythmic effort to reduce the flood level in the invert. The miners and their labourers shovelled oakum and clay into the earth voids to seal the gaps. The bricklayers abandoned their work to assist in the efforts of quelling the flow and stabilising the work face by drilling relief holes in the completed arch to allow the water to escape. Cast iron pipes were squeezed behind the poling boards to divert flows to the already flooded floor and to prevent the further dilution of the silt and clay.

The din, compounded by the noise of the water now issuing from the new drains and crashing some 22 feet onto the shoe plates of frames 6 and 7, was astonishing. The ground was being tamed; the work relentless. Supervisors barked commands; men bellowed orders and reiterated instructions for clarity, bodies shifted all over the shield face, like ants; the tumultuous effort reaching a crescendo.

Suddenly, the water stopped. Total silence prevailed.

All looked to Isambard for further instruction. Time stood still.

Then came a rumbling from above, followed by gurgling noises. The men stiffened, fearing the worst. But then came the reassuring sound of water resuming its controlled course through the drains, accompanied by an audible sigh of communal relief. Work could now recommence unhindered.

And then, in the silence, the danger that had crept up on us all as the work progressed further and further under the river manifested itself. Like a mist gradually advancing over marshland, so the miasma of human excreta slowly increased to an all-pervading stench, infiltrating our nostrils and throats, invading our eyes. The open sewer that was the Thames was discharging its guts into the tunnel's confined space.

CHAPTERFORTY-FIVE

The Thames Tunnel, Rotherhithe to Wapping
October 1826—April 1827

IN THE ABSENCE of Isambard and Beamish, who had both fallen ill with vomiting and diarrhoea, I resumed my full-time duty with the shield; illustrating both our dire need of assistants and the new problems presented by the excavation. Around one in ten miners were falling sick. The number of men now employed on the project had swelled from 180 to 467; the costs rising to £150 per week with some 40 feet of tunnel completed.

The new Irish labour force—enlisted by the directors to save cost and 'speed up' operations against my wishes—were doing the best they could, but were not used to this manner of work. Open countryside and fresh air were their habitat—this environment was far too oppressive for them. They would often take flight from the face at the hint of a ground slippage or merely from the sound of gravel scraping against the staves as the frames pushed forward. The Irish foremen, Munday and Lane, spent most of their time cajoling their men and thwarting their all too regular rush to the safety of the shaft. There had been instances when mere rumours of water flooding in, put about by watchmen and operators distant from the tunnel face, had caused a minor panic amongst the foremen and engineers—including myself on one occasion—when in actuality all was in control.

As a precaution and as a result of recent experiences of flowing ground, I instructed stockpiles of straw, clay and oakum to be kept in all the top boxes of the frames, ready for ramming into the voids behind the poling screws, if and when the occasion arose. I had also already made provision to supplement the hand pumps with a horizontal-engine-driven one.

Gravatt and I had committed to alternate day and night shifts; Gravatt more than once operating thirty-eight consecutive hours. God forbid that he succumbed to the illness too. Riley moreo- ver looked particularly unwell; his face so grey and drawn that I suspected early stages of the onset of fever and requested he leave and return after receiving rest and treatment.

"Mr Brunel, as I take my leave of you, may I respectfully remind you that the visitors will be arriving soon."

I had not forgotten. "Yes, thank you, Gravatt. I am more than aware," I uttered through clenched teeth.

My anxiety levels were now even higher than usual as The Company had resolved to invite the general public to visit the western archway at a charge of one shilling per person. Extra revenue was needed, they said. I could not object even if I wanted to, which I obviously did.

In an hour, by my pocket watch, I would make my way to the timber barrier that formed the partition between the completed brickwork section of tunnel and the manned frames one hundred feet distant, in the gas-lit gloom. The public would be able to spy upon the works if they had the patience to stand for long enough and stare through the apertures deliberately formed in the brick and timber partition. My own dear wife, with Emma, Sophie and her three little children were amongst the first, excited at the experience. The young actress Fanny Kemble, destined for great stage success, no doubt, judging by the refreshing, energetic and confident character I met on her visit with her charming father, wrote to the national press:

> *"But I must tell you what the tunnel is like, or at least try to do so. You enter, by flights of stairs, the first door, and find yourself on a circular platform, which surrounds the top of a well of shaft, of about two hundred feet in circumference and five hundred in depth. This well is an immense iron frame of cylindrical form, filled in with bricks; it was constructed on level ground, and then, by some wonderful mechanical process, sunk into the earth. In the midst of this a steam engine, and above, or below as far as your eye can see, huge arms are working up and down while the creaking, crashing, whirring noises, and the swift whiling of innumerable wheels all around you, make you feel for the first few minutes as if you were going distracted. I should have liked to look much longer at all these beautiful, wise, working creatures.*
>
> *On turning round at the foot of the last flight of steps through an immense dark arch, as far as sight could reach stretched a vaulted passage, smooth earth underfoot, the white arches of the roof beyond, the whole lighted by a line of gas lamps, and as bright,*

almost, as if it were broad day. It was like one of those long avenues of light that led to the abodes of genii in fairy tales. The profound stillness of the place, first broken by my father's voice, to which the vaulted roof gave extraordinary and startling volume of tone, the indescribable feeling of subterranean vastness, the amazement and delight I experienced, quite overcame me, and I was obliged to turn from the friend who was explaining everything to me, to cry and ponder in silence.

Mr Brunel, who was superintending the works, came to my father and offered to conduct us to where the workmen were employed—an unusual favour, which of course delighted us all. So we left our broad, smooth path of light and went into dark passages, where we stumbled among coils of ropes and heaps of pipes and piles of planks, and where ground springs were welling up and flowing about in every direction. An iron frame has been constructed—a sort of cage, divided into many compartments, in each of which a man with his lantern and his tools is placed—and as they clear the earth away, this iron frame is moved onward and advances into new ground.

The appearance of the workmen themselves, all begrimed, with their brawny arms and legs bare, some standing in black water up to their knees, with the red, murky light of lanterns flashing and flickering about them, made a most striking picture.

As we returned, I remained at the bottom of the stairs last of all, to look back at the beautiful road to Hades, wishing I might be left behind."

Although the workforce was rapidly becoming experienced in overcoming the difficulties that beset them, through experience and effective drilling and instruction, the operations would never be entirely free of risk. The public would be blissfully ignorant; but my conscience was not.

Isambard had returned in good health.

Beamish reported on his arrival back that he had been overcome by a haze rising before his eyes, which left him blind in his left eye. His treatment was active and immediate but succeeded in only partially restoring his vision.

Riley too had become delirious, and tragically died from the fever. He was twenty-four.

The silt was still persistently permeating the ground. It was now becoming so easy to remove the spoil that, after removal in sections of the poling boards, the saturated earth could be scraped away with the miners' bare hands. The straw, wedges of timber and oakum proved their worth in stemming the ground flow but the poling boards themselves became unsteady and often fell off. Stones, brickbats, pieces of coal, bones, and fragments of glass and china also fell through, indicating to me that we were very close to the river bed.

I had repeatedly asked the directors for the use of a diving bell to inspect the area of excavation from the top (river) side, and eventually my demands were met.

* * * *

I felt the hairs stand up on the back of my neck. I had designed these contraptions but had yet to experience one. A strange feeling overcame me, compounded by claustrophobia. My anxiety was matched by the excitement of adventure. The murky brown Thames came up eerily to meet us as the heavy bronzed bell was slowly lowered. Incarcerated with Isambard, I lost my frame of reference completely; it was not like me to lose my bearings. Was it my age bringing on premature anxiety?

My normal good sense of direction did not count here as this was verticality; plunging into a world where another kind of logic takes over. To have water at your feet and air around you and above your head with no obvious barrier of separation was bizarre.

My only protection against total disorientation was to look out from the small porthole at the familiar, but slowly disappearing, city buildings on the bankside before the water engulfed the bell completely.

Isambard and I were lowered slowly into the river by the ship's steam hoist, the connecting lines pumping air into our cylinder of containment to equalise the internal pressure and force down the water level at our feet. It was low tide now, and it did not take long until the riverbed was reached. The ground over number one frame was considerably depressed. Isambard reached for the iron rod and poked at the ground—it was very loose, and it was not long before the rod struck metal.

"That must be the top staves of the frame!" He declared.

"Yes, let us insert the iron pipe and attempt to speak to Gravatt below us!"

It was incredible to think that we had come so near to the surface of the riverbed. But this was the lowest point of the river cross-section, made worse as some of the gravel had been dredged away for ballast, and the clay disturbed by ships' anchors.

"We will need to cast a steening in concrete over this depression to protect the works from further ingress." That should surely improve matters. I silently prayed to God that the worst of our difficulties would be behind us.

Just then a mumbled voice echoed along the length of the pipe followed by a clanking sound of metal upon metal. A small package issued from the end of the pipe, which I snatched before it had time to sink back, and opened in haste. Inside were a number of gold pins with the tag 'to the friends of Benjamin and Sophie Hawes to commemorate this fine and astonishing occasion'.

CHAPTER FORTY-SIX

The Boardroom, Thames Tunnel Company, London
May Day 1827

"THE TUNNEL HAS been closed for seven days now, but I believe the miners are yielding. We shall not give in to them."

Smith and the Board were adamant and were, for once, all united.

I was naturally dispirited and very disappointed with the workforce—some of whom I had made the briefest of acquaintances with during the course of the works. I felt that we had a bond through shared experiences and the spirit and willingness of overcoming difficulties; good men like Phelan, McGraw and Keene. I'm sure that their like would have disapproved of the men's decision to strike for better pay. However, as it stood, the majority had won the day and the shaft lay empty and silent, apart from the men standing guard at the tunnel entrance, taking it in turns to prevent workers returning.

They were holding us to ransom, but would not succeed. From three shillings and threepence to three shillings and ninepence a day did not appear to be, on the face of it, an excessive claim, but it would set a precedent for future wage demands if we yielded now.

"Mr Brunel, what have you to say?" I was starkly reminded of the time I was at The King's Bench Court when sentence was passed for my debts. Smith would make a good magistrate.

I sat back in my chair, and gazed up at the ornate white plastered ceiling of the conference room of the Thames Tunnel Company.

"I have it on good authority that some of the men are very discontented with the current cessation. They have families and mouths to feed. The longer this unacceptable situation continues, the more likely that the men will see the light. This action will hit them hard in the pocket."

"Hear, hear," was the resounding collective voice around the long beechwood table.

"That is all very well, Mr Brunel, but we cannot wait forever. If you are correct, we need to resume activities as soon as possible. There have been many problems, not necessarily of our own making, that have thwarted progress and cost the company more money. I am conscious that we have now completed approximately five hundred and forty feet of tunnel, which is in some ways creditable, given the problems encountered to date, but we do not have a bottomless pit of finance and cannot allow this situation to continue."

I was pleasantly surprised that Smith would give some credit to the progress made on the project so far. This was a rare event indeed. The after-dinner brandies probably helped.

"I am aware of that. I am also aware of the identity of the ringleaders. I suggest they are not re-employed when this dispute is over and the men return to work."

This was met with nods of approval.

My main concerns, although I did not air them here, were related to the condition of the works now left unattended for some time. The silty gravels would have settled more under the weight of the saturated ground—particularly at high tide, when the pressure would be greatest. Top staves and poling screws could have rusted. The frames might well be distorted under prolonged stress not allowed for in my design and would now require more force to drive them forward. A full survey would be needed before we recommenced.

* * *

The Thames Tunnel, Rotherhithe to Wapping
17th May 1827

"I am pleased to see them all back and working as diligently as ever."

"Yes, indeed, Father. You were correct in your assumptions regarding the condition of the frames. We have made extensive repairs, and are now making steady progress again."

Isambard, Gavatt and I looked on from the rear of the timber gantry just as the seepages in the exposed ground above the top cell of number 6 frame suddenly became stronger. Grey-brown streams issued forth, carrying with them clumps of clay. Both miner and labourer shovelled away with haste. A piece of brass and old shoe buckle fell through from no 9 upper box.

"Make for the baulking timbers and wedges to strut this as before!" Beamish bellowed. "And then abandon this area until the water eases."

Isambard nodded and then turned toward me.

"The silt is now overlaid with a yellow mottled clay, which often separates in lumps when subjected to strong water flows."

This was not looking at all good.

"Might I suggest we now restrict the forward movements to seven inches at a time, due to this new risk of collapse. I don't like what I'm seeing."

"Yes, we will do so, Father."

The shining metal blade end of a shovel, wrapped in clinging silt and clay, was suddenly laid bare through the exposed roof. It carried the inscription 'TTC'.

"I recognise that as the shovel that we lost when we were placing the concrete steening on the river bed some sixteen days ago!" Isambard was surprised.

Could that be a lucky omen?

* * *

Engineer's Diary
Richard Beamish
Thames Tunnel
18th May 1827

At two o'clock in the morning, I relieved Isambard Brunel in the superintendence of the working. At five o'clock, as the tide rose, the ground seemed as though it were alive. Between nos 6 and 7 frames there were occasional bursts of diluted silt, which subsided, however, as the tide ebbed. The men who came on at six in the morning exhibited extreme reluctance to go to their work, hanging about the engine house, where arrangements had been made for them to dry their clothes. The day passed on with not more than the usual amount of alarm; but, as the flood-tide returned, the same general disturbance of the ground was observed as had occurred in the morning.

The visit of a dear friend, Lady Raffles, with a large party, about five o'clock pm, did not tend to allay a strong feeling of apprehension which took possession of my mind. No sooner had she taken leave than I prepared myself for what, I was satisfied, would prove a trying night. My holiday coat was exchanged for a strong water-proof, the polished wellingtons for greased mud boots, and the shining beaver for a large, brimmed sou'wester.

The tide was now rising fast. On entering the frames, nos 9 and 11 were about to be worked down. Already had the top polings of no 11 been removed, when the miner Goodwin, a powerful and experienced man, called for help. For him to have required help was sufficient to indicate danger. I immediately directed an equally powerful man, Rogers, in no 9 to go to Goodwin's assistance; but before he had time to obey the order, there poured in such an overwhelming flood of slush and water, that they were both driven out; and Corps the bricklayer who had also answered to the call for help, was literally rolled over onto the stage behind the frames, as though he had come through a mill sluice, and would have been hurled to the ground if I had not fortunately arrested his progress.

I then made an effort to re-enter the frames, calling upon the miners to follow; but I was only answered by a roar of water, which long continued to resound in my ears. Finding that no gravel appeared, I saw that the case was hopeless. To get all the men out of the shield was now my anxiety. This accomplished, I stood for a moment on the stage, unwilling to fly, yet capable to resist the torrent which momentarily increased in magnitude and velocity, till Rogers, who alone remained, kindly drew me by the arm, and, pointing to the rising water beneath, showed only too plainly the folly of delay. Then ordering Rogers to the ladder, I slowly followed.

As a singular coincidence, I may here remark that this man, Rogers, who showed such kindly feeling and devotion, had served with me in the Coldstream Guards.

As I descended from the stage, the water had so risen in the tunnel that all the loose timber near the frames, the cement casks, and the large boxes used for mixing the cement, were not only afloat, but in considerable agitation.

The light was but barely sufficient to allow me to grope my way through these obstructions, which, striking against my legs, threatened to arrest my progress. I felt that a false step could not be retrieved, clad as I was, and with heavy boots quite full of water. After a short struggle, I succeeded in gaining the west arch, luckily comparatively free. The water was noticeably rising; it had already reached my waist; still I did not venture to run, feeling that a stumble might prove fatal. If I could only gain the barrier which limited the ingress of visitors, I should be clear of the floating timber which must be there arrested!

As I approached this barrier, the sight of some of our most valued workers cheered me. Not understanding the cause of procrastination, they could not withhold their expressions of impatience, Mayo and Bertram swore lustily at my apparent tardiness. At the barrier, four powerful hands seized me, and in a moment placed me on the other side. On now we hurried. At the bottom of the shaft, we met Isambard Brunel and Mr Gravatt. We turned. The spectacle that presented itself will not readily be forgotten.

The water came on in a great wave, everything on its surface becoming the more distinctly visible as the light from the gas lamps was more strongly reflected. Presently a large crash was heard. A small office, which had been erected under the arch, about a hundred feet from the frames, had burst. The pent air rushed out; the lights were suddenly extinguished, and the noble work, which only a short few hours before had commanded the homage of an admiring public, was consigned to darkness and destruction. It only remained to ascend the shaft, but this was not easy. Men filled the staircase and, being themselves out of danger, they entirely forgot the situation of their comrades below.

For the first time, I now felt fear, as I dreaded the recoil of the wave from the circular well of the shaft, which, if it had caught us, would inevitably have swept us back under the arch. With the utmost difficulty, the lowest flight of stairs was cleared when, as I had anticipated, the recoil came, and water surged under our feet. The men now scrambled up the stairs, and though nearly exhausted, I was able to reach the top. Here a new cause of anxiety awaited us. A hundred voices shouted, 'A rope! A rope! Save him! Save him!' How anyone could have been left behind puzzled and amazed me. That someone was in the water was certain. With that promptitude which ever distinguished Isambard Brunel, he did not hesitate for a moment. Seizing a rope, and followed by Mr Gravatt, he slid down one of the iron ties of the shaft.

The rope was quickly passed round the waist of the struggling fellow, who proved to be old Tillett, the engine man. He had gone to the bottom of the shaft to look after the pumps He would have speedily disappeared under the waters had it not been for the presence of mind and chivalrous spirit of his superiors.

The roll was now called, when to our unspeakable joy, every man answered to his name; and we were thus relieved from the painful retrospect that must have followed any sacrifice of life.

To convey the news of the disaster to Mr Brunel was our next objective. Taking a pony belonging to Isambard, I hastened to town; but Mr Brunel had gone to dine with a friend, and it was not until ten o'clock that night that I was able to execute my painful mission.

After the first shock, and upon receiving the assurance that no life had been lost, it was marvellous to witness the ease with which he took part in the preparation of a letter to The Times. *This missive would convey to the general public correct information as to the nature of the catastrophe, and inform them of the methods with which he would overcome the effects of the misfortune.*

Finally at one in the morning, I threw myself on my bed. I breathed a grateful thanksgiving for the protection which a beneficent Providence had extended to me and to those placed in my charge and sunk, utterly exhausted, into a profound sleep.

* * *

The Rotherhithe Church had a full attendance today. Its modest nave and delicate stained-glass window lay testament to the outpouring of gratitude from the congregation; Godfearing working men, supervisors and women amongst them giving praise to the Highest.

As I stood close to my beloved Sophia, I considered that Beamish and many others were fortunate to have escaped from the inundation. The curate, however, was less than gracious in his sermon, citing the accident as a fatal one and a 'just judgement upon the presumptuous aspirations of mortal men'. There was little I could do to repudiate the error in his dialogue or address his attitude here in this, God's house. I felt a little wounded, but my faith in the Almighty and the tunnel project remained untarnished.

CHAPTER FORTY-SEVEN

Bridge Street, Blackfriars, London
19 May 1827

"I FEAR THE hole in the riverbed is deeper and more extensive than we first considered, Father."

Isambard and Beamish had just returned from the diving bell inspection the day following the inundation. It was important to survey the area as soon as possible to determine the degree of damage and instigate remedial work to the river bed in order to get the works moving again. Any delay would prove costly both in morale and finance. The directors were continually placing me under pressure and questioning my every move, every decision—engineering, build practice, coordination of management and workforce, resolution of problems—nothing escaped their scrutiny and almost incessant interference.

"The depression extends from where the shield last penetrated the ground eastwards for some few yards, marked with almost vertical sides. We could see little gravel present, even in the lowest undisturbed bed which must have been previously dredged out. In discussion with the captains of coal barges on our return to shore, we were informed that they have had to move to another section of the river as their anchors would not hold."

"Did you manage to inspect the top of the shield frames from the riverbed side?"

"Yes, although our enterprise was daunting, our anxiety was more than compensated for by the excitement and sense of adventure both Beamish and I experienced. We were able to venture forth and drop down out of the bell and actually place one foot on the back of the staves and the other on the completed brickwork of the arch. From what we saw, the shield is holding up well under the pressure and extreme circumstances."

I smiled, sharing my son's enthusiasm. I was also naturally very satisfied that my design was holding fast under stresses not originally allowed for.

"Your input and observations are extremely valuable, Isambard, though there is a thin line between bravery and foolhardiness. You should not put yourself at undue risk. Diving bell design is still very much in its infancy, subject to error and possible failure that would lead to problems."

Isambard's expression changed from wonder to concern.

"We will need to plug the hole as soon as possible and effectively arch over the void made by the huge influx of water. Bags of clay with connecting iron rods may well be the best method," I ventured. "These measures should ensure that the gaping hole in the riverbed is finally sealed off, and we can then look forward to priming all the pumps ready to suck out the water within the tunnel so work can resume. This operation may take some days, though, as it would appear from your observations that hundreds, maybe thousands of cubic feet of clay bags and hazel rods will be needed. We will need to be patient and pragmatic at a time when the pressures to recommence early will override good sense."

"I have had word, sir, that the directors are suggesting a timber raft filled with clay be laid over the infilling to provide extra security against further water ingress, particularly at high tide," Beamish intervened.

The incorrigible attitude and false wisdom of the directors continued to be a thorn in my flesh. I said nothing, as I did not wish to reveal my frustrations to these young, impressionable engineers and thus undermine their enthusiasm and vigour. They were committed to the cause, and my guidance and experience were key to maintaining morale and supporting their continued efforts.

"Then we shall do as they ask, but I have my doubts as to how effective this application will be. In fact, I consider that this may hamper things further."

* * *

The Thames Tunnel, Rotherhithe to Wapping
31 May 1827

The pumps were working well. The water level in the tunnel was beginning to subside, as I observed from the relative safety of the old, damaged timber staging some forty feet back from where the brick-work arch had at last been completed. It would not be long before we would be able to venture further along the tunnel and inspect the frames and my mighty shield at close quarters. The dim light from our hand-held gas lanterns was all we could rely upon to give us some semblance of vision into the eerily quiet chasm ahead of us. A trickle of water could be heard as my junior engineers, clerk of works, charge hands and foremen took it in turns to swing their lights to and fro to cast as much light in as many directions as possible in an attempt to illuminate the gloom. But we waited. We needed to be sure.

"Shall I make arrangements to procure a small boat so that we may inspect further ahead?" Gravatt was keen, but I remained cautious. After the recent flooding, I was no longer prepared to take any unnecessary risks. Patience was of the utmost importance.

"It is now four o'clock. Let us return at nine and see."

Our discussions on the events experienced so far, speculation on the success of the huge clay plug in the riverbed and progressive talk on the best way forward, continued in the comfort of the King's Head Inn as we ate heartily and quenched our thirst with the best of London's ales.

* * *

Pinckney was an experienced diver. Muddy waters and the experience of descending into the gloomy depth of the Thames did not daunt him. As Isambard's companion on this, the final inspection of the riverbed, the many mounds of clay bulging out from the bed had become almost commonplace to him. He had witnessed at first hand the laborious process when many barges and men had worked all the daylight hours for five days to seal the vast underwater aperture. The bell had risen and plunged many times over this period; and not without incident. Links in the chains that supported the heavy buoyant bell had fractured on two occasions. Had it not been for the quick thinking of the barge captain in replacing these components with spares he had on board, and the experience of the ship's hands, the bell would have almost certainly had capsized with the unfortunate Pinckney inside it.

There were other causes for concern. The Thames was a very busy shipping lane and the docks on the north shore in particular were permanently clogged with ships of all displacements and denominations awaiting on- or off-loading of their cargoes. So much so that many vessels anchored midstream, vacant and vulnerable to petty theft. It was not uncommon for crews to grow impatient and bored, as the worth of their cargo diminished and cost of their stewardship increased. Many attempted to manoeuvre their vessels into more favourable positions, jostling for the right to berth first and deeming the presence of a mere barge or two carrying out duties less important than theirs.

Collisions were therefore difficult to avoid, and the hole-filling operation therefore became even more hazardous.

As the bell came within a few feet of the riverbed, Pinckney could see one of the uppermost bags bloated by expanded clay. The surface of the bed looked firm and steady as the bell swung gently with the tide and the rocking of the barge above. He had the confidence to take a step out to prove that this man-made platform was now stable enough for him to impose his full weight and demonstrate the job was nearing completion, the ground sufficiently compacted. Isambard thought otherwise.

"What are you doing, Pinckney?"

"Don't be concerned, sir. I have carefully surveyed all these bags being placed over some days, with the connecting iron rods inserted rigorously and accurately. I have therefore great faith in your father's method and feel that I need to prove that to you and others."

Before Isambard could stop him, Pinckney leapt forward off the footboard and into the murky depth up to his waist before his feet slipped as the ground gave way under him.

It was a foolhardy and unnecessary act. Discretion is the better part of valour and Pinckney was taken by the moment; overconfident and spurred on by the presence of Marc Brunel's son.

Isambard scrambled to the edge of the footboard of the bell in an attempt to reach out and grab whatever appendage that came to hand—a shoulder, arm, even Pinckney's head—in a desperate effort to prevent him disappearing into the depths. As the man coughed and spluttered, thrashing around, it was Isambard's left leg that came to his rescue as Pinckney stretched every sinew of his long arm to grab hold of it. Isambard, in return, fought hard to pull the man up with one hand whilst anchoring himself to the bell's nearest safety handle with the other to prevent himself slipping and getting into the same serious predicament as the man he was attempting to save. The timber footboard broke off in the struggle and slowly floated upwards and away from the bell.

From his vantage point on the starboard stern of The River Queen, Beamish looked on at the scene unfolding before him. Boats full of clay were still arriving and docking alongside the barge in readiness for hoisting up and plunging into the rippling water. He had tallied in excess of 19,000 cubic feet of clay and gravel bags that had now been deposited on the river bed and was attending to the signalling of operations, including the contact with the bell below via a length of connecting tube and hailer.

Suddenly, a timber board splashed its way to the surface next to where Beamish was standing. He could not believe his eyes as he recognised that this was no innocuous flotsam, but the timber footboard from the diving bell. Isambard was in danger. Beamish scrambled for the communication tube but immediately received the signal from below the waters that a slight mishap had occurred and that all was well, much to his relief; although he would not feel entirely assured until his friend emerged unscathed from the depths.

The prepared matting to cover the newly replaced ground was readied to be lifted into place and secured by anchors and chains; another ploy from the directors which met with little approval as to its success from Marc Brunel himself. The diving bell came slowly into view, water cascading from its surface and the faces of Isambard and Pinckney peering out of the small rounded portholes. Beamish breathed a sigh of relief as Isambard stepped onto the awaiting deck and shook his friend's hand.

"All seems successful. The vast hole is plugged. We must now venture forth on the underside of the tunnel to inspect the shield and surrounding area once the pumps have been in full operation for a few days and the flood water in the tunnel has subsided sufficiently to gain access by boat."

"I will go, Isambard. You have had enough anxiety to last you some time, and now need a rest. I will take two of the more experienced and capable miners, Woodward and Pamphilon, with me."

* * *

Beamish recounted this boat journey to me in the tranquil surroundings of Bridge Street office. Isambard also attended.

"The pumps had been working hard and the tunnel was effectively dry for the first one-hundred-and-fifty feet, but by the time we had arrived at the frames' down gradient, the water surface was within three feet of the top of the arch. We could go no further than within one-hundred-and-fifty feet of the frames as there was a great amount of silt, clay and gravel brought in from the water course and engulfing them. So I had to clamber out of the boat, with a small lantern in hand, and scramble over the frames on hands and knees to get a better view."

I shook my head at the bravery and commitment of this man.

"To my amazement I discovered that the frames remained in a good upright condition with little or no damage to the top staves, rollers or bolted connections, but full of soil. I shone my light upward and could see the bellied-out bags of clay forming the new soffit and replacement riverbed. There was a steady stream of water in the east corner."

"Then we must put work in hand to secure the area now, and drive on."

"Father, now that we are able to envisage an early restart, the journalists are pressing to make a full story on the progress and problems of the tunnel to bring reassurance and hope to the public attention. The public and key figures remain compelled to read about our success and would want to share and rejoice in this great project."

"I will find time to speak to them."

"The directors are now also interested in inspecting the works and the damage that may have occurred. They wish to examine at first hand the problems encountered and to regain confidence in the shield moving forward."

Again, these most interfering of men wished to meddle in matters of no direct interest. Could they not simply be satisfied with reports and communications from myself and my fellow engineers, showing the efforts we are making to resolve this problem? Visiting the temporarily abandoned tunnel by boat is hazardous enough when undertaken by capable and experienced men, never mind the prying eyes of ones not suited to the conditions and environment. I could, and would, oppose such a proposal, but knew too that I was unlikely to prevail.

***

Engineer's Diary
Richard Beamish
The Thames Tunnel
27th June 1827

Two of the Directors, Mr Martin and Mr Harris, having expressed a wish to inspect the shield, proceeded with Mr Gravatt and two miners, T Dowling and Samuel Richardson, in the small boat down the western arch. Richardson, though not called upon by Mr Gravatt, insisting upon getting in at the stern of the boat when he had shoved it off. The weight proved too great. The water came in; and though one of the gentlemen was requested to go forward that the boat might be balanced, neither was willing to stir until Mr Martin, feeling the water inconvenient, and forgetting that as the boat made progress down the archway, the headway rapidly diminished, suddenly stood up, and striking his head against the tip of the arch, fell backwards amongst the others.

The boat filled, and the party were at once plunged into water about twelve feet deep. The only swimmers were Messrs Gravatt and Dowling. The directors clung to Mr Gravatt, who could only release himself by diving. Swimming out, he quickly returned with a second boat. Meantime Mr Martin and Mr Harris had succeeded in getting hold of the plinth in one of the side arches, and there supported themselves until relieved by Mr Gravatt; but there was no account of Richardson. A drag was procured, and his body at once found. It was conveyed to my bed as the nearest; but although every means was resorted to that science dictated, all proved in vain—life was altogether extinct.

The shock was to Mr Brunel far greater than the eruption of the river. For that, a remedy was at hand; but who could call back a departed spirit? It must be ever remembered that one of the most striking characteristics of Brunel's inventions were sage means provided for the protection of life; and not withstanding all the difficulties by which the operations of the tunnel were beset, no life had yet been sacrificed where the necessary care had been practised.

* * *

Work finally resumed, tentatively at first, as the miners were ill at ease and expected the worst, despite assurances from all senior management figures including myself. It would take only one man to speak of impending doom for the entire workforce to down tools and hastily beat a trail to the shaft. Isambard informed me of one such instance when, solely through the outbursts of a miner who was sleeping between shifts on the gantry of frame number 6, loudly uttered in his sleep, "The water's in again, the water's in!"

This alert had reached Gravatt and Isambard via the night watchman just as they were changing shifts at the shaft head and compelled them to make haste to the head of the tunnel workings. When they arrived, they witnessed a scene of calm and normality and a dry tunnel base, the guilty man somewhat red-faced and other miners looking exceedingly relieved.

The shield was holding fast, despite the influence of the tides and accumulated silt and gravel in and around the west frames. Men were working day and night shifts to remove all the debris carefully and systematically to minimise any movement or damage to the frame staves and poling board screws.

My young, capable team of Gravatt, Beamish and Isambard continued to direct the necessary operations so that the whole tunnel end could be cleared and work resumed; but the menace had crept up on us again as the filthy river oozed forth its disgusting, gut-wrenching stench. In the few hours I was at the shield, my eyes and nose dribbled, and the back of my throat grew dry and sore. I noticed a black deposit around the men's eyes, nostrils and mouths.

"Has that awful reek persisted on our return, my son?"

"I'm afraid so. It seems to have worsened. The river bed here is at a low point, so presumably the solid human effluent has settled out more here and permeated the ground and water. Many men have had to retire because of headaches, vomiting and giddiness. The situation has been exacerbated as the ventilator built into the central pier was blocked by the irruption. We are digging it out to replace it with a timber one, but this will take time."

Suddenly a bright light flashed before us, closely followed by a shock wave or air riding on a large 'bang' We temporarily lost our balance on the staging. A cry of anguish was heard coming from a miner in number 9 frame.

"I will attend, Isambard." Gravatt rushed to the scene with a pail and dampened cloth.

"And that is another peril we now experience from time to time, Father. When the stale pungent river air builds up, there is a risk that combustion will occur with the portable gas lanterns. The effect never exceeds that of a minor burn to the skin, but the event in itself is disturbing and is affecting morale."

"The quicker that ventilation shaft is back in operation the better."

* * *

I was the first to succumb. The ghastly conditions and the oppressive heat of July turned my insides to liquid and my skin to a heavy wet hide; my head throbbed incessantly. 'Nature, long oppressed, commands the mind to suffer with the body.'

I found myself incarcerated in my bedroom again for many days as a result of my weariness; able to summon only enough energy to rise for my ablutions. I partook of minimal simple food and fresh water, though it would not guarantee nourishment as it was soon evacuated from my body. My loving Sophia was my only regular attendant, the doctor visiting once a week.

I was told, in no uncertain terms, to abandon any plans I might have had of returning to the tunnel, until such time that the doctor deemed me well enough. I would nevertheless receive daily bulletins on the tunnel progress from my trusted engineering lieutenants. Sophia read these to me when my mind was too weak with fever and my body too unpredictable of constitution to be able to do so myself.

I returned to examine my magnificent shield after several weeks of absence, and experienced once more the elation that comes through hard work and concerted effort. I was further encouraged by the application and commitment to the cause of the labour force and management.

"I am sorry to hear of Beamish's illness and absence, Isambard."

"Yes, Gravatt and I feel his absence, not only as a reliable engineer, but as a friend and confidant. He has pleurisy, I understand. When I visited him on Friday, his condition seemed to be improving. Sadly, however, 'Old Greenshield', one of our key men, passed away yesterday. The work is now back on track, but slower without him."

"I am naturally sorry to hear that. I did not know the man of whom you speak. But shall pray for his soul."

"And you, Father, are you fully recovered?"

"Sufficiently to attend today and regularly from now on, as the sight and sound of this great iron structure thrusting forward lifts my spirits and excites my very being."

* * *

"Do not despair that you are unable to attend the tunnel as much as you would like to, Marc. As you can see from the reports from Beamish, Gravatts and your son, all is being done with the best will and knowledge in your absence."

Sophia picked up the newspapers lying on my writing desk.

"People all over the country are in wonderment over this enormous undertaking, and the press, even *The Scotsman* newspaper, reports 'no stronger proof could be adduced of the great anxiety and interest entertained by the public generally in the success of this great undertaking, than the fact that £62 was received, during the last week, as admission money from visitors, great numbers of whom were scientific foreigners, whose visits are made almost weekly'."

I had mixed feelings on that news. I did not agree with the public visiting at this particular time, but the increased revenue was welcome and would help to keep the directors at bay despite our apparently slow progress. But, if one takes into account how much work has been done, all tasks executed in a very confined situation with water occasionally bursting upon us and the ground running in like slush, it is truly remarkable to have arrived at the point where the public pay to view what they consider to be a wondrous creation. My concern, however, is that, despite the constant reverberations of the pumps and the crashing of large pieces of iron breaking off, these people are completely unaware of the danger they court by their presence here. Unfortunately, I no longer have any say in this matter; my hands are tied.

CHAPTER FORTY-EIGHT

The Thames Tunnel, Rotherhithe to Wapping
10 November 1827

THERE WAS GOOD cause for celebration. The halfway point of the tunnel had been reached—five hundred and fifty feet of double-arched, central pier brickwork lay testament to the tremendous effort and the qualities of human endurance to overcome devastating odds over many weeks.

The entrance to the western archway of this bold and strik- ing structure now took on a totally new aspect in preparation for the scene of a banquet. Crimson drapes adorned the walls; a white damask cloth covered a long table; four huge decorative candelabra, mounted on tall ceramic pedestals, stood at each corner courtesy of the Portable Gas Company, and places were laid for fifty specially invited guests.

Conditions in the tunnel had much improved. The recent exceptionally high tides had tested the men and engineers; the threat that all the works would be submerged became a reality as all toiled in haste to surround the Rotherhithe shaft with a raised bund or levee of clay to prevent the river flowing into the works. And yet, through all the difficulties and setbacks in competing with the constantly changing properties and character of the saturated soil as works progressed, in addition to the almost constant influx of the dirty brown Thames water, the shield held firm, but many weeks had passed before this point had been reached.

Friends and dignitaries alike were in attendance, headed by Mr Bandinel of the Foreign Office, supported by Captain Stevens, Equerry to HRH The Duke of Gloucester, Captain Codrington and Mr Benjamin Hawes, junior. The Band of the Coldstream Guards, Beamish's old regiment, whose attendance he had successfully requested, struck up the national anthem. The sound of their instruments was made even more impressive by the reverberation around the tunnel walls. This grand occasion was intended as a showcase tribute to miners and managers alike but also, to some extent, as an act of defiance to some of the more pessimistic and interfering directors of the Thames Tunnel Company. The man of the greatest importance in the enterprise was sadly not present. His place was ably taken by his young and capable resident engineer son, Isambard, who was the first to propose a toast to the King, the Duke of Wellington and Marc's health. All raised their crystal glasses towards the fine brickwork arched roof and drank as the band played.

Mr Bandinel, as Marc's distinguished and valued friend, stood and proposed a toast to the health of Admiral Sir Edward Codrington, a vigorous supporter of the tunnel project.

There followed a confidently delivered speech which was met with great cheers. The band of the Coldstream Guards then struck up 'See the conquering hero returns', followed by 'Rule Britannia'.

"May I also make a toast to the health of Woolaston, the deputy chairman of the Thames Tunnel Company and to my own absent father, who regrettably is still recovering from a persistent malady and cannot be with us today."

Enthusiastic applause rippled through all the assembled.

Meanwhile, in the adjoining eastern arch, over one hundred leading workmen, miners and bricklayers were also gathered for a modest feast in similar celebratory mood, with free ale and pies being enthusiastically consumed. The leading hand, Thompson, requested a toast be offered up for their tools.

When the applause subsided in the adjoining west archway, a special delegation of four of the workmen presented Isambard with a specially inscribed pickaxe and shovel with the letters 'TTC' to mark this grand occasion.

* * *

I was naturally very disappointed that I was unable to be present at the ceremony, but being still confined to my bed with sickness and fever, that was impossible. However, the full story of events and a description of the occasion were brought to life at my bedside by my ever-reliable and loyal son. I was delighted that everything had gone well and to plan. All my plans had come to fruition, it seemed, particularly when I read the summary of the minutes of the meeting of the proprietors of the Thames Tunnel on 20th November, who reported, "The difficulties which had arisen, and the effectual manner in which they had been overcome, proved to demonstration the entire practicability of the undertaking."

The directors expressed the hope that, notwithstanding the excess of the cost beyond the estimate, "the work would be deemed by His Majesty's Government so far of a national character, that there would be found a disposition to afford such further assistance as could, with propriety, be granted. That the interest is so general, that the success of the work will be regarded as a national benefit and honour; but, its abandonment, while practicable, a national misfortune and disgrace."

Heartening and encouraging words indeed. I slowly closed my eyes and drifted off again. The report letter dropped to the floor as I entered into another slumber to dream of the resumption of operations on my shield.

CHAPTER FORTY-NINE

The Thames Tunnel, Rotherhithe to Wapping
12 January 1828

AMIDST THE GLOOM and the eye-watering, gut-churning stench, the dull sound of picks and shovels perforated the air. The men knew the routine.

Muscular navvies, their sweaty clothing clinging to their darkened skin, toiled at the face; hacking great lumps of sodden soil away and then inch by inch forging the great wrought iron shield relentlessly forward. Most of them worked in silence; the only human sounds reverberating through the confined space were the repeated grunts and occasional raised voices of instruction. The dim tunnel was lit merely by a series of portable gas lamps meandering back down the bricked-up walls to a small oval of natural light at the entrance to the main shaft, some five hundred feet away. The gangs continued to work under the threat of regular explosion, from the exposure of flame to the ever-present methane gas emanating from the detritus of the open sewer that was the Thames.

Once the tunnellers had done their job and the shield had advanced once again to expose a thin crescent of freshly excavated soffit, and once the labourers had barrowed the spoil away, the bricklayers set to work off huge timber trestles, lining the tunnel with kilned clay and mortar, thus creating an unrelenting production line.

Outside, in the cool clear air, the steam pumps rattled and hissed their rhythmic refrain, sucking the foul river sewer water from the excavation sump into the bright London sky.

"It seems more than a trickle now," Collins observed from the upper cell of number one frame. The bilge pump was beginning to labour with the pipe running full bore. To move this end frame forward as excavation was completed now required the removal and reinstatement of the timber side shoring. Ball came to assist, and both men struggled around the poling screws and boards supporting the front face, as the lateral support timbers were painstakingly removed ready for repositioning.

Isambard stood on the timber platform behind the network of wrought iron frames that made up the west shield and watched as the men slowly but surely advanced. His eyes were circled by the residue of London's excrement. He could hardly keep awake; he had had a disturbed night lying fully clothed on the scaffold boarding in readiness for the early shift. Rubbing his eyes, he realised they were not deceiving him as he noticed a swelling in the silty clay around the area where Collins and Ball were now working.

Without warning, a column of ground ten inches in diameter burst through. A torrent of water followed immediately behind it, cascading with some force and knocking Collins clean out of his cell and onto the timber staging where the bricklayers were building the arch. Ball hurried to assist Collins and together they attempted to replace the timbers, with Isambard in close attendance. They called furiously for more men, but it became abundantly clear that their efforts were proving futile against the now violent and significant flow of water. An unexpected whistling rush of air extinguished all the gas lights, leaving the men thrashing blindly up to their waists through the rapidly rising tide.

Isambard's voice could just be heard above the anguished cries of men and the deafening surge of water as he urged them to abandon the workface and make their way back to the main shaft immediately. No sooner than he had bellowed the orders than the staging gave way under his feet and he was hurled into the water. He managed to stay upright, and fought to keep his balance whilst wading through the putrid flow carrying with it loose timbers and cement barrels that buffeted his body. Then he could move no longer. A large baulk timber was trapping his right leg. In desperation, he tugged and twisted for what seemed like an eternity. By sheer persistence, he managed to dislodge the obstruction and struggle on to the relative safety of the east arch, the water lapping ominously around his chest.

"Collins, Ball. Are you with me?"

Isambard's repeated cries were unanswered. He half-waded, half-swam, in an attempt to avoid being driven into the walls of the tunnel whilst being forced forward by the turbulent fast-flowing current. The crescent of light from the main shaft grew larger as he reached the bottom of the workmen's staircase and into a chaos of men and activity; some were descending ready to return to work for the day shift, others ascending from the night shift, all in a desperate scramble to get away from the rising torrent.

He glanced down to see the swirling mass of water increasing below, filling the tunnel. His passage blocked, he attempted to make for the visitors' stairway in the west arch but was suddenly propelled upwards, surrendering to a huge vertical wave of water which brought him to the top of the rim of the shaft. He grabbed at a dangling rope and the waiting arms of Beamish hauled him to safety. Three men below him, attempting to climb a ladder lying against the shaft, were not as fortunate; the back surge of the same wave that had inadvertently saved Isambard crashed into the ladder and lower section of the staircase, smashing it to pieces and sweeping them under the arch as the churning, seething mass immersed all before it.

* * *

Beamish came to me at Bridge Street; but this was no routine visit to enquire after my health. Nor was it a report of progress on the tunnel as he had related to me on other occasions. I could see from his distraught expression as he strode into our drawing room that this was a much more serious incident than those that had previously befallen us. My eyes filled with tears as he carefully recounted the severity of the events. This new flood had resulted in loss of life, and serious injury to my beloved son.

"What is the extent of Isambard's injury? Where is he now?"

"He has a deep gash to his right knee which he badly twisted making his escape. Otherwise, he is conscious and in good spirits. Despite having difficulty in walking and being in some pain, he remains undaunted and has refused to leave the works. He is already making plans and relaying instructions for the necessary diving operations to determine the extent of the cavity on the riverbed."

I grimaced and held my head in my hands as the dreadful story unfolded. There was silence in the room as I reflected on this most recent and disastrous episode in the Tunnel's short history. I had designed the shield to protect and preserve life firstly and foremostly. It had not failed in that respect; but was it my overconfidence in the shield's ability and purpose that had extended the boundaries of risk? My fever, although on the wane, was fuelling my uncertainty and doubts.

"I must prepare myself and see him straight away."

* * *

My son lay asleep in his bed. The doctor had visited. Isambard had badly damaged his knee and had suffered some internal injuries. He would need to rest for some weeks to recuperate. Sophia and I were very pleased and thankful to see him and know that he had survived almost intact. I was confident he would make a full recovery with his mother's loving care, but it would take time.

With Isambard's permission, I had earlier consulted his record of the event, and was somewhat surprised at his attitude. It was written with youthful vigour, genuine excitement and sense of adventure, but also with sympathy for those committed and spirited men we had lost:

Here I am at Bridge House

I have been laid up quite useless since the 14th January. I shan't forget that day in a hurry, very near finished my journey then; when the danger is over, it is rather amusing than otherwise—while it existed I can't say that the feeling was at all uncomfortable. If I was to say the contrary, I should be nearer the truth in this instance. While exertions could still be made and hope remained of stopping the ground, it was an excitement which will always be a luxury to me.

When we were obliged to run, I felt nothing in particular; I was only thinking of the best way of getting us on and the probable state of the arches. When knocked down, I certainly gave myself up, but I took it very much as a matter of course, which I had expected the moment we quitted the frames, for I never expected we should get out. The instant I disengaged myself and got breath again—all dark—I bolted into the other arch—this saved me by laying hold of the rail rope—the engine must have stopped a minute. I was anxious for poor Ball and Collins, who I felt too sure had never risen from the fall we had all had and were, as I thought, crushed under the great stage.

I kept calling them by name to encourage them and make them also (if still able) come through the opening. While standing there, the effect was—grand—the roar of the rushing water in a confined passage, and by its velocity rushing past the opening was grand, very grand. I cannot compare it to anything, cannon can be nothing to it. At last, it came bursting through the opening. I was then obliged to be off—but up to that moment, as far as my sensations were concerned, and distinct from the idea of the loss of six poor fellows whose death I could not then foresee, kept there.

The sight and the whole affair was well worth the risk and I would willingly pay my share, £50 there about, of the expenses of such a 'spectacle'. Reaching the shaft, I was much too bothered with my knee and some other thumps to remember much.

If I had been kept under another minute when knocked down, I should not have suffered more, and I trust I was tolerably fit to die. If, therefore, the occurrence itself was rather a gratification than otherwise and the consequences in no way unpleasant, I need not attempt to avoid such. My being in bed at present, tho' no doubt arising from the effects of my straining, was immediately caused by me returning soon to a full diet. Had I been properly warned of this, I might now be hard at work at the tunnel. But all is for the best.

When I gaze down at his face, I still see the innocent look of a boy who would sit on my knee and ask many questions of my designs and innovations; apply himself to mathematical methods under my assistance; sketch and watercolour many illustrations of architectural features, horses and the like, just as I did when I was a youth in France; hold my hand on all too few days we spent out along the river—the river that so nearly took his life.

It will not win. The Tunnel will prevail.

APPENDIX

Reproduction of the report 'Documents relating to the Thames Tunnel'. United Kingdom: n.p., 1829.

THAMES TUNNEL.

PREFATORY REMARKS.

PROCEEDINGS AND RESOLUTIONS
OF THE PUBLIC MEETING
Held at the Freemasons Tavern, July 5, 1828.

REPORT OF THE DIRECTORS
Of the Thames Tunnel Company, of the 11th June, 1828, on the Income to be expected from the Tunnel, when completed.

REPORT OF THE ENGINEER,
On the Practicability of the Completion of the Tunnel.

RESOLUTIONS OF THE PROPRIETORS,
June 11, 1828.

RESOLUTIONS OF THE DIRECTORS,
June 12, 1828.

FORM OF DEBENTURES UNDER THE ACT OF PARLIAMENT.

LONDON:
Printed by ARTHUR TAYLOR, 40, Basinghall street.
1829.

Title page of Documents relating to the Thames Tunnel

The Committee which was appointed at the Public Meeting of friends to the undertaking of the Thames Tunnel, to assist in raising funds for the completion of the work, deem it incumbent on them to put the Public in possession of every information bearing upon the object in question.

With this view they publish the following series of documents, in the earnest hope that they may be found deserving of attentive consideration.

The proceedings of the Public Meeting; and the rank and character of the parties composing it, show that the Thames Tunnel is regarded as a national work; as one honourable to science, and useful to the country, and not a mere experimental effort of ingenuity, though highly to be esteemed in that view: but, that it is chiefly to be considered as a WORK which is likely to confer a real benefit on this country by the establishment of communications between the shores of rivers where the navigation of large ships and the depth and violence of the current render a bridge in its erection difficult, and in its expediency doubtful: and that it is a work, in the words of His Grace the Duke of Wellington, important in a commercial as well as in a military and political point of view.

The advantage of it in a *commercial* point of view is obvious since everything that facilitates intercourse and communication must be beneficial. In a military point of view, it has over bridged the important advantage that it may be rendered impassable without injury to the structure. In a political point of view, the advantages just described are doubly evident.

The annexed Report of the Directors of the Thames Tunnel Company assumes the perfect practicability of the work, upon the unanswerable fact of the Tunnel having been made complete to the extent of 600 feet, and of its having withstood two irruptions of the river. The Report then proceeds to consider the adequacy of the future annual amount of Tolls to pay the interest on the money to be raised, *viz,* £200,000. The Directors state the ground of their opinion to be the following.

1. That there is *no* bridge to the eastward of the Tunnel, nor any westward nearer than London Bridge, which is *two miles* distant.

2. That the character of the neighbourhood is highly commercial, as is evinced in the immense number of ships which are lying on each side of the river above and below the Tunnel; the vicinity of the London Docks, the East and West India and St Katherine's Docks, on the north bank of the river, and the Commercial, the East Country, and Grand Surrey Canal Docks, on the south side.

3. That the surrounding population is dense, and that the commercial establishments surrounding the Tunnel are various in nature, many in number, and great in extent.

4. That a more immediate communication will thus be opened between the counties of Middlesex and Essex, Surrey and Kent, four of the most populous counties.

5. That the communication thus afforded will he commodious the ascents and descents not being steeper than Ludgate Hill.

A comparison is then drawn between the neighbourhood of the Tunnel and that of Waterloo Bridge: and an expectation is declared by the Directors, and grounded by them on the great preponderance of trade and population surrounding the Tunnel, and on its distance from any bridge, that the tolls of the Tunnel must exceed those of Waterloo Bridge, which amount to 13,688*l. per annum*; this sum would allow a large deduction to be made for the various expenses of maintaining the works, *&c,* and yet leave a balance more than sufficient to pay the interest on the capital now required *viz.* 200,000*l.*

The Directors also express an opinion that the gradual increase of Tolls, and the improved value of their property, will produce a fair income divisible amongst the original Proprietors.

The Engineer to the work, Mr. Brunel, in his Report declares his unhesitatingconviction that there is nothing to prevent a completion of the work as far ashe is concerned as Engineer; and he remarks that the sound and perfect state of the Tunnel after the accidents which have happened afford at once a proof of its solidity and durability.

The Committee, whilst they present this short abstract of the documents they now publish, are aware that there are very many individuals who regard the Tunnel, quite independently of pecuniary considerations, in a purely national point of view, and to them the Committee now particularly look for that countenance which will re-encourage the Proprietors, and for that support which will enable the Company to proceed through the only remaining portion of difficulty and danger.

The Committee hope that they may be the channel through which this end may be attained; and that a work which will do honour to the enterprising spirit of the Country, and be both beneficial and useful to commerce and to science, may not be abandoned through the inefficiency of the funds necessary for its completion.

Committee Room,
29, Bridge street, Blackfriars.

Proceedings at a Meeting called respecting the Thames Tunnel, at Free-Masons' Tavern, Saturday 5th July **1828.**

It being moved by His Grace The Duke of Wellington and seconded by His Royal Highness The Duke of Cambridge, that Charles Nicholas Pallmer, Esq. M.P. do take the Chair, the same was agreed to unanimously, and Charles Nicholas Pallmer Esq, M.P. took the Chair.

MR. PALLMER rose, and said:

I can assure your Royal Highness, my Lords, and Gentlemen, that I feel deeply my own unworthiness to fill the high and honourable situation to which you have been pleased to call me upon the present occasion. Having had that honour at your hands it shall be my humble endeavour to perform the duties of it to the best of my ability. My Lords and Gentlemen, I will not detain you by any observations of mine from proceeding to the more important business for which we are assembled this day, knowing as I do, how valuable the time of the illustrious individual on my left is, and how badly spent your time would be in listening to any observations of mine.

Permit me, however, just one word, to say that I congratulate this country on seeing so respectable and numerous an assemblage for the purpose of upholding an undertaking calculated to be the admiration of the world in the present day, and to go down, as I trust it will, in the history of this country, as one of the proudest monuments of English enterprise and English science. [Applause.]

My Lords and Gentlemen, for this undertaking I derive the most auspicious hopes, not merely from the assemblage which I have the honour and pleasure of seeing before me, but because I have the honour of having on my right hand a Member of that Royal Family under which the arts, as well as the liberties, have flourished in this country [Applause], and have ever been patronised; and I have on my left hand an individual who, happily, not only manages the public interests of this country with great talent, but, with respect to whom, Englishmen have from experience been accustomed to think that everything which he undertakes is likely to succeed. [Applause.]

I thank you, my Lords and Gentlemen, for having heard me so long, and I will detain you no longer.

THE DUKE OF WELLINGTON:

I assure you, Gentlemen, I am exceedingly flattered by the honour which has been done me by being called upon by certain Members of this Association to propose the Resolutions which I shall presently have the honour of reading to you; and, Gentlemen, I sincerely hope that the predictions of the Honourable Gentleman now in the Chair, that this work will succeed in consequence of my being the individual fixed upon to move those Resolutions to you, will not be disappointed. [Applause.]

At the same time, Gentlemen, I cannot but feel that there are many here present, who, although not more zealous in the cause than I am, and not more sensible than I am of the advantages which will result to this Metropolis, to this country, and to the world, from the performance of this great work, are yet much more capable than I am of displaying to you all its advantages, and of exciting toward and it your interest. [Applause.]

Gentlemen, there are in this country many works of extraordinary utility, beauty, and magnificence; but what is still more extraordinary is, that they are the works of individual enterprise. The sagacity of individuals has suggested to them the utility, or their taste has suggested to them the beauty and magnificence of those works, and they have not been deterred from undertaking and completing them by the risk and expense to be incurred by carrying them into execution; but, Gentlemen, I speak from my own knowledge, and I could appeal to others now present more capable than I am of stating what is the opinion abroad upon this subject, I speak from my own knowledge when I tell you that there is no work upon which the public interest of foreign nations has been more excited than it has been upon the Tunnel [Applause]; every man feels not only the benefit which will result from it to the intermediate neighbourhood, to the populous district in which it is established, to the counties of Surrey, Kent, and Essex, between which it will establish a short and convenient communication, but likewise, men cannot but see the great political, military, as well as commercial benefit that will be derived from the example of such a work, by the establishment of others in other places, and in other countries in which such works may be absolutely necessary.

Under these circumstances, Gentlemen, I cannot but congratulate you upon the enterprise which has induced you to undertake this work, notwithstanding its novelty and all the disadvantageous circumstances under which it is undertaken; and I now call upon you to assist in carrying it into complete execution, of which completion there is at present so fair a prospect. Gentlemen, at the risk of fatiguing you, I will now call your attention to some of the financial details attending this measure. The original estimate was for £200,000, of this sum of £200,000 the sum of £193,000 was subscribed; of the sum of £193,000 subscribers failed to pay their deposits to the amount of £13,000; there remained, therefore, £180,000, and of that £180,000 £170,000 has been expended.

Gentlemen, it is not extraordinary that mistakes should be made in the formation of the estimate upon which this work was founded;—the novelty of the work, the difficulties of ascertaining the nature of the bed of the river through which it was to be carried, or the accidents to which it was liable, and which have occasioned a considerable expense, all tended to increase the expense of this great undertaking; but, Gentlemen, I beg particularly to can your attention to this fact, that the work itself has cost only £ 120,000, the remainder has been the purchase of machinery and the purchase of premises, and of the ground which is absolutely necessary upon one of the banks of the river in order to carry the work on, and I beg you to observe that in proportion as that expense, particularly the expense of the premises and of the ground, has been large, in the same proportion does the work promise to be useful, and promise to be profitable in case it should be completed. [Applause.]

Gentlemen, the sum now necessary in order to enable the Directors to complete the work is still £200,000, of this sum £98,000 will be required to complete the Tunnel across the river; of the remainder £45,000 will be required to purchase the ground and premises on the left bank of the river, together with salaries of officers and other contingent expenses of the undertaking, and £50,000 to make the ways up to the Tunnel on both sides of the river, making altogether a sum of £191,000, and leaving (if £200,000 should be subscribed) a sum of nearly £20,000 in hand, including the sum of £10,000 which now remains in hand.

Now, Gentlemen, I will beg to observe that the proposition I have to make to you is this, that this sum should be lent on Debentures of from £20 to £100, the holders of these debentures being to receive their interest in priority of all the claimants for Subscriptions up to the present moment. You must see as well as I can detail to you what the chances are of the success of this undertaking; this I will say, that if this money is found it is quite certain that the Tunnel must be completed. [Applause.] The accidents which have occurred, and which appear to have occurred only to demonstrate the enterprise, the genius, and the ability of the Engineer who has conducted it [Applause], have proved to a certainty that it is absolutely impossible that the work should not be completed. They have also proved this, that the work itself is excellent, and that if once completed it will be durable in proportion as the honour of having completed it will be durable to this country. Gentlemen, under these circumstances I have only to conclude by moving these Resolutions, and by earnestly entreating you to give your assistance to carry on this great work. [Applause.]

Sir Edward Owen seconded the Resolutions, which were carried unanimously.

Several Gentlemen successively addressed the Meeting; after which His Royal Highness The DUKE of CAMBRIDGE rose, and said:

Gentlemen, though little in the habit of public speaking I have undertaken the honourable office which has been entrusted to me, which is of returning thanks to His Grace the Duke of Wellington for his attendance here today; I am sure that no one feels more gratified than I do that it falls to my share. It would ill become me to make a long speech upon such an occasion; everyone knows the services the Duke has rendered to his country, and it would be even indelicate in his presence to say more, but I have the happiness to see the situation hi which he now stands, and I trust and feel that we shall see him as great a man in the Cabinet as we have seen him in the Field [Applause]; that is the *ne plus ultra* of greatness, and more I cannot say.

Allow me to say a few words more upon the subject of this Meeting; having lived several years upon the Continent, I am aware what is the sentiment throughout the Continent relative to this great undertaking; it is looked upon as the greatest thing that ever was done, therefore I feel pride as an Englishman in recommending the thing, for I am convinced it will succeed if we can find the means to finish it. Our national pride is at stake, and I am sure this country will never suffer such a noble undertaking to be abandoned for want of means. Gentlemen, I do assure you that it is a pleasure and a pride to me, who have been so many years away, to have the pleasure of speaking to my countrymen again, and if the few words I have said can advance this cause nobody will be more happy than myself.

The Earl of Powis seconded the Motion.

The Duke of Wellington returned thanks.

The Chairman of the Company, W. SMITH, Esq. M.P. remarked that this was not a meeting of the Thames Tunnel Proprietors, far less an exclusive meeting of the Directors.

The thanks of the Meeting were then proposed to the Chairman for his services in the Chair, which were unanimously carried; and the Meeting separated, after Subscriptions to the amount of £8000 had been entered into, which have been severally advertised.

The following were the Resolutions moved by His Grace the Duke of Wellington:

That this Meeting being of opinion that a Tunnel under the Thames in that part of the river where the commercial intercourse is considerable, and where regard for the navigation must preclude the erection of a bridge, would be a work of eminent utility, and that the completion of such a work would not only be honourable to science, but would reflect credit on the country through whose means and continued encouragement the work was produced, and that the undertaking at Rotherhithe, of which a large portion is now accomplished, and which has excited at home and abroad an unusual interest, is recommended by all these characteristics, and that the abandonment under these circumstances of that work, which is now stopped for want of money, would be discreditable to the country: Resolved,

1. That the prosecution of the work in question merits and demands the support of the British public.

That the present Meeting being of opinion that, as the irruptions of the river have on both occasions been overcome by simple means, and have left the structure of the works undisturbed throughout the whole length of the part already finished, and assurance bas been thereby acquired that the plan of those works is good, and is deserving of public confidence, and that although the enterprise was, at its beginning, of that peculiar nature as almost to baffle accuracy of estimate, yet the completion of one half under circumstances in which a variety of difficulty was encountered and surmounted, has given from the experience of the past reasonable grounds for forming a conclusion as to the expense of the future; and that it appearing by a statement of the Directors, that the premises on one side of the river, with machinery and other expenses, have cost £50,000, and the actual progress of the work (including the accidents) has cost only £120,000, making a total of £ 170,000 for the whole of the present expenditure:

Resolved,

2. That the amount of £200,000 more, which the Directors under the authority of Parliament are permitted to raise, does appear to this Meeting to promise to be more than equal to all the future probable exigencies of the work.

That this Meeting coinciding in the expediency of the plan put forward by the Directors, of raising this sum by borrowing it upon Debentures which shall bear interest at five percent, *per annum*, to be charged on the tolls and other revenues arising from the estates and property of the Company, and to be paid in priority to all claims under the original shares; and being of opinion that the plan is further entitled to public encouragement and support by the pledge to which the Directors bound themselves not to re-commence active operations until subscriptions for £ 100,000 are received, and not to call for any portion of that sum until the whole of it be subscribed, and then only by monthly instalments not exceeding ten percent.

Resolved,

3. That this Meeting do accordingly earnestly invite the public at large to support the plan proposed for the completion of the work, and to subscribe their names for Debentures which are issuable towards it in sums of £20 and upwards, and for Donations, which Donations are to be applied at the discretion of the Committee for the payment of interest on those Debentures, or otherwise.

Resolved,

4. That Books be now opened at this Meeting for the Subscription for the Loan in question upon the plan proposed, and also for Donations, and be likewise left at the Tunnel Office, and at the Houses of Bankers in London and in the Country; the Subscription and

Donation Books to be examined, from time to time, by a Committee, and when the sum of £ 100,000 shall be subscribed, to be delivered over to the Directors of the Company for the prosecution of the works; and the Committee in question to consist of the following persons, viz,

C. N. Pallmer, Esq. M.P.
William Smith, Esq. M.P.
James Bandinel, Esq. F.L.S.
Simon Cock, Esq.
Bryon Donkin, Esq.
Benjamin Hawes, Esq.
Benjamin Hawes, Jun. Esq,
Robert H. Marten, Esq.
Frederick Perkins, Esq.
David Pollock, Esq.
George H. Wollaston, Esq.
W. H. Wollaston, M.D. V.P.R.S.

who do forthwith proceed with the object of this Meeting.

Copy of a Resolution of the Committee appointed at the Public Meeting of the 5th July 1828.

Resolved,

That the sums to be received as Donations and Subscriptions for Debentures be vested in Trustees and deposited in the Bank of England.

Resolution of the Court, 1st of July 1828.

Resolved,

That the money received from visitors to the Tunnel previously to the 11th of June last, as well as the money which has since been and shall hereafter be received from the same source, be appropriated as a fund to assist in paying the interest on the Debentures.

Report of the Directors of the Thames Tunnel Company, to a General Assembly of the Proprietors, convened at the city of London Tavern, on Wednesday, the 11th day of June 1828.

YOUR Directors have the satisfaction to report, that the late irruption of the River Thames into the Tunnel has been overcome, and that the works may proceed so soon as the shield is put into a working condition. Your Directors, however, intend to delay the prosecution of the works until a sufficient part of the further capital authorised to be raised by the Act of Parliament recently passed shall have been obtained.

To enable you (the Proprietors) as well as the Public; to form a judgement as to the completion of the Tunnel, your Directors called upon Mr. Brunel, the engineer of the Company, to report upon the past operations, present state of, and future plan of proceeding with, the Tunnel; and Mr. Brunel has accordingly reported—That the unanswerable fact of the Tunnel having been made perfect and complete to the extent of 600 feet, and of its having withstood the destructive impetuosity of two irruptions of the river, cannot but satisfy you, as well as the public, of the sufficiency of the construction, and of the reliance which may be placed upon the works when completed: that the late irruption has been effectually overcome, and that the arches and works completed before that irruption have been found in a sound and perfect state, so that when the shield shall be restored to a working condition, he (Mr. B.) will be ready to proceed as usual: that the Tunnel has approached to within 350 feet of low-water mark on the north shore of the river, having been already completed to the extent of 600 feet from the shaft on the south side of the river: that he feels perfect confidence in being able to overcome every obstacle that may oppose itself to the progress of the work, and finally to complete the remaining part of the Tunnel in the same perfect and substantial manner in which the 600 feet have already been completed: that when the increased resources contemplated by the recent Act of Parliament shall have been raised, and the Company shall have at their disposal the means of enabling him to have recourse to additional precautionary measures, he shall propose to have a diving bell with a proper vessel at all times ready to enable him to examine and probe the bed of the river above the shield; also to make an artificial bed if, and when, found wanted, over that part of the ground under which the shield will traverse: and that this bed, consisting simply of bags of clay, he shall be enabled, by the experience of the past, to effect upon a scale of expense within the scope of the finances of the Company. " *Mr. Brunel concludes his Report by expressing his decided and firm conviction, that he shall meet with no obstacle which can prevent the perfect execution of the works, and the completion of the Tunnel.* This Report is annexed for your consideration.

Assuming that you will rely upon the Report and decided conviction of Mr. Brunel, as to the completion of the Tunnel. Your Directors have agreed to recommend for your consideration and adoption a plan which they deem to be the best calculated to raise the funds necessary to complete the undertaking; but before they state this plan, they request your particular attention to the probable adequacy of the annual amount of the tolls, not only to pay the interest on the money to be raised, but also to yield an ultimate remuneration to the Proprietors.

Your Directors would in the first instance remark, that the tolls of the Tunnel are likely to amount to a much greater annual sum in consequence of there being no bridge to the eastward of the Tunnel, nor any bridge to the westward nearer than London Bridge (which is two miles distant), than they would amount to if there were a free bridge, or any other bridge, on each side of the Tunnel and near to it. Your Directors would further remark that the amount of tolls which are annually taken on one of the bridges over the river Thames (although there is a free bridge very near to each side of it) is not generally known, and is hardly to be credited.

The Waterloo Bridge has Blackfriars Bridge near to it on the east, and Westminster Bridge near to it on the west, and, notwithstanding the proximity of those two free bridges, and the apparently few passengers, *the tolls actually taken on Waterloo Bridge during the last year,* viz. *from August* 1826 *to August* 1827, *amounted to the very large sum of* £13,688. Now when the situation of the Tunnel, with all the advantages incident to it, is compared with the situa- tion of the Waterloo Bridge, your Directors are of opinion that the annual amount of the tolls of the Tunnel will most probably exceed the annual amount of the tolls actually taken on the Waterloo Bridge, which latter are a fair criterion by which a judgement may be formed of the amount of tolls which may be expected to be taken at the Tunnel. In order, however, that you may know the grounds on which the opinion of your Directors is formed, they proceed to state them.

The great distance of the Tunnel from any bridge is an important advantage in its favour; and it will be recollected that an immense number of ships are constantly lying on each side of the river above and below the Tunnel; *that on the north side* are the London Docks, the Saint Katherine Docks (now in progress), the West-India Docks, the East-India Docks and Warehouses, the Regent's Canal, *and a dense population* inhabiting Wapping, Ratcliff highway, Shadwell, the Commercial road, Mile-end road, Whitechapel road, Poplar, Limehouse, and Stepney; *that on the south side* are the Commercial Docks, the East Country Docks, the Grand Surrey Dock and Warehouses, and numerous wharfs, including those to which nearly the whole of the coasting and Irish trades are confined, numberless granaries and warehouses for wheat, flour, hemp, &c., *and a dense population* inhabiting Bermondsey, Rotherhithe, Tooley street, the Borough of Southwark, Deptford, Greenwich, and the Kent road; *and that on the north as well as on the south sides* there are numerous manufactories, foundries, shipbuilders' and shipwrights' yards, ropemakers. sailmakers, and ship handlers. It will also be recollected that the *Tunnel will open a land communication, two miles below London Bridge, between the counties of Middlesex and Essex and the counties of Surrey and Kent and the borough of Southwark;* that a considerable part of the traffic over London Bridge cannot fail of being diverted from thence to the Tunnel, owing not only to the present circuitous route over London Bridge to and from the various docks and wharfs on each side of the river, and to the stoppages and interruptions which at present take place in the crowded streets, but also owing to the distance that will be saved by going through the Tunnel, and to the facility which it will afford to waggons and carts when loaded, in making two or more journeys in one day, to and from the Docks, through the Tunnel (the descents and ascents to and from which will not be greater than Ludgate hill), whereas waggons and carts going over London Bridge to and from the Docks loaded, generally make only one journey.

These advantages are not equalled by those connected with the situation of the Waterloo Bridge, and hence the conclusion to which your Directors have come that the tolls of the Tunnel will exceed the tolls of Waterloo Bridge.

But should the tolls of the Tunnel be only equal to the tolls of Waterloo Bridge, then, allowing for an annual expense of £3000 to light and watch and keep up the Tunnel, there would remain an annual balance of tolls of £10,688, which would be more than sufficient to pay the interest of £200,000 at 5 *per cent.* The surplus of the probable tolls, added to their gradual increase, and the revenue from the estates of the Company which will not be required for the purposes of the Tunnel, will, it is hoped, produce a fair income divisible among you as Proprietors, in return for your money invested.

Your Directors having thus laid before you the confident opinion of your Engineer as to the completion of the Tunnel, and their own opinion as to the adequacy of the tolls to pay the interest on the moneys to be borrowed besides the prospect of an income to the Proprietors, your Directors now request your attention to the Act of Parliament which, in conformity with the resolutions of the 20th November last, they applied for and obtained.

By this Act of Parliament, the Company are authorised to raise an additional capital of £200,000 over and besides the capital and money authorised to be raised by the original Act of Parliament, and the modes which Parliament have sanctioned for raising money are,

1. By the creation of new Shares of £50 or less, which shares the Company are authorised to issue and sell-the Act also authorising the Proprietors to give such privileges and advantages to such new shares as they shall think fit.

2. By Mortgage of the undertaking, or of any part of the property, estate, or effects of the Company.

3. By Annuities for life or lives, or for terms of years, upon such terms as the Proprietors shall think fit to grant.

4. By Debentures payable to bearer, entitled to an interest of 5 *per cent.* charged on the tolls and other revenue arising from the estate and property of the Company.

Taking into consideration the best plan to be pursued in order to raise the necessary funds to complete the undertaking, your Directors recommend that you should authorise the issue of debentures bearing an interest at 5 *per cent.;* which debentures, according to the Act, will be payable to bearer, and charged upon the tolls and other revenue arising from the estates and property of the Company, and will have a priority over the Shareholders. The Act of Parliament gives to persons who may hold debentures an option of substituting a share in lieu of any debenture, within six months after tolls have begun to be taken.

This plan of raising the necessary funds is so comprehensive and so convenient, that your Directors trust that the Proprietors and the Public will be glad of an opportunity of further manifesting that national interest which has been excited in favour of the completion of the Tunnel, more especially if you and the Public shall concur in their opinion, that the tolls will be fully adequate to pay the interest on the money to be raised, and leave (with the revenue of the estates of the Company) a fair income to be divided among the Proprietors.

As the Act of Parliament authorises the raising of £200,000 your Directors propose to create debentures to that amount, in order that the whole sum which may from time to time be raised upon such debentures shall be upon an equality; but your Directors think it proper to state to you distinctly that they do not intend to proceed with the works, or to appropriate any sum which shall be advanced upon debentures, until £100,000 shall have been subscribed for, and when that sum shall have been secured, your Directors are of opinion that every financial obstacle will have been overcome in regard to the completion of the Tunnel.

Your Directors have thus presented to you the result of their deliberations, and they trust that the spirit of the Proprietors will be aided and assisted by the British Public in a work which, when completed, will be an honour to the United Kingdom.

(Signed)

WILLIAM SMITH,
Chairman.

AMOUNT of all the Disbursements hitherto incurred by the Company, in the purchase of Premises at Rotherhithe, and Overcoming the irruptions from the River, and in the completion of 600 Feet of the Tunnel.

Cost of Premises, and Expenses relating thereto	£30,000
Cost of Machinery, Building, Stores, and Parliamentary Expenses	£20,000
Expense of the Shaft and of 600 feet of Tunnel, including all the Expense hitherto incurred in repairing the irruption from the River	120,000
Total present Expenditure	£170,000

Report of Mr. Brunel, the Engineer of the Thames Tunnel Company.

To the Directors of the Thames Tunnel Company.

Gentlemen,

In conformity with the Resolution of the Committee of Directors calling upon me to report on the past operations, present state of, and future plan of proceeding with, the Tunnel, I have to report,

First, as to past operations. The unanswerable fact that the Tunnel has been made perfect and complete to the extent of 600 feet, and that the arches and works have withstood the destructive impetuosity consequent on two irruptions of the River into the Tunnel, cannot but satisfy you as well as the Public, of the sufficiency of the construction, and of the reliance which may be placed upon the works when they are completed. I have therefore not deemed it necessary, after the reports already made, to go into a detail of operations so far as regards the past.

Secondly, as to the present state of the Tunnel.—Having heretofore laid before you an account of the irruption of the river into the Tunnel, which took place on the 12th of January last, I have now to report that this irruption has been effectually overcome, and that the arches and works (completed before that irruption) have been found in a sound and perfect state; so that when the shield shall have been restored to a working condition, which is now in progress, I shall be ready to proceed as usual.

Thirdly, as to the future plan of proceeding. The Tunnel has approached to within 350 feet of low-water mark on the north shore of the river, having already been completed to the extent of 600 feet from the shaft on the south side of the river. I feel perfect confidence in being able to overcome every obstacle that may oppose itself to the progress of the work, and finally to complete the remaining part of the Tunnel in the same perfect and substantial state in which 600 feet have already been completed.

When the increased resources contemplated by the recent Act of Parliament shall have been raised, and the Company shall have at their disposal the means of enabling me to have recourse to additional precautionary measures, I shall propose to have a diving-bell, with a proper vessel at all times ready to enable me to examine and probe the bed of the river above the shield, and also to make an artificial bed, if, and when, found wanted, over that part of the ground under which the shield will traverse. This bed, consisting simply of bags of clay, I shall be enabled, by the experience of the past, to effect upon a scale of expense within the scope of the finances of the Company.

Having thus complied with the Resolution of the Committee of Directors, I conclude by repeating my decided and firm conviction, that I shall meet with no obstacle which can prevent the perfect execution of the works; and that the Tunnel now in progress may be safely and securely completed.

I have the honour to be,
Gentlemen,
Your very obedient servant,

(Signed) M. I. BRUNEL.

May 29, 1828.

Resolutions passed at the Special General Assembly of Proprietors, held at the City of London Tavern, on the 11th of June 1828.

Resolved,

I. That the Reports now read be received, entered upon the Minutes, and printed and circulated.

II. That the Tunnel having been completed to the extent of 600 feet from the shaft at Rotherhithe, and there remaining only 350 feet to arrive at low-water mark near Wapping, this Meeting receives with satisfaction and confidence the expressed opinion of Mr. Brunel, the Engineer of the Company, that the Tunnel may be completed.

III. That the Directors be, and they are hereby, authorised to raise, under the authority of the Act of Parliament recently passed, such sums of money as they may deem necessary for the completion of the undertaking, not exceeding £200,000, with power to make such allowances as they may consider reasonable to those who may assist in raising the same.

IV. That the amount of the Tolls of the Tunnel, estimated upon the principle of their exceeding the tolls taken annually on the Waterloo Bridge (which in the last year amounted to £13,688) will, in the opinion of this Meeting, be more than sufficient to pay interest on the money to be raised, and leave, with the revenue from the freehold property and other effects of the Company which will not be required for the purposes of the Tunnel, an income for the Proprietors in respect of the capital invested.

V. That when a sum of £100,000 shall have been agreed to be subscribed, the Directors do proceed with the works, and commence making their calls on subscribers, this Meeting being of opinion that when that sum shall have been secured every financial obstacle in regard to the completion of the Tunnel will have been overcome.

VI. That all persons who have voluntarily contributed to this undertaking, and who may be desirous of taking a debenture or debentures to be issued under the Act of Parliament, shall be allowed the amount of their subscription in part payment of such debenture or debentures, if applied for within a period to be fixed by the Directors.

VII. Thanks were voted to William Smith, Esq. M.P. the Chairman of the Meeting, and to the Court of Directors of the Company.

Resolutions of the Court of Directors of the Company, passed 12th of June 1828.

Resolved,

I. That the sum of £200,000 be raised by the issue of debentures bearing interest at 5 *per cent. per annum,* such interest to be charged on the tolls and other revenue arising from the estates and property of the Company, and that the money which may be agreed to be advanced be called for by the Directors in such sums, and at such times as they shall think proper: but that the Directors shall not be bound to call for any part of the sum agreed to be advanced, unless £100,000 shall be agreed to be advanced in the whole, by a day to be fixed by the Directors for that purpose.

II. That the debentures to be issued be in sums of £20, £30, £40, £50, and £100 or upwards, and that every debenture-holder have the option of taking a share in the Company for each £50 of debentures held by him if he shall require the same within six months after the Tunnel shall be completed and open to the Public.

Under the Act of Parliament holders of Debentures are to have a priority over the Shares.

N. B. The instalments on Debentures will only be called for at the rate of 10 *per cent. per* month.

DEBENTURES.

Extract of the Act of Parliament relating to Debentures.

AND be it further enacted, That it shall be lawful for the said Company to raise all or any part of the said further sum hereby authorised to be raised, by the issue of debentures, charging the tolls and other revenue of the said Company with the sums of money for which such debentures shall be respectively issued, and interest thereon at any rate not exceeding five pounds *per centum per annum,* which debentures shall be granted under the common seal of the said Company, and may be in the form, or to the effect following; (that is to say,)

"We the Company of Proprietors of the Thames Tunnel do hereby by virtue of an Act of Parliament passed in the ninth year of the reign of His Majesty King George the Fourth, intituled [*here insert the title of this Act*] charge all and singular the tolls and other revenues of the said Company, and all the estate, right, title, and interest of the said Company, and of their successors and assigns, of, in, and to the same, with the payment to the bearer hereof, of the sum of together with interest for the same in the meantime after the rate of *per centum per annum,* such interest to be paid half yearly on the twenty-fourth day of June, and twenty-fifth day of December in every year, [*or on such other day or days as shall he agreed upon*] and the first payment to be made on [*here specify the day on which the first payment of interest is to he made*]: in witness whereof the said Thames Tunnel Company have hereunto affixed their common seal, this day of one thousand eight hundred and ."

COURT OF DIRECTORS.

Chairman.

WILLIAM SMITH, Esq. M.P. Upper Seymour street.

Deputy Chairman.

GEORGE HYDE WOLLASTON, Esq. Clapham Common.

Directors.

TIMOTHY BRAMAH, Esq. Pimlico.
THOMAS BRANDRAM, Esq. Sise lane.
THOMAS BRUNTON, Esq. 12, Park square, Regent's Park.
BRYAN DONKIN, Esq. 80, Great Surrey street, Blackfriars.
HUGH GRAY, Esq. 27, Mincing lane.
RICHARD PECKOVER HARRIS, Esq. Union court, Broad street.
BENJAMIN HAWES, Esq. Russell square.
ROBERT HUMPHREY MARTEN, Esq. Mincing lane.
FREDERICK PERKINS, Esq. Park street, Southwark.
W. H. WOLLASTON, Esq. M.D. V P R S. Dorset street, Manchester square.

Engineer.

M. I. BRUNEL, Esq. F.R.S. &c.

Solicitors.

Messrs. Sweet and Cars, Basinghall street.

Clerk.

Mr. Charles Butler.

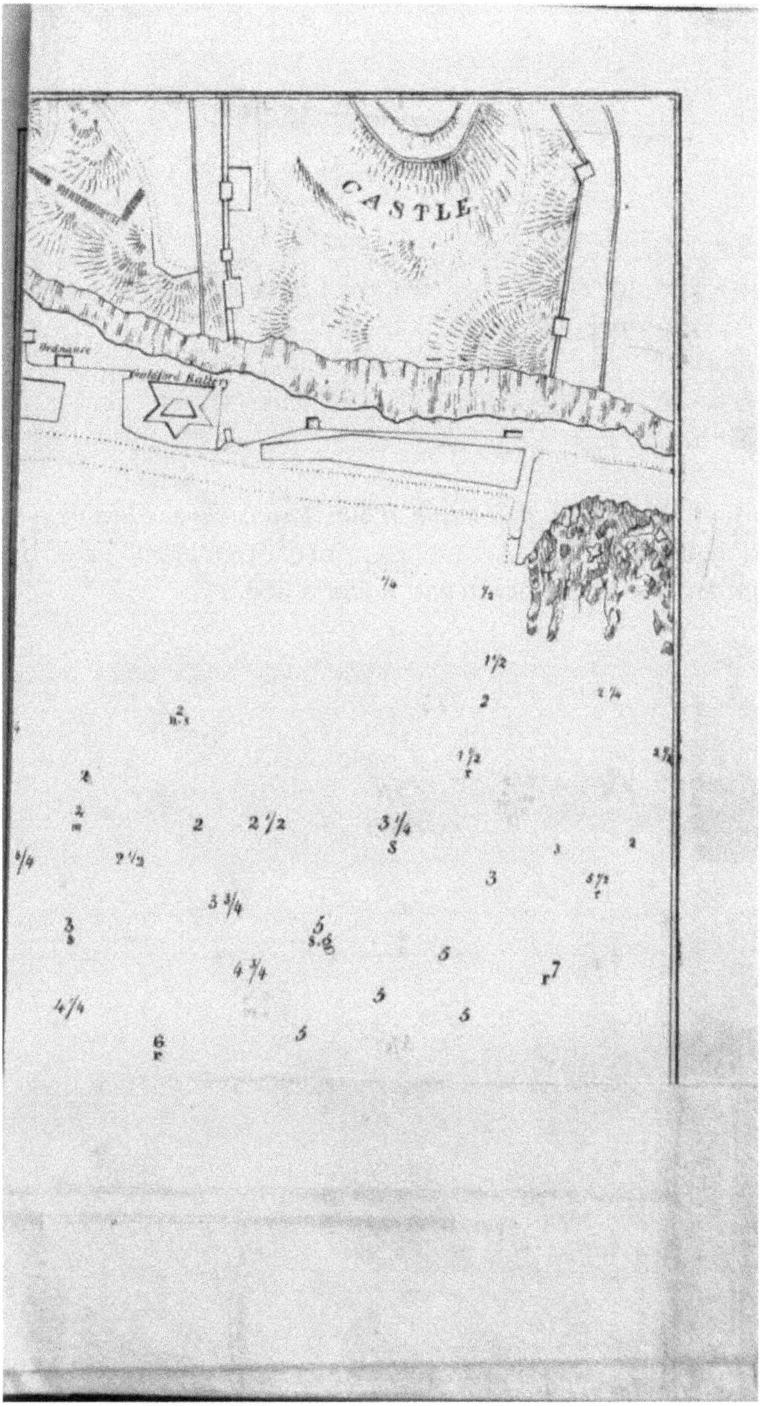

Map from Documents relating to the Thames Tunnel

FURTHER READING

Bagust, Harold. *The Greater Genius? A Biography of Mark Isambard Brunel.* London, Ian Allen Publishing, 2006

Mathewson, Andrew, Laval et al. *The Brunels' Tunnel.* London, ICE Publishing, 2006

Beamish, R. *Memoir of The Life of Sir Marc Isambard Brunel.* London, Forgotten Books. Date? (reprint of original published by Longman, Green, Longman and Roberts, 1862)

www.ingramcontent.com/pod-product-compliance
Lightning Source LLC
Chambersburg PA
CBHW071948270125
20929CB00005B/115
* 9 7 8 1 0 3 5 8 0 7 8 3 3 *